GUATEMALA IN MY BLOOD

How nursing in remote jungle villages revolutionized my life

BY ELIZABETH DESIMONE

Published in the United States of America by
Travels In Guatemala Press
4244 University Way N.E. Seattle, WA 98105
www.JungleNursing.com

First edition, August, 2009 Printed in the U.S.A.

Chapter Nine was previously published as "The Gift: La
Cumbre, Guatemala" in *Between the Heartbeats: Poetry and
Prose by Nurses*, University of Iowa Press, 1995.
Chapter Eleven was previously published as "A Recipe for
Humble Pie" in *Clinician Reviews*, June, 1998.

Photo on front cover and photos on pages 25, 86, 90, 109, 117,
137, 184, 185, 190, 195, 207, 209, 211, 212, 217, 219 and 230
are © copyrighted by Eric Wheater; all others are ©
copyrighted by the author.

Cover and book designed by Oriana Green

With gratitude, this book is dedicated to the Kek'chi Maya, the spirited people of the Petén

ACKNOWLEDGMENTS

The path to this book dipped and turned in ways never imagined. I didn't set out to write when I went to Guatemala, but the story needed telling and I felt compelled to write it.

I thank my dear Mama, who showed by example how to work hard, have faith and help others.

I appreciate my patient, darling daughter Maria (below), who loved unconditionally throughout my distracted putting together of this book.

Along the path, I met many writers, writing instructors and joined several writers groups. For reading and listening to endless versions and helpful criticism, support and encouragement, I thank Irene Wanner who edited the next to final version; Jessica Maxwell, whose feedback enlivened my writing; Seahurst writer friends Betty Sorrels, Barbara Benepe, Gerri Sorenson, Debbie Alexander, Kathy White (deceased) and Mary O'Malley. Muchisimas gracias to Father Fern

Gosselin who supplied many details, especially in the chapter Another Trip, Another Massacre. Thanks to precious friends Fay Hauer and Kay Studer who shared photos and memories of the Petén. Much praise to Oriana Green, who expertly did the graphics and designed this book. Many friends encouraged me to finish and publish this book. Thank you everyone.

I have great affection for the many priests, brothers, sisters and lay missionaries of Maryknoll, who've helped and inspired me through the years.

I gratefully acknowledge the inspiring people of the Petén, especially the Kek'chi. There wouldn't be a story without them. Many thanks to faithful companion, Tox. I hope to see you again someday. To the current health team: Chabela Reyes, Domingo Pop, Elvia Milian, Father Demetrio and especially Carmen Ché, my love, gratitude and admiration. We'll be in touch.

Finally, I thank the people of our community in Poptún, 1977-80; Fay and I would never have come to the Petén were it not for the vision of Mo Healy. He had the brains and chutzpah to begin everything. I thank Father John Fay (deceased), Father Fern Gosselin, Brother Leon Cook, Brother John Blazo, Pastora Lira and Aidé (Maria Dolores) Cheng for unforgettable memories.

TABLE OF CONTENTS

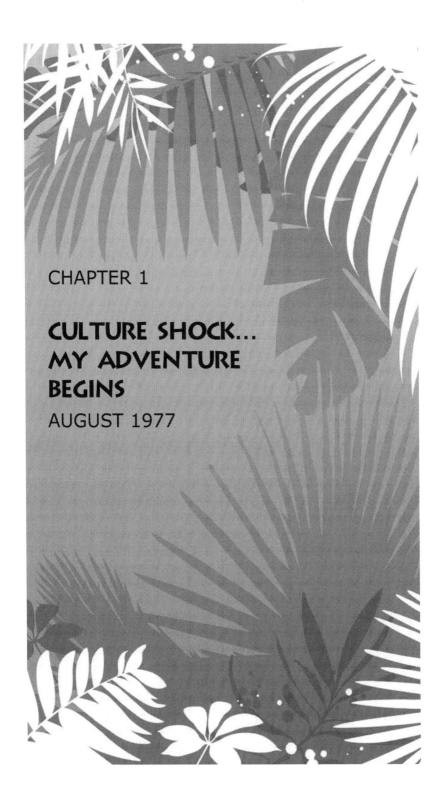

CHAPTER 1

CULTURE SHOCK... MY ADVENTURE BEGINS

AUGUST 1977

I first arrived in Guatemala in August of 1977, dragging my old army duffel bag, plaid suitcase and a guitar in a black case. I stayed in the Maryknoll Center House, in *Zona* 10, an area of Guatemala City where the affluent lived. Houses were set back from the streets behind concrete fences or wrought iron gates.

Though I was a world traveler and 35 years old, not knowing anyone, I felt lonely in a place with no women except the cook and laundress. My friend Fay Hauer, with whom I would begin to administer the health program, had already gone to Poptún, the town in the jungle of the Petén where we would live. It's a good thing I didn't know it would be an all-day trek on a rough dirt road.

I didn't then appreciate the oasis qualities of the Center House. Only after I'd lived in the Petén awhile, did I understand how heartening it was to have such a place to rest. In its quiet, hotel-like comfort, Maryknoll priests and brothers who worked in El Salvador, Nicaragua and Guatemala enjoyed the company of fellow missionaries who spoke their language, luxuriated in the feel of hot showers and ate ice cream from big tubs stocked in the freezer.

Trying to summon the courage to go to Poptún, I hung around. Normally I have no trouble venturing places on my own. I had no idea why I lacked the motivation. Now I know it was the beginning of culture shock.

Thinking back, I can't imagine why I thought someone would escort me to the Petén, but that is exactly what I expected. Finally I called Poptún, which had only one public telephone. A messenger, whom I later learned delivered messages by motorcycle, sped off to locate Fr. Maurice Healy, the Maryknoll priest who had requested nurses. Fr. Healy called back an hour later.

"Hi there Liz, welcome to Guatemala. How was your trip?"

"Just fine, thanks." I tried my best to sound just fine.

"Sorry I can't come to meet you," he went on, "but I'm heading out today for a course with Maria Dolores. We should be back in a few days. Probably the best way to get here is fly to Flores and then take the bus. It leaves from San Benito and comes straight here."

"Oh..." I said, trying to hide my disappointment. "See you in a few days." I didn't know it could have been worse—I could have been unlucky enough to take the bus from

Guatemala City to Poptún, a journey of 15 hours, if there were no mishaps.

Fr. Ron Hennessey, who lived at the Center House, a lean man with graying hair and an easy way about him, was regional superior of Maryknoll in Central America. Ron had the habit of falling asleep almost as he was talking to you, but just when you thought he hadn't heard a word you'd said, he opened his eyes and nailed you with some wry observation. If Ron hadn't been a priest, he would have made a great peacemaker for warring nations, because he could see both sides of situations and bring the most unlikely people together. He treated me very kindly, but every now and then he asked gently, "Uh, when are you going to uh, Poptún?" Ron didn't say it, but I suspect he wondered when I was going to get a move on.

"What kind of boots should I get?" I asked him. Ron must know as he had worked in the jungle too. For some reason, I imagined myself in fishermen's hip boots.

"Well, uh...about any kind you can find," Ron answered.

"Where should I buy them?" I persisted.

"The *mercado,* the market, or you can wait till you get to Poptún."

I never bought boots in the city, because even setting out to shop at the mercado alone required more initiative than I could muster.

One night, a week after I'd arrived in Guatemala, Ron stopped by my room. "Liz, Fern Gosselin has come today from vacation in the States," he said. "Maybe you could go with him to Poptún."

What a relief! Now I wouldn't have to travel alone.

I liked Fern immediately. A quiet man with curling hair and a warm smile. He had that big-guy look, more like a trucker than a priest. We made plans for the flight the very next day. Then Fern spotted the guitar case lying on the floor.

"Do you play?" he asked.

"No. How about you?"

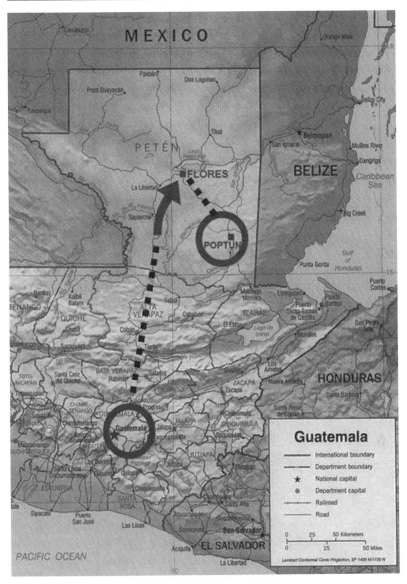

"I just fool around a little." He was being modest because later on I found out he played quite well and had a Johnny Cash kind of voice.

"Here, why don't you play something?" I bent down to open the case, forgetting what I had used to pad the guitar for the flight from Bolivia. Panty hose, bras and underpants tumbled out on the floor in front of the two priests.

I turned red with embarrassment. "Oops," I giggled. But Ron and Fern only laughed. Fern strummed the guitar while I hastily stuffed my underwear back into the case.

"How did you happen to bring a guitar when you don't play?" Fern asked with a twinkle in his eye.

I stammered an explanation. When I had been planning with Fay and Mark to come to Guatemala, the nurses I would be working with, we bought a guitar thinking music might help us form a community. But when Mark changed his mind, and Fay departed from language school early, they left me the guitar. Now, listening to Fern's soft strumming, I felt reassured that our idea had been a good one. Maybe I could learn to play, too.

The following day, with Fern and his friend Father Joe Morris, I left for Flores by a World War II propeller plane, which dipped like a crazed ferris wheel. I'd been told to expect a spectacular ride, as we would fly close to the ancient Mayan ruins of Tikál (below). Fr. Joe Morris and Fern sat in front of me, but it was almost impossible to converse above the ancient engine's roar. They had known each other in seminary days.

Fr. Morris now worked in Kenya and had come to visit Fr.
Fern. Fern's full name was the French—Fernand. He had lived
and worked in the Petén for a year.

I watched the dark green, almost black, hills flowing by in
an impenetrable wall. I had known nothing like this detached
feeling before, as if this flight was happening to someone else.
In Bolivia, where I studied Spanish from January to June of
that same year of 1977, that culture had been strange too, but
because I knew my time there was short, the adjustment wasn't
difficult. I lived as the natives did, in a rented house with Tom
and Chris Amato, a lay mission couple, in a house overrun by
ants, coped with a toilet that wouldn't flush, but none of it
bothered me. Now that I'd arrived in Guatemala where I'd live
for the next two and a half years, I was already having second
thoughts. Part of me wanted to board another plane and leave.

Once I deplaned, my nausea passed. From Flores, an
island with pastel houses and winding streets, we rode a bus
across a spit of land to San Benito. There we learned the bus to
Poptún wouldn't depart for three hours. (On the road, below.)

I restrained a groan. It was only ten o'clock, but hotter than any place I'd ever had the misfortune to be. By one o'clock, I would be cooking. I tried not to think about it.

"Let's get something to eat," suggested Fern.

We trudged the bustling streets of San Benito to a row of stalls. Between two—one selling shoes, the other with polyester fabrics hanging on a rope like gaudy flags—was an open-air diner. The walls leaned, as if someone had halfheartedly tried to knock it over.

We sat at a table covered by a faded oilcloth, littered with crumbs from previous customers. My chair rocked in the dirt. I could almost see the heat waves roasting my head from the tin roof. Perspiration beaded my upper lip and I longed for a fan. Not a breeze stirred the air.

Scrawny dogs sniffed our feet, cringing, miserable creatures who snarled as if they would love to bite our well-nourished legs. The dogs settled down to wait for scraps under the table. A circle of gnats hovered in the air above them. Bony chickens pecked under our table.

Buses and a few '50s vintage cars raised dust and made me cough. Flies picked at the crumbs on the table. The air smelled like a sauna equipped with a festering compost pile.

A woman in a polyester dress appeared, soiled apron bulging over her stomach. Her bare brown legs were patterned with tortuous veins. She swatted at flies with a towel, rattled words at Fern, nodded to Joe and me, then disappeared behind a string of beads screening a doorway.

I had understood nothing. "Don't they have a menu?"

"There's only one plate a day," explained Fern. "Today it's beef soup."

The string of beads flipped aside and the woman reappeared bearing a steamy bowl of meat, potatoes, rice and chunks of zucchini-like squash. She served Fern first, then Joe and finally me. She slapped hot tortillas wrapped in a stained towel on the table. Flies immediately congregated on the towel.

I tried to eat, but couldn't. It must have been well above a hundred degrees in the diner, and the grease on my soup nauseated me again.

Something had to stimulate me out of this sluggishness, so I ordered coffee.

The woman brought a cup, coffee sloshing onto the saucer. In those days I didn't drink sugared coffee, but it was already sweetened. At least the flavor was good.

After lunch, we walked the streets crowded with travelers, to the *terminal de bus*. The *terminal* was in the middle of the business district.

I found a seat while Fern, Joe and the driver heaved my suitcase, duffel bag and guitar case to the rack on top. We still had two hours to wait, but didn't dare get off or we'd lose our seats.

I had never felt so overheated. Sweat streamed down my back. I wanted to sleep, but could hardly breathe. I drifted, my head against the window.

It was a good thing we claimed our places when we did. An unbelievable number of people crushed in. I shared my cracked, green-upholstered perch with a woman and her two children. Others braced on the edges of seats and clung to the overhead poles, even spilling onto the steps of the open door. I stared at them and they stared back. Maybe my short hair and jeans amazed them, because all the other women had long hair and wore dresses.

When we finally advanced down the road, dust gusted in the open door and windows. They rattled. Always a reader, I couldn't open a book while the bus shook us like rag dolls.

The passing scenery was a dense green tunnel with no end (next page). We rocked through potholes the size of cars. Children with watermelon bellies on stick legs waved at us. From their delighted expressions, I guessed this to be an exciting event of their day, watching the bus go by. Here, as in town, gaunt chickens scuttled across the road almost under our

wheels, but the driver never even swerved or slowed. Malnourished dogs raced beside the tires, then splayed down panting in the middle of the road.

When we stopped an hour later, the driver and his helper hurled huge sacks of corn and packages bound with rope to the top of the bus. More passengers wedged themselves on board. I couldn't believe the driver would continue with the door open, passengers hanging on doggedly, enduring the clouds of dust enveloping them.

At one stop, a young girl boarded, balancing a basket of plastic bags with red liquid, like Kool Aid, on her head. Straws were stuck into each bag. She rode the bus a few minutes shouting, "*Cookos!*"

People around me bought those drinks. The bus was filled with sounds of noisy sucking. I resisted trying one myself, as the water was probably contaminated.

At another stop, I could hardly see out the window for all the women with baskets on their heads, yelling, "*Compra mis mangos*, buy my mangos." Some sold juicy papaya slices. Another woman begged, "*Por favor, seño, taquitos, bien ricos,* please miss, tacos, very delicious." The tacos looked yummy, crisp corn tortillas sprinkled with white cheese. I almost bought one until I realized sprinkled on them were tiny pieces of cooked beets.

Through the window, which I'd wrestled with but not been able to close, fried food smells drifted in. I felt guilty I hadn't bought something, but worried I'd get sick. The thought of what their kitchens might be like or whether they'd washed their hands, made me resist their fervent sales talk.

At last we jerked ahead again. I hadn't gone to the bathroom since early morning; it was now three o'clock and I'd seen nothing resembling an outhouse. We did pass villages from time to time, but there were no gas stations and most houses had no facilities either.

We continued on our way at perhaps 15 miles an hour. The road was rocky, causing the overloaded bus to lean as if it would tip at any moment.

The driver and his helper sang with the Mexican ranchero music blaring on the radio, which sounded to me mostly like static. Printed in red letters above the driver's head were the words, *Dios es Amor,* God is Love, and next to that a brightly painted Barbie form. A crucifix swung crazily above the dashboard as we careened along.

I clung to the rail and slid into the little boy crushed between his mother and me every time we rounded a curve.

Fern turned in his seat and said, "We're almost there, Liz," but I was too overcome by heat to respond.

Immersed in misery, I was only vaguely aware of the other people. They seemed happy, laughing and chattering. I strained to understand them. Their Spanish was not the same language I'd studied, but a dialect, filled with colloquialisms.

The woman next to me said something. I caught only a few words, but nodded as if I understood. Her little boy's dark brown head felt like a heating pad on my ribs.

"*Mucho calor,* very hot," she said, smiling, and fanning herself.

"*Sí,*" I agreed, feeling like an idiot but grateful to understand at least that.

I had spent five months learning Spanish at the Instituto Lingüístico in Bolivia where Maryknoll sent all its missionaries bound for Latin America. Our teachers spoke clearly and slowly. Now I found the words around me incomprehensible. Maybe Poptún would be better, I tried to console myself.

What have I done? The question ricocheted in my mind. My contract was for three years. The reality of my commitment dawned on me in this sweltering bus, as I smashed along in profound discomfort toward a town I did not know, among strangers I couldn't understand. The words from orientation in New York...*sharing my abilities...witnessing my faith...*seemed unreal to me now. How could I accomplish anything when it took all my energy to breathe? This was no two-week vacation.

I could not head home after enjoying the tourist spots. The task before me seemed insurmountable.

The bus ride lasted five hours. I felt like I'd gone from one world to another. The sky had darkened and the lights of the town beckoned when we arrived in Poptún.

CHAPTER 2

SETTLING IN
AT THE MISSION
IN POPTÚN

1977

My behind was numb when I stepped stiff-legged off the bus. Maryknoll brother John Blazo (right) met us. His spectacles gleamed in the dark and I felt his warm greeting.

"Welcome to the Petén! Glad youse finally made it," John said in his Bronx accent. He grabbed our bags and limped toward the Toyota jeep. The limp had been caused by polio, but he never let it stop him.

"You're gonna love it here." He grinned. "Everybody's

sick!"

Lights shone from individual houses, but there were no other lights. Poptún had the same unpaved streets as the road we had just survived.

"Good to see you Fern. Maria Dolores and Mo are at a course in La Libertad," John went on. "They should be back in a couple of days."

"Where's Fay?" I asked.

"At the house waiting for you," he replied.

"Everybody's been asking for you, Fern," John said. "And guess what? We have a new cook! Her name's Betty. Really cute. She's not too bad...a cook, I mean. She makes spaghetti."

"Is it good?" I interrupted, perking up. Growing up Italian, food was very important to me, especially Italian food.

"Well, not bad." The way he said it made me doubt Betty's cooking abilities.

"Are you Italian, John?" I asked.

"Part," he said. "The other part's Polish."

Along the road, chickens pecked, and we barely missed hitting the horns of a cow lumbering by. Some soldiers carrying guns stumbled past as if drunk.

We stopped at a bulky wooden gate. John jumped out and swung it open. It dragged on the ground. He carried it to the side, then climbed back in the jeep. Once we were through, he jumped out and shut the barrier again. Nothing in this country seemed simple. At the U-shaped rectory, a light from the kitchen illuminated Fay running toward me.

I realized I had been feeling alone. Now that disappeared. Here was a familiar, loved face. "Fay," I said and hugged her.

"Oh Lizzie, I'm so glad you're here." Her fine features were animated. Arm in arm, we entered the dining room. "Are you hungry?" she asked. "We saved you some dinner."

The dining room had no windows. A single bulb cast shadows on the walls. On the table a plate of greasy scrambled eggs mixed with something green would have been unappetizing even if I'd been hungry. One of the rolls was moldy. The air smelled like a garbage dump. Maybe I was lucky the heat and long ride had left me no appetite.

"I'll show you where we'll live, Lizzie," Fay said.

We crossed to the old convent. A horse munched grass by the light of the moon. The silhouette of a well appeared. A tapestry of stars blinked across the black sky. I had never seen so many. They appeared so close, I might have been walking among them. When we stepped into the convent, I was at once aware of its musty smell. Our footsteps echoed on the tile, which felt gritty underfoot. Fay led with her flashlight and showed me my room across the hall from hers.

"It's full of termites, Lizzie, and needs painting, but we can fix it up. I'm buying a Guatemalan bedspread as soon as I go to the city. It'll be neat. I'm going to paint the walls yellow and white. Will you help?"

"Yeah, sure," I replied, feeling like my body was here, but my mind was viewing all this from a distance.

My room could use painting, too. The floor tile needed a wax job. Faded wood covered the top half of the walls. The bottom was mahogany, with a chewed-on appearance. Below those spots termite shavings mounded.

Painting would help, but what about the termites?

I left my suitcases on the floor and slipped into my nightgown, then sank into the bed Fay had made for me. The rough cotton sheets were too short to cover the mattress. It smelled of mold and the tufts dug into my back. The stiff blanket had the consistency of cardboard.

I couldn't sleep right away. The mustiness made my nose itch and I sneezed three times in a row. I thought back to my home in Seattle, and the chain of events leading to this moment.

Fay (left) and I met in 1974, when both of us were attending the University of Washington. Though she was a nursing student and I was a graduate student in the nurse practitioner program at the same school, we were both already in our mid-30s. I'd been nursing for eleven years, in all sorts of positions, including being in the Army Nurse Corps in Korea. When Fay and I met, I was working in the emergency room at University Hospital, which was at that time a major trauma center.

Prior to graduate school, I had experienced a spiritual crisis and didn't like my lack of purpose. I was a "cradle

Catholic," i.e. born into a Catholic family, but I'd never developed a personal relationship with God until then. My spiritual quest revealed to me that I'd been hungering for a deeper purpose for my life. Dreams of adventure and a life of giving myself to others struggled to surface. I didn't know what I wanted to do exactly but knew there could be more to life.

When I was growing up and reading voraciously, I devoured every book I could get my hands on about nurses in the boondocks. I longed to do something similar some day. But I never had. Now, fired by my spiritual awakening and my closer relationship with God, I dreamed of doing something special.

No one at school knew of this desire of mine. I hardly knew it myself. It was so unclear, what I wanted to do.

One day, I sat in my advisor's office, discussing my thesis.

"Liz, have you ever thought of working overseas after you graduate? There's a nursing student I think you should meet. She babysits for me. She has connections with missionaries in Africa, and I think she plans on going there herself. Would you like her phone number?"

"Yes, please," I said. I felt so excited that I could hardly wait to get home that night to call the student she had mentioned, Fay Hauer. Although overseas work appealed to me, I was reluctant to go anywhere alone. I longed for someone to go with.

A door opened for me when I met Fay. We had much in common. Both of us had grown up with traditional Catholic values. We were the same age, and above all, we wanted to work in the third world. At the time I met her, Fay was still a nun in the religious order of the Holy Name Sisters in Seattle. She was an experienced teacher and in her final year of nursing school.

Fay, I soon found out, was a "character." Our friendship

grew rapidly. She was a pretty, tall, slim woman of 34, with a mobile, expressive face. She was always fighting for some cause or another. With Fay there was no chance of avoiding the limelight. She persuaded me to speak before groups, soliciting funds for a woman doctor from Seattle who worked in Vietnam, Dr. Pat Smith. Fay helped me shed a few inhibitions in speaking to all kinds of groups.

Cynthia, my advisor, had been mistaken though. Instead of Africa, Fay planned to go to Vietnam and help Dr. Pat when she finished nursing school. Dr. Pat was famous for years of work with the Montagnard tribe in the Vietnam highlands. I joined Fay in fundraising activities for Dr. Pat's work. Fay introduced me to another friend of hers, Mark Kirsch, also a nurse. The three of us met often, and mostly we talked about overseas work.

Living in a third world country seemed adventurous and exciting. That it would be difficult, hardly entered my mind—like a teenager who dreams of romance and doesn't know the reality of marriage.

I prayed, read the Bible, talked with the pastor of my church, and agonized. Finally, I decided to go with Fay and Mark to Vietnam, which was still very much a war zone.

The only hurdles left for me were finishing school and telling my family. My only sibling, my sister Angie, was married and had three sons. She thought it was a wild idea, but gave her full support, because a part of her wanted an adventurous life too. I knew my mother would never understand. An Italian from the old country, she thought unmarried daughters belonged at home. They were supposed to care for their mothers, even if that mother was able to care for herself. And typical of many daughters of Italian mothers, I had never quite cut the apron strings. I dreaded telling her. My mother was formidable when it came to me leaving to go anywhere. I was right. She didn't understand, or accept. But my decision was firm. In spite of disapproval from her and guilt at leaving my mother, I knew this was what I had to do. Nothing had ever seemed so right for me. I was very excited about this new life I would be entering.

Our plans were to leave for Vietnam in June of 1975. In April, Vietnam fell to the Viet Cong, and Dr. Pat left Vietnam and returned to Seattle. We were very disappointed, but determined to find another way to follow our dreams. During the following year we explored other possibilities for work. Dr. Pat told us she might find work in Guatemala. We wanted to work with her. We had to find a way to go there too. We contacted every missionary and humanitarian organization we could think of, from the Catholic Medical Mission Board to Medico.

During that time, I received Maryknoll Magazine, published by the Catholic Foreign Mission Society of America. Every month I poured over pictures of missionaries in faraway places. Someone told me there was a Maryknoll House in Seattle, where Maryknoll priests stayed who did mission promotion and fundraising work. We lost no time in contacting the priests there. I was tremendously impressed by the ones we met, Fr. Dick Clifford, and Fr. Jim Connell. Fr. Dick told us about a new program Maryknoll was starting for lay people, that is people who were not priests, religious brothers or nuns.

"Why don't you write?" Fr. Dick suggested.

So we did. A letter came back saying that although Maryknoll was starting such a program, it was in the beginning stages, and there was no place for us. Undaunted, we met again with Fr. Dick and Fr. Jim at the house in Seattle.

Surely Maryknoll had a place for us somewhere.

Maryknoll seemed an ideal organization, not only because of its goals and work, but because it took care of its people.

I wanted nothing to do with groups that sent missionaries to some isolated post to fend for themselves. Too often I had learned, these missionaries returned ahead of schedule, often ill, disillusioned, and having accomplished little, if anything.

Fr. Dick and Fr. Jim suggested we write to the regional superiors in each area of the world where Maryknoll had missionaries. Maybe someone, somewhere, had a job.

Fay, Mark and I each took the names of two regional superiors. I wrote to the superiors of Africa and Central America. The only positive reply came from Fr. Ronald Hennessey, regional superior of Maryknoll in Central America. He proposed two possibilities, one in El Salvador, and another in the Petén, the jungle area of Guatemala. He promised he'd speak to priests in those areas.

In the end, **Fr. Maurice Healy** (left) in Guatemala wound up saying yes. He wanted nurses for work in the Petén, although three were more than he'd asked for. We notified Maryknoll at their headquarters in Westchester County, New York. We had found ourselves a job.

A long process followed. I got recommendations from co-workers, and my pastor, Fr. Joe Kramis. We had physical exams, psychological testing and an interview with a psychiatrist. I was afraid they'd refuse me, because everything I saw on the Rorschach ink blot test seemed sexually suggestive. Despite all my travels and experiences in nursing, nothing in my life so far had spoken to my spiritual quest to be of service. I remember the plane ride to New York, and thinking that at the age of 35, my life was just beginning.

Being at Maryknoll, New York, for three and one half

months, with so many interesting priests, brothers and nuns
who had worked in China, Tanzania or Peru, was a stimulating
time of orientation and reflection. The final decision of whether
we would go or not was made jointly between the program
directors and we lay people. *Yes*, I would go to Guatemala!

From New York, we flew to Cochabamba, Bolivia
where Maryknoll ran a world-renowned language school. I
studied Spanish for almost six months along with Fay and
Mark and others from our lay mission group. One-on-one
classes took half a day. Then I listened to tapes until 4 or 5 p.m.
I lived with a middle–class Cochabamban family for the first
months and then moved in with a lay mission couple, Tom and
Chris Amato. By the time I left Bolivia, I was proud of how
easily I'd learned Spanish and enjoyed what I thought was a
proficiency in the language. For some reason, I didn't suffer
much from culture shock in Bolivia. Maybe because I didn't
have to stay there, it was Guatemala I was heading toward.

The last month in Bolivia, when I lived with Tom and
Chris, I discovered a little of what it really meant to live in
Latin America. Before, I had been insulated from daily
realities, such as flies on the meat at the market. We cooked our
own food and had trouble making the oven work. The toilet
wouldn't flush and the house was full of ants, but we loved the
challenge of being on our own.

Fay and Mark and I exchanged letters with Fr. Healy.
Fr. Healy was a progressive thinking priest unafraid to start
something new. His vision was to start a training program for
lay people who were the church leaders. He wanted a team
approach to minister to the immense educational, spiritual and
health needs of the people. He told us about the Petén, in
Northern Guatemala. It was less populated than other parts of
the country, with a wild jungle terrain and climate and far from
everything. Fr. Fern Gosselin had begun a Maryknoll mission
there one year before. Although Fr. Healy described it, I
couldn't imagine what it would be like. I had traveled all over

the States, to Europe, Korea, and Argentina where my mother's family had emigrated, but nothing could have prepared me for the Petén.

Lying on my lumpy bed, it felt unreal to be in Guatemala. But that bus ride today had been all too real and wretched. This was going to be a hard place to live. And I hoped all the food wouldn't be like what I'd sampled earlier.

The night had cooled. Motorcycles roared past on Fay's side of the building, where her room faced the street. I wondered how I was going to like staying in a convent. I had hated the one at Maryknoll, New York, and briefly in Cochabamba, Bolivia where I felt obliged to greet others even on the way to the bathroom. As far as I was concerned, convents had too many rules.

Through my open window came the chirp of crickets. How would I light the kerosene lamp on the bedside stand if I had to go to the john? I'd find matches and buy a flashlight tomorrow. Fay and I were alone here. The facility reminded me of a dingy warehouse. Scurrying sounds across the room made me sit up and yell across the hall. "What're those noises, Fay? A rat?"

"No, they're just *cucarachas*. They won't bite."

I shuddered and tried not to think of cockroaches I had seen in Hawaii, huge black bugs that loved dirty places. There weren't any cockroaches in Seattle.

What would Mama do if she could see this place? I remembered our good-bye and how upset she'd been. Maybe she was right and coming here had been a mistake. I felt homesick. Maybe a letter would come soon. Here, I knew no one except Fay.

Lord, what have I *done*, I wondered for the millionth time that day. In spite of my anxiety of what the next years might be like, I finally slept deeply through the night.

In the morning I woke up refreshed—to the sounds of roosters crowing, dogs barking and trucks rumbling past the convent.

CHAPTER 3

JUNGLE LIFE IN POPTÚN, POP. 6,000

1977

The next weeks I felt as though I was being smothered. Humidity hugged me like a moist blanket. The smell of rotted vegetation hung in the air, as strong as an open garbage can. Sweat gathered on my upper lip and neck, trickling from my underarms, down my back, and into my jeans. I'd always been an active person, but couldn't get myself going. I complained of being tired, and took naps during the day.

I felt as only a person who's entered a new culture feels,

that devastating sense of being surrounded by others, yet
suffering alone. I missed Kay, a fellow student with whom I
had become close during orientation at Maryknoll, New York.
Her father had died while we were studying Spanish in Bolivia.
She wouldn't come to Poptún for another month, which
seemed like a year away.

Every day, I waited for mail to soothe the loneliness.
Nothing came for weeks. I felt forgotten by my friends and
family. I'd regressed to an elemental level of neediness.

The postal system was unbelievable; letters accumulated
in piles and when they became huge, mail was simply
discarded. I warned people not to send gifts, as I'd heard they
never arrived. Friends sent my favorite Estee Lauder perfume
for my birthday in 1977. It arrived in 1978.

I'd been proud of how fast I'd picked up Spanish in
language school. Here in Poptún though, locals stared in
confusion every time I opened my mouth. I constantly repeated
myself. *Peteneros*, people from the Petén, slurred the last
syllable. I was forever saying, *"Como?"* or *"Repite, por favor."*

At night, I gingerly lay down to sleep in my cockroach-
infested room, which was littered with termite shavings no
matter how many times I swept them up. The floor-to-ceiling
closet smelled like a dank cave. I was afraid termites would get
into my clothes so I kept them in my suitcase, like a guest who
wasn't staying long.

The convent faced the street on one side. Motorcycles
roared, children yelled and cargo trucks rumbled past at all
hours. My apartment in Seattle had been quiet. It took getting
used to, this noisy town.

The rectory, where the priests and brothers stayed, a one-
story U-shaped building, was a quick walk across the grass
from the convent. Church records were kept in the office.
People from town and the *aldeas,* the small villages, came to
schedule marriages and baptisms or just talk with Fern, John
Blazo, Fr. Healy or John Fay, another Maryknoll priest. Next to

the office was a small receiving area where people could wait. Following the U around the corner was the dark dining room, the *comedor*. Fr. Healy and John Blazo had bedrooms on that side; John Fay and Fern had rooms on the *sala*, dining room side. Two bathrooms with rust stains in the shower stall flanked John Fay's room.

Globs of grease smudged the kitchen walls. A hot plate was sticky to the touch. There was no oven or stove. Stained curtains drooped from the lone window. The edges curled up from someone repeatedly pulling them aside to glance out to the road. I vowed to sew curtains if I could make the treadle machine function.

I feared the *agua potable*, the drinking water, reputed to be swimming with parasites, so I spent a lot of time boiling water to sustain my coffee-drinking habit.

Betty, our cook, was a girl with sad, puppy dog eyes and warm ways. She was often depressed. Her baby's father, to whom she was not married, must not have treated her kindly, because tears welled when anyone mentioned his name. Her

From left, back row: Maria Dolores, Fay, Mo, Fern, Tox, Kay; seated: Betty, John Blazo

cooking reflected her moods. I'll never forget one soup she made. Overcooked greens and a few lonely hard-boiled eggs bobbing in broth. And I hated her spaghetti sauce: watered-down tomato paste. Ugh! I couldn't believe John Blazo when he said, "*Aye...Betty, que rico,* how delicious!"

Bugs and insects jumped everywhere. At night, cockroaches scurried over dishes in the sink. When I opened the refrigerator, they leapt out. Sometimes at night I felt something crawling and woke up screaming. In the morning, smashed innards stained my sheets. I stored a broom behind the bedroom door and when a cockroach skittered across the floor, I'd crush it as hard as I could.

And the ants! They made their home in the dining room, swarming on the honey jar in large alive spots.

For meals, Betty set the table ahead of time. Ants whizzed over the plates and glasses. In desperation, I scrubbed the tablecloth, only succeeding in making the pattern fade. The ants remained. They also lived in the cupboard. I talked the ant problem over with anyone who would listen. But no one was as bothered by them as I.

"I hate those ants crawling on the bread," I said to John Blazo one day. "Isn't there anything we can do?"

"Well, they don't do any *harm*." Then, seeing my appalled look, John continued, "I heard of putting dishes of water under the cabinet legs. *Theoretically*, they can't climb up."

"Hmmm, I'll try. Could you help?"

"Anything for one of our lay missioners." He grinned. Poor John. He had a job keeping us happy in those early days.

I removed everything from the cabinet, scrubbed and replaced them. John lifted while I slid dishes of water under each cabinet leg. That night when I checked, there were just as many ants racing around. I gave up, but wrote a poem and hung it in the dining room.

ANTS, ANTS, ANTS
I have a tale to tell
Of a house and people known well.
They had in their kitchen
Some things I won't mention.
Would you believe—their roaches were never in need?
The refri was their main feed!
And I am told as well
That the ants rushed around pell mell,
Why, I even heard one day
Of a tale told to me by Kay
That she baked a cake
And failed to take
All the bugs and ants out first!
By then they had died of thirst!
If you should chance to be
In that house in Poptún for tea
Don't be too alarmed—
Even tho you've been fully warned—
You may find in the sugar jar-
More ants than you've seen by far.
Ants, ants, ants
The only place they're **NOT**
Is in my pants.

As long as I lived there, I always shook the ants off the plates first before eating.

Ants weren't the only nuisance. The old refrigerator functioned on kerosene. Every month, Fr. Maurice Healy stretched his long torso on the floor and refilled the tray underneath with kerosene. "Friggin' tray," he complained, as he maneuvered his long arms in a working position.

"Everyone calls me Mo," Father Healy told me when I first met him. It was easy to call him that, an over-six-foot

string of a man with a weird sense of humor and irreverent attitude.

The refrigerator door wouldn't stay closed, so **Mo** (left) and Fern soldered a belt to the sides. Opening the door required wrapping one's arms around the refrigerator to unhook the buckle. Usually the buckle clanged to the floor while I hugged the refrigerator to bring the ends together. The struggle probably wasn't worth the effort as it never kept things cold. My attempt at making jell-o turned to slosh.

Fay and I had the convent to ourselves those first days, until Sister Maria Dolores Cheng returned from teaching a course with Mo. Maria Dolores and I shared a bathroom. She had taught school in San Marcos, Guatemala, but took a leave from her community to follow her dream of becoming a missionary, then shed her nun's habit and was experimenting with clothes and hairdos.

The convent was a dour building with long empty hallways and dark rooms. When it rained, the sound on the corrugated tin roof was like tapping shoes that in time soothed me. Eventually I planted philodendrons and other plants in clay pots and lined them up on the outside patio. I've never had a green thumb, but everything grew so speedily and luxuriously that I had to cut shoots and transplant them.

There were four bedrooms with tall ceilings and offices where Mo's team planned classes. Later on, Fay and I used one room for our office and pharmacy.

I scrubbed the toilet with the brush I bought in the

mercado, poured down bottles of bleach, but the rusty stains stayed. I never sat on there for long, afraid the cockroaches in the floor drain would jump on me.

We had no hot water. After a few shocks of stepping into the cold shower I decided this was one discomfort I wouldn't tolerate. I began boiling water in the kettle for a sponge bath, then washed my hair in rainwater which drained from the gutters into the *pila*, a huge outdoor sink. When I saw the worms, leaves and dirt floating in the pila, I hesitated to shampoo there, but the rainwater made my hair soft and curly. After a while, I scooped out most of the debris, bent over the pila and poured the cold liquid over my head, which never failed to send shivers down my body.

The pila was a marvelous invention, a concrete laundry tub, but much grander, with a washboard surface in the center, ideal for scrubbing.We had no washing machine! You could always tell when we'd returned from an aldea trip by the basins in the pila, ringed with scummy soap, soaking muddy jeans and grimy t-shirts. After we began staying in the aldeas, no one had time to wash clothes, which took several hours. John Blazo hired Doña Hortensia, a sweet and pious widow to do laundry.

One day I handed Doña Hortensia my best jeans, filthy after I'd slid down a muddy hill in the aldeas. *"Se puede quitar estas manchas?* Can you remove these marks?" I asked.

"Como no, Seño Liz, no se preocupa, Sure señorita Liz, don't worry." said Doña Hortensia with her sincere smile. She soaked them first in a plastic basin, scrubbed them with a coarse brush, rinsed them repeatedly and laid them to dry on the grass. I didn't see her remove the grass stains by dousing them with bleach, leaving big white splotches. I was relieved when Doña Hortensia started teaching first communion classes and John Blazo hired young Marina, a less dangerous laundress.

Doña Hortensia stacked everyone's clean clothes on the dining room table. She ironed and meticulously folded Fern's clothes, who was the pastor in Poptún. The other men's laundry were folded neatly but never ironed. The women's clothing she rammed into a pillowcase.

One morning, I awakened at five, as usual. No one else was up. I stepped across the dewy grass to the rectory, filled the kettle to heat on the hot plate and made a cup of Nescafe. Then I slipped into the chapel. The place was termite-infested. Someone had tried to disguise holes in the wall with weavings and bright red floor cushions, but the place stank of mold.

I liked to read and pray before starting my routine. In a few minutes, I returned to the kitchen. The kettle was empty.

"Who stole my bath water!" I hollered.

From his room on the patio, John Blazo yelled, "Don't get mad. I thought it was for the Thermos," he confessed. "I'll boil some right away, OK?" Poor John. I got upset about everything those first months.

Until I lived in Poptún, I never knew I was such a private person. My room overlooked the patio. People stood under my window and peered in. Even after I sewed curtains, someone might pause there and try to see in when the breeze lifted the curtain.

Mo, Fern, John Blazo and John Fay had lived in Central America for years. They no longer noticed things that were driving Fay and me crazy. Once we started aldea trips, Fay and I didn't care much either, but in those first months, everything annoyed me.

I agreed with Fay who pronounced, "Just because we're supposed to live a simple life doesn't mean it has to be ugly!"

I felt guilty, though. Part of me argued I shouldn't bother with material things. My other self was outraged by the ugliness.

Fay and I painted her room, then mine. I liked my new curtains and the fresh yellow and aqua paint on the walls. I bought frames in the mercado, and hung pictures of my family and friends. We attacked the rectory next, assuming everyone would welcome our efforts. With all the white paint available in Poptún, we swabbed the kitchen and dining room cupboards. Soon we ran out of paint, but there was still a lot to do. But at least painting made me feel I had accomplished something.

One day, Fern returned from a long aldea trip and had to step around us while we painted cupboards on the patio. "Should be working instead of wasting time painting," he muttered.

Fay, if she heard, said nothing. He had his nerve, I seethed. Weren't we making this dump look better?

I did like our yard, a fenced, two-acre compound. A carpet of apple-green grass reached to my knees, under the orange, lemon and grapefruit trees. After Brother Leon joined the community, he picked oranges from our trees daily and squeezed the sweetest juice I've ever tasted. Papaya bushes sprouted along the patio at the rectory (above and right). Across the yard was a slumping storage shed and the *champa*, a gazebo with a thatched roof.

Enrique, whom Mo nicknamed "Henry the Horse,"

tethered his horse on our grounds. Henry's horse was our lawnmower. One night, I rushed from the convent and smacked into Henry's horse. I'm afraid of most animals, so I leaped back and stumbled. Fresh manure squished around my thongs onto my toes. From then on, I trod cautiously and carried a flashlight.

Poptún's electric plant was frequently on the blink. Sometimes, in the middle of some project like sewing, the lights faltered then flicked off. Then the men cranked up our generator. Usually, when the town lights went off at nine, we went to bed.

We kept lamps, flashlights and candles in our rooms for those frequent times when the electricity failed. I often felt lonely in my room, so would don my housecoat and speed across the grass to "the guys' house," sit on the mahogany bench outside the kitchen and read or write letters home. Fern played tapes of Johnny Cash, Merle Haggard or Willie Nelson, or picked sad country tunes on his guitar.

We women tried using our hair dryers, bought an iron and pressed clothing at the convent, shorting the electricity and irritating the guys no end.

Poptún was unlike any pictures of jungles I had ever imagined, except for banana palms in people's yards; purple plumeria and lilies thrived without care. Poinsettia bushes climbed roof high. Surrounded by pine-covered hills, the town

was home to 6,000 people and rose from a plateau. To me,
Poptún resembled Dodge City, 1850. Wood buildings had been
put up in a hurry. Men rode horses or mules. Pigs, cows and
chickens grazed along the streets. Bicycles and noisy
motorcycles churned up the dust. Eventually, I bought a bicycle
and found the level roads ideal.

A huge primitive outdoor laundry (*pila*) area sprawled
along the creek near the bridge in the middle of town (below).
Women congregated there to gossip, scrub clothes and lay
things out to dry on the grass.

Most people were Ladino, the mixed race of Guatemalans
descended from the Mayan Indians and Europeans. A few were
Kek'chi and Maya Mopan families, Indian groups who had
long lived in the Petén.

I liked walking to the mercado, the most lively place to
visit. During the rainy season, it was like shopping in mud
puddles. Paths were slippery and even inside the low concrete
building, aisles were pure mud. The place smelled of herbs,
flowers and slaughtered meat. Stalls on the outside sold

everything from rope hammocks to boots. There in Poptún's mercado, I finally bought knee-high black rubber boots. After only a few days in Poptún, I realized my leather shoes were useless and switched to blue, rubber sandals. My leather shoes gathered mold and rotted. I threw them out when I left.

On the outskirts, beyond camouflaging pines, lurked the town's reason for existence, a large military base (shown below is the airstrip). Soldiers patrolled with guns cocked. They carelessly waved their weapons and provoked the people, fell into drunken heaps and lay there until morning. No one dared say a word to them, no matter how obnoxious they acted. Everyone knew who wielded power in Poptún. Whenever I saw a soldier, I felt fear.

Like any military town, Poptún had prostitutes. They were checked monthly at Poptún's community hospital clinic for sexually transmitted diseases. This way of life was accepted as a matter of fact.

Two blocks from the convent, the Catholic church—Parroquia San Pedro Martir—dominated the skyline with two tall spires. (The church is pictured on the next page.) Someone had painted its stucco exterior a dour black and gray. Cows grazed in front; we had to shoo them away and step around manure piles before entering.

Besides painting and sewing curtains, we soon began advising the sick who came to us for medical help. (The girl

below was suffering from anemia, probably caused by worms.) Fay and I also visited the Poptún hospital daily to get to know the local medical staff. The first time, I fled in a hurry, completely overwhelmed by the cockroaches, dingy bed-sheets, the stink of urine, garbage and death.

Children with measles mingled in the same room as kids with no contagious disease.

Bored nurses sat idle. No one hurried like in American hospitals. I had been a nurse for 14 years, but I had to force myself to visit there every day. Several children lingered on the verge of dying, yet an air of indifference pervaded. I returned to the convent in despair. Everything needed changing, but how could Fay and I do it all?

We met Dr. Zepeda, a teddy-bear type of man who ignored our derogatory remarks about the hospital and patiently taught us about diseases like leishmaniasis, a skin ulcer caused by flies. Children with the bloated abdomens of malnutrition, listless with anemia, saddened us terribly. Nothing was done for them except a dose of worm medicine and vitamin shots, when what they needed was clean water and a decent diet.

Some scabbed spots were spreading on my skin, making me scratch, especially at night. I asked Dr. Zepeda, "What is this rash? It's driving me crazy. It's so itchy."

"*Es la sarna*," he said, matter-of-factly. If he was surprised I had scabies, he didn't show it. But I was ashamed, as I assumed only "dirty" people got scabies. Now I know the disease spreads by close contact from others with scabies. The mite burrows, lays its eggs and multiplies under the skin.

One day, a family came to the rectory with a seven-month-old infant who weighed seven pounds. She resembled a skeleton more than a baby, her skin tightened like an old woman's.

Fay and I rushed her to the hospital where the admitting doctor stared at her and said, "It's too late. We have to save the bed for someone we can help."

There were plenty of beds in the hospital, just no money to care for the sick. The cruel fact of life here was that there were no such things as health insurance or charity wards, and all patients were expected to pay for their own treatment, including IVs and x-ray plates. Despite being in Guatemala as part of a Catholic mission, we had no money in our budget for such things.

"But you *must* admit her," I pleaded, close to tears.

"She *has* to have IV fluids," Fay said in such a way that hardly anyone could refuse her.

We argued a few minutes. "I guess we could bring her in for a day," the doctor finally said, with little enthusiasm. People said he was an alcoholic, put in charge of the hospital because of his influential family. People didn't gain position through their expertise, but by whom they knew.

Prior to Maryknoll, I'd worked six years in an emergency room where we tried everything to save lives. To me, this attitude in medical care was incomprehensible.

Walking back to the convent, Fay and I were still upset. "I can't believe he resisted admitting her," I said.

"He just didn't care!" Fay cried.

But in one way he'd been right. "She probably won't make it," I said, "but we couldn't just let her die, could we?"

We looked at each other, too sad for more words. We were learning a grim lesson; we had to cut our losses and accept certain realities.

Our powerlessness was becoming clear. By insisting, we might help a few people. The system was terrible. People from rural villages (*aldeas*) were ignored, as they waited patiently for hours outside the hospital, resigned to their fate. Middle-class Ladinos in town got immediate care. Those with money went to the doctors with private practices, but the poorest people had no healthcare. This lack of respect toward the poor made me want to protect those powerless people.

We would need the services of this facility in the future, no matter how incompetent we deemed it. We must not make enemies.

I hated how the poorest were treated, particularly the **Kek'chi**, the largest group of Mayans in the Petén. (The child at right was suffereing from malnutrition). Most spoke no Spanish and were illiterate. The Kek'chi and poor Ladinos

traveled for hours, sometimes days, spending most of their money on bus fare to Poptún. They came only after trying the *curandero's* remedies, the witch doctor. Usually the trip was too late. So they thought of the hospital as a place to die.

The doctors and nurses could have asked a woman who worked in the hospital kitchen that spoke Kek'chi to translate but rarely did. Instead, they pointed to body parts and guessed what was wrong with a patient. I didn't blame the poor for distrusting the hospital and coming to see us first.

Fay and I visited the baby every day and watched her deteriorate. Each time I saw her, helpless anger grew within me.

Getting used to the hospital and health care system weren't the only adjustments. The group I lived with was as varied as riders on a train, though we were bound for the same destination. We represented different countries, lifestyles and theologies.

CAST OF CHARACTERS

To help readers keep track of the people in my story, here's a bit of information about each of us, along with our ages at the time my adventures began.

Liz Desimone (Elizabeth), 35. Seattle, WA. The author. Short-statured coffee drinker and giggler.

Fay Hauer, 35, Spokane, WA. Tall, slim, animal lover and champion of the underdog.

Kay Studer, 37, Wesley, Iowa. Warm brown eyes, skilled at listening, haircutting and cooking.

Mo Healy (Father Maurice Healy), 45, Long Island, NY. Tall, thin, loves tobasco sauce on everything and corny sayings.

Fern Gosselin (Father Fernand Gosselin), 34, Newport, VT. Twinkling eyes, loves onion sandwiches, tinkering with machines and playing guitar.

John Fay (Father John Fay), 55, Massachusetts. Thick white hair, loves peanut butter and the Bible.

John Blazo (Brother John Blazo), 32, the Bronx, NY. Limp from childhood polio never stops him, hospitality plus.

Maria Dolores Cheng, 37, Santa Lucia Cotzumalguapa, Guatemala. Irreverent humor, raucous laugh and a comic strip artist.

Pastora Lira, 28, Ocotal, Nicaragua. Petite, calm and good with children.

Leon Cook (Brother Leon Cook), 59, Michigan. Balding, humble, and a butterfly and insect collector.

Tox, (Salvador Tzi Bác), 17. Chacté, Petén. Quiet charmer, with intelligence and potential.

Lico Retana, 26, Poptún, Petén. Come-hither smile and the zeal of a missionary.

Carmen Ché, 15, Tanjoc, Petén. Shy Kek'chi girl in our first class of promoters.

I had never been around "religious" folks daily. The talk at meals frustrated me. Usually, John Blazo or Mo dominated the conversation and they usually talked about the weather or how many people had attended mass. I longed to complain about mission life, but was embarrassed. No one seemed to be having the trouble I was. At least no one else admitted it.

I loved to express my feelings, yet the others never mentioned feelings. I expected us to be close, but we were only acquaintances.

At Maryknoll, New York, we students had spent hours talking about community. No one told us when a community jelled; it was unplanned, a deep connection between persons with like minds. No one mentioned that unrealistic expectations could destroy it. I wanted to celebrate mass together. These men prayed privately, and said mass for the people of Poptún; there was no separate mass for us.

For both Fay and I, our idea of being missionaries was to minister to the poor with healthcare, not to proselytize for Catholicism. Happily, each of the brothers and priests ministered to the people in the way they worked best. Leon with his garden, John Blazo with his friendliness and making everyone feel welcome, Mo with his ability to teach leaders, John Fay through administering the sacraments, and Fern for his caring acts for those in need.

I sensed wariness in the men when they looked at us women, and presumed they disliked us. Whenever I expressed how I felt about something, they changed the subject or suddenly invented an appointment they'd forgotten. I felt rejected and nursed hurt feelings.

Maryknoll sent men to isolated parishes, where they worked alone, like the Lone Ranger, but even he had Tonto. One or two priests might live together, with no women except a cook. It is amazing to me now that it never occurred to me living with men with celibacy vows might be difficult. Priests and brothers vowed to abstain from intimacy with women, not only sexual relations, but even friendship, which might tempt them. Although the men were kind and in many ways thoughtful, they kept their distance. I was frustrated, because these were men with ideals like my own.

In Poptún, I could relate to few people. In time, I grew close to Tox, our seventeen year-old Kek'chi translator, and others, but at first I relied too heavily on these folks at the rectory.

As for "the guys," as I came to call Mo, John Fay, Fern and John Blazo, they weren't prepared for us either. When Mo proposed our coming, they all said yes, never imagining we would expect so much in friendship. Only later did I find out what a shock it was for these men to have women around. We were, after all, the first women to live at the mission. Even

though Fay was great company, this wasn't exactly the close-knit community I'd imagined.

Our motivations were the same, and, in that sense I felt at home as never before. Each of us burned to help people, and felt God had called us to this work.

Later that September, **Kay Studer** (left) arrived from studying Spanish in Huehuetenango. She was like a second sister. Intuitively, when we first met at Maryknoll, New York, I knew ours would be a lifelong friendship. She was a strong woman, intense but very warm. She lived simply years before joining Maryknoll, so our surroundings didn't shock her. We talked about everything for hours in her room, discussing Jungian psychology and analyzing everyone. With so many odd characters in our

community, we had a field day. **Kay** began working with Mo
and Maria Dolores in the leadership program (below).

Meanwhile, Fay and I spent our time planning. What to do
first? What was most important? People arrived daily at the
rectory seeking medical help. We could only offer a diagnosis.
Our job descriptions called for us to start a health promoter
program. Health promoters, or *promotores de salud*, were
villagers trained like mini-doctors. Mo, who had written our
job descriptions, hadn't a clue how to start this new project, nor
did Fay or I. We had no idea how to proceed and there was no
one to tell us, either.

One day we sat down in the sala with John Fay and Fern.
John had worked in Central America for 25 years, saying mass,
administering the sacraments of marriage, communion and
confession in each aldea he visited. We hit it off instantly. He
was quiet and private, but steamed into anger whenever the
poor were treated disrespectfully.

While we talked, Fern took a swig of his favorite bottled
drink, *agua mineral,* carbonated water. "Here in town people
have more medical help than the aldeas," he said in his
thoughtful way.

"If I were you, I'd work in the aldeas," said John Fay, his
Irish blue eyes twinkling. "Harder than here in town, but you'd

be needed more. Come on our next trip. See what it's like."

"There's a lot of programs in the country. Some nuns run one near Santo Tomás. Why don't you visit them?" said Fern.

Fay and I mulled over John Fay's and Fern's suggestions. It was scary to be responsible for developing the whole health program. At the rectory and in the convent, I doubt if we even had some band-aids or aspirin. There was no equipment to examine patients, no medicines, not one single item to stock a clinic or to provide care. We had to start from scratch. First though, we had to educate ourselves on the scope of problems and learn from other missionaries who had started similar programs.

Two weeks after I arrived in Poptún, Mo announced, "I'm going to the city for supplies. You girls wanna come?"

A trip to Guatemala City? Did we!

"We can buy more paint," Fay said with glee.

"Twelve hours if all goes well," Mo said cheerfully.

Still, I looked forward to it. I got a kick out of Mo's sense of humor.

Mo was proud to be from "The Big Apple." He loved reading *The New York Times*, though it arrived a week late. Whenever any of Woody Allen's movies hit town, Mo found an excuse to get to the city. On his return, he entertained us with hilarious descriptions.

He invented names for everyone. For instance, I was titled "Elizabeth of Simon, whither goest thou," a take-off on my last name, Desimone. Fay was dubbed "Faysie," and Fern got stuck with "Fernie Boo, how are you?" When Brother Leon Cook joined our group, Mo called him, "Leon the Seetz." Maybe even Mo didn't know what *that* meant.

Mo repeated corny sayings like *"Otra gran dia en la vida de Ivan Ivanovich,"* which meant, "another great day in the life of Ivan Ivanovich," and "Another biggee." After I'd been in the Petén a while, I knew better what the phrase signified; the sameness of each day, with no entertainment or distractions.

The others in our community rolled their eyes when Mo repeated himself, but I always laughed.

I did thank God I didn't live in the rectory the first time I heard him chant, "Oooooooooooooooooommmmmmmmmmm shhhaaaannntyyy at 5:30 a.m. when he practiced yoga. Then he listened to the English newscast, *"Buenas Dias, America,"* full blast on the radio.

After Mo's invitation, we left for Guatemala City early one September morning, Mo in cut-off jeans, white T-shirt and a straw hat over graying hair.

We lurched along in Mo's broken down green pick-up. I felt happy leaving Poptún.

Although the sun burned us now, rain like a giant faucet had gushed daily from the sky, making the roads into mud soup.

Three hours later, the way ahead became lakes. We grew quiet. I tensed. Mo drove through one huge puddle after another, and cursed as we slammed against the ruts. His swearing had no underlying anger. He sounded, if anything, cheerful. Then, we arrived to water across the whole road. My first thought was, Oh, no! We'll have to go back.

But Mo climbed out and stuck his long legs into high black boots. "I'll see how deep it is," he announced. I giggled, thinking how comical he looked with his hollow-looking stomach and that hat perched on his head like a plate. With the first step, he sank several inches. With each step, he bogged down further. Partway across, he turned and clomped back to the truck.

"We should make it if I don't stop."

Fay and I looked doubtfully at each other. He must have done this before, I reasoned.

Slowly, he drove into the water. I sat by the door, mesmerized by the water sliding around the tires, covering them inch by inch and rising with a soft slap-slap. It seeped into the truck, swirling at our feet. Fay and I removed our shoes and put them on the dash along with our feet. Half-way across, the wheels went THUD.

"Friggin' water!" muttered Mo. He accelerated. A wave of brown sludge splashed over the hood, streaked the windshield and rushed up the door. The engine died.

"****!" said Mo. "Everyone out. Let's push it across."

I had my doubts about how we would escape this mess, but Mo seemed so calm I wasn't afraid. I slipped on the boots I'd bought in the mercado. Fay and I pushed open the door without much water rushing in. We waded into thigh-high murk that resembled crankcase oil.

Some *campesinos,* farmers, miraculously appeared and waded out to us. Funny how in Guatemala, someone always popped up. With six of us pushing, we moved the truck across.

Fay and I giggled to relieve the tension. How amazing we had managed to get out! Mo was unfazed, as if getting stuck happened every day.

He tried to start the truck. It refused to turn over.

"Something must be wet. We'll have to wait till it dries," he said. With that, he disappeared into the bushes.

Deep greenery and tall pines enclosed us. There was not a house to be seen. I wondered what would happen next.

A campesino peered under the hood. He began scraping a wire with a three-inch-wide machete blade. I felt as though I was watching a scene from Abbott and Costello. Where was that Mo!

"My God," said Fay. What was that man trying to do?

Mo appeared, adjusting his pants. He rushed over to the man with the machete. "Hey, wait a minute!" he yelled in English. For the first time, Mo was flustered. He gently took the wire. "*Muchas gracias,*" he said to the man. "I have a pocket knife."

Fay and I couldn't restrain ourselves. Whether we were

reacting from the strain or just getting hysterical, I don't know, but we laughed until tears came. Perhaps the man had tried to scrape a wet spark plug. Who knows? We waited another half hour before Mo could start the truck.

In Guatemala City, we loaded up on paint. I bought a blue bedspread, woven with yellow, red and white designs and enjoyed a warm shower in the Center House.

Mo went to see the Woody Allen movie, *Annie Hall*.

Back in Poptún, we could hardly wait to tell everyone about our 17-hour trip and the 16 gallons of paint we'd bought, but we never got the chance, because John Fay announced, "Fern and I are heading out to the aldeas tomorrow. Wanna come?"

Fay nodded, with her little smile of anticipation.

"Sure," I said. This was our chance to learn what health problems existed in the aldeas. After what we'd just been through, I must have been crazy, but the adventures I'd been dreaming about all my life beckoned.

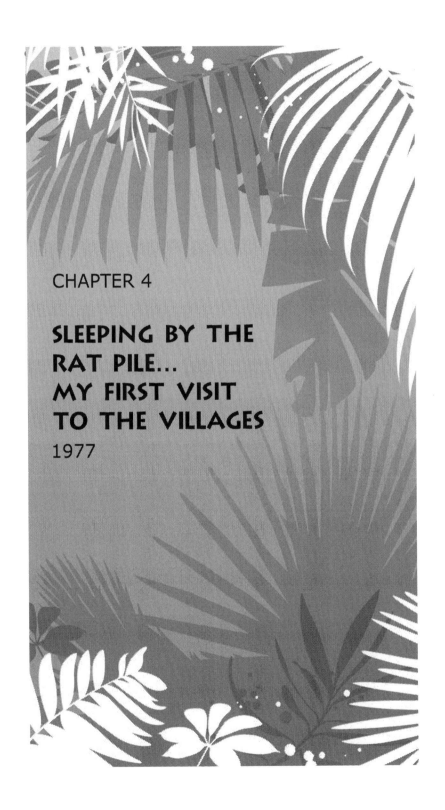

CHAPTER 4

SLEEPING BY THE RAT PILE... MY FIRST VISIT TO THE VILLAGES

1977

We left the next morning, while it was still dark. By dawn the land cruiser was climbing the hills above San Luís, the largest town south of Poptún. Cotton candy clouds puffed across the sky. Jagged rows of corn, broad-leafed palm and banana trees dotted the hills on both sides of the road. We drove past houses of narrow vertical branches and thatched roofs. Barefoot children stared as we passed. Except for an

occasional truck going by, ours was the only vehicle.

Farmers (*campesinos*) trudged up the hill, machetes swinging from their belts. Little boys ran alongside them, carrying red or yellow plastic canteens of water strung over their shoulders.

John Fay drove. Fern rode beside him. Fay and I, seated on the metal seats in back, tried to keep our heads from smacking the roof every time we hit a rut.

"Where are they going?" I leaned forward to ask Fern.

"They're on their way to the *milpa*, corn fields," he said. (above)

I thought of kids in American schools and couldn't help comparing their lives with these kids. (Pictured left is a typical rural school.)

"Why aren't they in school?" Fay wanted

to know.

"Can't afford it. Everyone's needed to make a go of it."
Fern sighed. "Boys get maybe one or two years of school. Girls
don't get sent at all, usually."

"How unfair," said Fay.

A bony chicken squawked as our wheels barely missed it.
Behind us, a cloud of dust lingered above the road where we
had passed.

The strange terrain of the Petén loomed in the distance, as
if a hand had swept through making ice cream cone peaks.

Fern pointed towards the hills. "That may be a Mayan
ruin." It stood out from the rest of the peaks, green to the top,
then a giant finger of granite. The ancient Mayans built altars
on mountains to be closer to the sun god. Many such ruins
studded the hills.

In front of me,
John's snowy mound
of hair rose above his
blue shirt. Even now,
at 55, he was an
attractive man. (**Fern**,
left with **John**, right.)
Every shirt John
owned was blue. They
matched his eyes and
had been given to him
as gifts. John was very
reserved, but on one
subject he expressed
passion: he hated the
military and what it
was doing to the
people.

I admired John. The most expensive items he owned were
second hand; a manual typewriter and his vehicle. He was one

65

of the least materialistic people I knew.

John visited the 25 road aldeas once each month in his white Toyota jeep. They were called the "road aldeas" because they were on the connecting route from Poptún. In some, he stayed overnight, sleeping in his hammock. All he carried was a book-size woven bag, containing his Bible, toothbrush and hammock. I loved hearing his explanations of the readings at mass. He really knew the Bible.

When the Maryknollers came, the people of the Petén were delighted to have a priest visit regularly. Some places had never enjoyed that luxury. When I saw how villagers responded to having a mass in their aldeas, I felt ashamed of my frequent complaints about priests back home whose masses had been boring or with whom I didn't agree. Here, locals attended mass once or twice a year, or whenever a missionary braved the impossible roads. Campesino families whose income averaged $350 a year, could rarely afford the bus fare to town for mass. Many earned even less or nothing at all.

John performed so many marriages, John Blazo dubbed him "Marrying Sam."

From June to January, the roads were muddy ruts. In the dry season, you could choke on the dust. In spite of the miserable conditions, John had only turned around and come home once during the three years I knew him. That was when the bridge to Chinchilá lost half its planks.

John was never late. He went to bed at nine and arose at five. He walked around town for exercise every day. In this culture, everyone was late. The unexpected happened every day. Guatemala was a mañana kind of country, where if a government office was closed when it was supposed to be open, people accepted the inconvenience as part of life. John lived daily the frustration of being an organized man in a disorganized country.

John and Fern enjoyed an easy rapport. Fern, in his role as pastor, occasionally visited the road towns with John. That was why Fern was with us today.

At that time, the Petén had over 90 settlements. Most were tiny hamlets, scattered in an area of nearly 20,000 square miles. People migrated from all over to settle one of the few regions with available land: the Petén.

Once they came however, new settlers found it difficult to obtain land titles, which required several trips to the *municipalidad*, the town hall. Army officers had already confiscated much property.

By mid-morning, we'd arrived at the southeastern boundary of the parish. Los Angeles had nothing in common with Los Angeles, CA, or maybe it did, since both were ugly and polluted. Los Angeles in the Petén lay on a flat, often flooded, green plain. Hordes of mosquitoes assaulted the villagers, bringing deadly malaria.

Few people here owned land. They worked it for large landowners, the Ladino people. The Petén had never been invaded, just settled as time went on.

Los Angeles served as truck stop for vehicles rumbling through with everything from gas to Coca Cola. On each side of the road perched *comedores*—open air diners. Comedores were shacks on stilts, leaning crookedly over the foul water beneath them. Rocks kept the tin roofs from blowing off.

I remember a very big and tall Latina woman who ran one. Fay and I ate lunch at her place one day and were completely disgusted when the woman scratched vigorously at her generous Marilyn Monroe butt just before she served our *arroz con pollo.*

Behind one comedor a long, raised walkway led to an outhouse (left). In a photo Fay took, I'm standing on the walkway, trailing a swatch of toilet paper. It's all too obvious where I'm heading. Below, were festering wetlands and the revolting sight of used toilet paper left by truckers.

Down the road was the Catholic church constructed of poles and branches between two houses. Los Angeles was too poor to afford a real church.

The altar was thick planks covered by blue plastic. In the center, stood a crucifix of Christ, red splotches dripping from the hands and feet. The crucifix was surrounded by yellow candles in coffee jars.

Fay and I watched people gather. Women wore black or white lace mantillas like the one I'd worn in the States before Vatican II in the 1960s. The parishioners brought lilies and purple plumeria, daisies and orchids and tangerine-colored hibiscus in tin cans. The beauty of the flowers made the containers unimportant. Women placed them around the altar, reverently, as if this were a cathedral. They murmured a shy, *"Buenos dias, padres,"* and smiled, happy to see the priests.

That day the catechist's daughter would marry. Catechists are the spiritual leaders of the community. We were invited to the celebration after mass. (Pictured below is a typical aldea altar.)

John sat on a stool by the altar. He bent his head and shielded his face with one hand. A villager circumspectly approached, sat and began whispering in John's ear.

This must be the confessional, unlike those in the States, with their wooden booths, padded kneelers and automatic light. One by one, the villagers went to confession.

Slowly, other people arrived. No one rushed; things flowed easily. Fern listened to the catechist, Don Miguel, voice his concern that so few attended mass and prayer meetings. He told Fern about a man who had deserted his wife and four children, and that parents were upset because the teacher didn't show up at school for weeks at a time.

Fay and I wore jeans, T-shirts, knee socks and rubber thongs. Sensible garb in this humidity. But we didn't fit in with the other women in polyester dresses. Their legs were bare, feet in falling-apart, black rubber shoes. The women and girls had long hair combed with water that shone in wet strands.

After three hours of riding over dusty roads, Fay and I looked like we'd been on a month-long camping trip without soap and water. People stared. I wasn't sure if they were amazed by our short hair, jeans, filth, or all three.

During mass, I couldn't help comparing their garish altar with the prayerful demeanor of the people. They prayed as if the Pope was sitting in their midst. Don Miguel led the singing, holding the only hymn book. Everyone belted out the words, even the littlest child, high-pitched voices strangely in tune. I liked the songs, *"Amar es Entregarse*, Loving is Giving Yourself, and *"Juntos como Hermanos*, Together, like Brothers." There was something sweet and joyful in their singing.

"How do they know so many verses when they're illiterate?" I whispered.

"Memorization, maybe," answered Fay.

During mass, John blessed the couple's marriage and their two children. They'd lived together for years. Now they could afford a wedding ceremony and celebration.

Afterward, the bride's mother, Doña Maria, led Fay and me to the long outdoor table covered by an embroidered cloth.

"Sientese aqui, señoritas...sit here, young ladies," she said, with a beautiful smile that showed her missing front teeth. We'd never met, yet she treated us like honored guests.

The bride and groom sat with their two children. John and Fern flanked them.

The priests were served first. Someone placed a bottle of Coca Cola in front of me and I took a sip. It was hot! I drank it down anyhow. True thirst makes you less particular.

Next came steaming potatoes and meat. The broth tasted like beef stew. I gnawed on a hunk of meat. Finally, I removed it secretly from my mouth. I was horrified to see black hairs sticking out. I laid down my spoon, restraining an impulse to spit, leap from the table and yell yuk. I looked around furtively. Fay grinned as she sipped her Coke.

"*Le gusto el caldo*, did you like the soup?" asked a lady.

"*Es delicioso*," said Fay, "but I have a stomach ache."

John and Fern guzzled the soup. Fern chewed as if this was the best meal he'd ever tasted.

I felt nauseated. "What kind of meat *is* this?"

"Tepiscuintle," Fern said, sucking on a piece of meat. "It's a delicacy. Everyone loves it...looks like a big guinea pig!" His eyes twinkled with a mischievous expression.

Guinea pigs resembled rats to me. I shoved my plate across to him. "Here, have mine too. I ate before I came. I'm very full." I patted my stomach.

Doña Maria nodded, accepting this excuse.

Fern finished his portion and tackled mine.

"*Una comida excelente*," he said, grinning up at the cooks. "An excellent meal."

"*Muy sabroso*," echoed John, "very delicious."

I ate several tortillas while Fern stacked tepiscuintle bones

on his plate. The tortillas were the best I'd ever tasted. Hot, thick and with a gentle corn flavor, they filled me up.

After lunch, I took pictures of the bride and groom with their family. They posed, hands on each other's shoulders, and gazed fixedly at the camera (left).

"Smile...please smile," I pleaded. Their reserve reminded me of photos my mother had of her family in Italy. Exactly the same serious faces.

Later, I photographed people when they were unaware to capture their joyful smiles. They were thrilled after they saw their pictures in the albums Fay and I brought with us every time we visited the aldeas.

After lunch, we headed for the next village. John celebrated mass in all three places we visited, with what seemed like thousands more baptisms and marriages. Fay and I felt exhausted from the heat and humidity and from bumping along the road between aldeas. My nose itched and my nostrils were full of dust.

Fern met with the catechists, men who led the churches in the priests' absence. They held prayer meetings, visited the sick and buried the dead.

Children hung on Fern, eager for attention. He wrestled the boys and teased the girls. People wouldn't leave him alone. But he was at ease, enjoying the company. Except for these occasional visits with John, he worked in aldeas inaccessible by road.

Fern was the first Maryknoll priest assigned to the Petén. He started in San Luís and Dolores near Poptún. Aldea work was perfect for Fern. He liked being with simple people. They were forgotten by everyone; their schools and clinics were empty. Some places hadn't had a priest's visit in years, if ever. Fern traveled on foot, by motorcycle or rode a mule, depending on the roads. Everyone worshiped him because he visited them through all sorts of weather, going where no other priest had ever gone.

He came home after weeks in the aldeas, reeking of sweat, his clothes and motorcycle caked with mud. He didn't talk about his experiences unless asked, but he knew more about the lives of the people, their culture and beliefs, than anyone else on our team.

Aldeas were either Ladino, like Los Angeles, or Kek'chi. The Kek'chi were descendants of the Mayans. The Kek'chi never did surrender to the Spanish conquerors in the 15th century—they were Christianized by the missionary, Bartoleme de las Casas because the Spaniards couldn't penetrate the jungle. In the Petén, although other groups had begun to settle the area, most were Kek'chi.

The Kek'chi fascinated me. I watched them file into church, each man followed by his woman. Almost every woman carried a baby on her back, slung in a woven cloth, (left) which was tied across her forehead, hanging onto her shoulders and down her back. Some girls with babies looked 12 or 13 years old. Men sat on the left side, the women on the right on homemade benches.

The men were under or barely five feet tall, slim and muscular. They dressed in green, blue or purple pants, or white pants made of sugar bags, patched in places. All sported white or colored shirts, and straw cowboy hats, which they removed before entering church. Hats were fashionable in the aldeas, providing protection from the blasting sun. In the interior, men wore no underwear, except for those who lived along the river, whose undershorts served as swimming trunks.

Kek'chi women were natural beauties without a trace of make-up. Full-breasted and slim-hipped, they had a reserved and graceful walk. They skimmed along the ground as if their feet knew the earth. Black hair in thick braids reached to their hips with a bright ribbon wound into the braid and tied in a bow at the end (left). Their faces were strong featured with high cheekbones and skin the color of clear coffee. They watched the world through serene black eyes, seeming unaware of their dignity and grace.

Right away, I noticed the women and the men, too, had an unspoiled appearance. Totally natural.

For mass, the women wore their finest *huipil*, the traditional blouse. The Kek'chi had especially beautiful *huipiles*, made of white, gauzy fabric, which floated above their midriffs. The neck and sleeve edges were embroidered in geometric designs in red and blue and magenta. Under these garments, so fine you could see through them, were cotton blouses of the same style.

The Kek'chi skirt, worn knee length, was yards of woven purple, blue or green plaid, gathered and tied with a string around the waist. The skirt contained enough fabric to do three turns. Dangling silver earrings and strings of silver necklaces sparkled from ears and necks.

Most women and many men went barefoot, their feet wide across the toes and slim at the heels. A few men wore black rubber knee-high boots, like mine. Some women carried flat rubber shoes in their shoulder bags. When they got to church, they slipped them on before entering.

We arrived in Chacté, an aldea of several hundred people, in late afternoon. It must have been well over 100 degrees with humidity to match. The inside of the church was shadowy—lit by the sun filtering through cracks in the wall and the open back door. The church perched on top of the highest hill. Chacté could afford a tin roof and walls of close-fitting wooden boards, but I liked the thatched-roofed churches better. They suited the climate. The tin-roofed building in Chacté would last longer, but it was more uncomfortable than the airy churches.

Confessions dragged on forever, even with both John and Fern hearing them. Children cried and people murmured in a low-pitched hum, the soft guttural tones or glottal pops, almost sung, of the Kek'chi language. Dogs lay in the aisles, fleas jumping on their bodies. Flies feasted on their open sores. Occasionally, a new dog wandered in, and one of the men would mutter and kick at it viciously. The poor dog would go yelping

out the door. Dogs weren't privileged pets in their culture.

Small children, some naked except for a shirt, (far left) sat bare bottomed, munching corn chips, discarding wrappers in the dirt. One little boy without pants peed in front of me. No one but me paid him any mind.

I was astonished to see women openly breastfeeding (left). There was no trace of embarrassment, nor did they attempt to conceal their ample breasts popping out of blouses, as in the U.S. Some continued breastfeeding with the babies sucking vigorously, while the women received communion. At times, a young woman left her whole breast showing, with its large protruding nipple. Older toddlers, still breastfeeding, handled their mother's breast as if it were no more than an appendage, twisting and turning and pulling the nipple until I felt like screaming. This was such a difference in body modesty that I could hardly absorb it. But by the time I'd re-visited the aldeas a second time, this behavior no longer shocked me.

"Do you think we should go to communion again?" I whispered to Fay.

"Maybe it would look funny to the people if we didn't."

"I've never received communion three times in one day

before, have you?"

"No," Fay whispered back. "This could get really old."

I knew what she meant. How repetitious it must be for the priests.

I could hardly breathe in the sweltering church. Would I ever get used to this heat? But there was nowhere to go. For the first time, I felt the burden of being a missionary, expected to endure hardship without complaint. I didn't know if I was up to it. Lord, help me, I prayed.

Mass took longer than usual because it was translated from Spanish to Kek'chi. More baptisms and more marriages followed. Sweat poured down John's forehead while he gave the homily. He wore a white vestment over his clothes, adding to the heat. Poor John. It must have been a sauna up there on the altar.

I noticed a bird with large black wings flying around inside the church. Poor bird, I thought, until I realized it was a bat. Then, before I could think *rabies* it streaked out the crack above the back door.

At the end of mass, Fern smiled at Fay and I and announced, "Today we're very pleased to have with us two *enfermeras*, nurses. They'll be outside after mass. Please ask them anything you want about your illnesses."

People turned to stare, shocked at our attire, as if we'd come from another world, which we had. I tried to smile. Fay and I exchanged looks of dismay.

"I hope they don't ask much. We can't do anything for them now," I muttered. This trip had been to see what the aldeas were like. We hadn't brought medical supplies or medicines because we had none yet.

After mass, we slipped out of church as soon as we could. At least outside I could breathe. But that relief was short-lived because in seconds I was surrounded by people.

A woman held up her infant, pointing to pus-filled scabs covering its body. I had never seen such a severe case of impetigo, a bacterial skin infection.

Before I could help her, another lady shoved a baby into my arms. The baby's skin was shiny and blotched. The eyes were sunken into its head. Pathetic whimpers escaped through its split lips. The child couldn't hold up its head.

A knot formed in my throat and I felt like crying. This baby resembled starving infants in Africa. Except those had been pictures and this one was in my own arms, a mere handful of bones.

I gave the tiny thing back to its mother, and touched her shoulder. We locked eyes and I tried to tell her without words how sorry I was.

More people pressed close to me, "*Seño! Por favor, ayudame!*" Miss! Please help me! What should I do? Oh God! Fay's head stuck up above the mob. She was surrounded by a mass of people begging for her help. Mentally, I was ticking off the supplies and medicines we needed to stock a clinic for these people.

"Fay," I shouted. "These babies. They need medical attention! The mother has no money."

Fay pushed through the crowd and handed me a wad of *quetzales*. I slipped it to the two mothers, but the other people saw me.

"*Aqui, aqui! Seño!*" The sight of the money had inflamed them. They pressed closer, begging me to see their child next. I felt claustrophobic, unaccustomed to people touching me on all sides. Where were Fern and John? I was in a mob scene with no escape.

Finally, people drifted away. Between the two of us we had doled out $25 of our own money.

Now I no longer wondered what we'd do for our job. The question was: how to limit it? Each aldea must have hundreds of needy people like these. We could never care for them all.

At nightfall, we ate supper at Teresa's house, a Ladina lady who owned a store on the road. Afterward, Fern rose quietly. "We're going to the church," he said. "You can spend the night with Teresa."

Fay and I frowned at each other. "Why can't we stay with you?" I blurted.

"I already asked Teresa. She'd feel badly now if you didn't stay." Not looking at us, he left with John. They climbed the hill to the church.

I resented the fact that Fern had decided our sleeping arrangements without asking us. I ached to talk over the day's events. I had so many questions. I'd been shocked by what I saw today. The starving baby and all the sick people kept flashing in my mind. Fay was unusually quiet. I sensed she was as stunned as I.

We set up folding cots and sleeping bags in the store by a pile of corn laid out to dry. The kernels were maroon, pale yellow and white and a deeper golden color. Some were even black. I had thought corn was yellow only. I learned that white corn was preferred because of its pure look, but the others were more nutritious. I slid into my sleeping bag. The night had cooled. The cot was amazingly comfortable.

"Why do you suppose the guys didn't want us up there with them?" I asked Fay.

"Who knows. They're probably afraid for their celibacy." Fay gave a disgusted snort and turned on her side.

"I'm so mad. I don't understand the big deal it would be to stay up there. We needed to talk." We were both quiet.

"Better not tell anybody we gave those people money," I said.

"Yeah, but there was nothing else we could do," Fay said. "Next time we're coming equipped."

I lay in the dark, listening to cars and trucks roaring by. How could I begin to explain all the impressions to anyone who'd never been here? I found myself slipping off to sleep.

I awoke with a start. Scurrying sounds came from the corn pile inches from my cot.

"Fay!" I whispered. "Did you hear that?"

"Yeah!" She sat up. "I bet it's a rat."

"Oh, no," I groaned. "What if one jumps on me?" I huddled there, trying to see the corn pile in the dark, tensed for something to land on me. I'm terrified of rats.

After a long time, my thudding heart slowed, I grew sleepy again and lay down. Minutes after I'd dozed off, I awakened to Teresa's baby crying. The baby fussed the rest of the night.

"I bet those guys are sleeping peacefully up there," muttered Fay.

I lay awake a long time, wishing I could ignore the scratching from the corn pile, the baby crying and the fact that Fay was undoubtedly right.

Fuming, I vowed to give John and Fern a piece of my mind the next day. However, I would never get the chance to talk about the horror. Until now, this story has never been told, because in Guatemala, something new always came up.

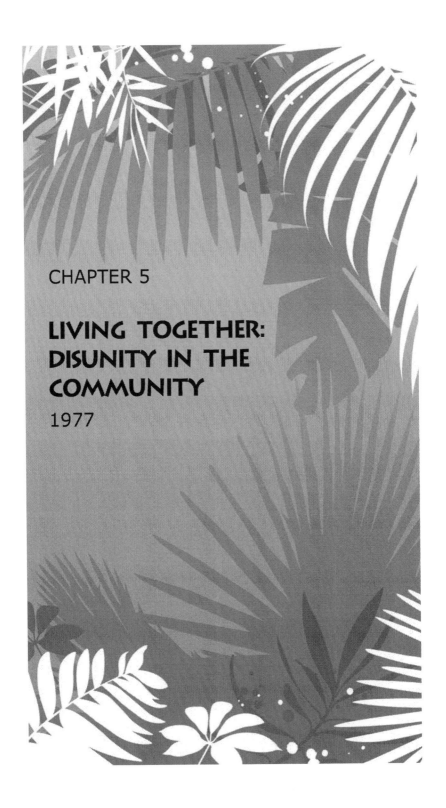

CHAPTER 5

LIVING TOGETHER: DISUNITY IN THE COMMUNITY

1977

Back at our home base in Poptún, black, shiny cockroaches clustered in the drain on the kitchen floor. Some hopped on the dirty dishes in the sink.

"Leon," I screeched.

He skimmed into the kitchen and swooped all six into a plastic bag.

"Ugh. I can't stand those things, Leon."

"*No problema.*" Leon smiled. "Thanks a lot, Liz," he said,

as if I had presented him with a gift instead of dead cockroaches.

Leon—Brother Leon Cook—joined our group after Fay and Kay and I had been in the Petén a few months. He had become a Maryknoll brother shortly after World War II. Unassuming and gentle, he lived close to the earth, like the Guatemalans. (That's us picking oranges in the convent yard, left.)

After years of tending the grounds at Maryknoll, New York, he came here, his first overseas assignment. He operated tractors to clear the 1976 earthquake rubble. At 58, when most people would be thinking of retiring, Leon studied Spanish at Maryknoll's language institute in Bolivia. He tried for six long months, but at the end he still couldn't speak more than a few phrases. *No problema* was one of them.

Instead, he communicated with gestures, most of all by simply being in tune with others. The people of Poptún understood Leon. He had a faithful spirit, like theirs.

Mo hoped **Leon** (left) would teach the aldea people to plant other vegetables besides corn and beans. Leon doubted he could start much of a "program," as Mo envisioned, especially if it involved formal classes. I couldn't imagine Leon teaching in a classroom. He was a one-on-one man.

Leon started by planting a garden at Incatep, the education center a mile from the rectory. He learned which vegetables could survive and thrive by exposing his plants to insects. He had success with okra, shell beans and greens.

When I'd first met him, I thought Leon was eccentric. After I got to know him, I appreciated he was truly himself, unafraid to be different. In his spare time, Leon collected cockroaches, scorpions, butterflies and every sort of bug (below). On Sundays, after mass, he slung his agile legs on a yellow-and-green Moped motorcycle and put-putted off into the jungle growth around town, his butterfly net posted like a flag at the back of his seat. He packaged bugs and sent them to companies in the States, where specimens were used in experiments. He earned several thousand dollars a year with his hobby.

He always had a plastic bag hanging from his back pocket, in case he found any flying things. He must have been in bug heaven in Poptún. He caught amazing numbers of cockroaches, scooping them up in swift motions without crushing them. They couldn't be sold if damaged in any way.

After a while, I no longer had to kill cockroaches. I called Leon instead.

Children in town discovered Leon's hobby. When kids came knocking at the rectory door or over at the convent, and asked for Leon—"*Esta el Hermano?...Is* the brother here?"— we knew some flea or termite rested in their cupped palms. Leon paid them a penny apiece. No wonder he was popular with the children.

Leon collected cow and horse manure for his garden in a wheelbarrow, which he pushed through the streets of Poptún. He simply wasn't embarrassed to do these kinds of things.

One Saturday afternoon, all the people I lived with gathered in the dining room for our community meeting. Looking around, I felt happy to be among such personalities. We'd grown into a group of nine.

I was enjoying getting to know **Maria Dolores**, (left) who worked with Mo and Kay. We hit it off immediately, gabbing about the people who made up our community. We admitted we were as odd as the rest for coming and staying.

"Leeez," she would call from her room next to mine. She suffered the loneliness of a nun who has left her order. Even so, she added zest to our group with her witty humor. Mo teased her, by calling her Maria Dolores "Chengke," a spoof on her last name of Cheng. Sometimes though, they had explosive fights.

Kay told me of one argument on the road to Flores. Mo drove, Kay sat in the middle, with Maria Dolores by the door. They started yelling at each other across Kay.

"You don't pay any attention to me," shouted Maria Dolores.

"Whaddya mean?" Mo said. He accelerated down the road, slamming every pothole in his agitation.

Kay bore it as long as she could. "I'm tired of your arguments," she cried. Things must have been really bad to get Kay so upset. (That's **Kay**, below, working in the leadership program.)

In those early days, there was always some fire of dissension burning in our community.

In the dining room where we met that afternoon in early

November, it was cold enough to wear my sweater. On the patio, rain fell from the gutters in ribbon-like sheets (left). I made myself a cup of Nescafe and grabbed a package of the creme-filled vanilla cookies

we kept in a tin on the cupboard.

"Attention please," John Blazo said. "We have a few things to talk about. Fay and Liz have some suggestions about the kitchen." John Blazo, God bless him, with four women in the community, had the misfortune to be in charge of the kitchen.

I began. "Betty *is* sweet, John, but I can't stand all that yucky spaghetti. I have to remind her to boil the water. The kitchen is filthy. No wonder we have cockroaches."

"I don't see anything wrong with her spaghetti," said John.

"Her food is bad enough, but all those weepy moods are getting to me," said Fay. "She's always crying about something." A crisis often disturbed Betty's family, who lived across the street. She was a single parent trying to support her little boy, Walter.

"Betty doesn't bother me, but we should be eating more raw vegetables, like carrot sticks and salads," said Kay. "We lose the vitamins if we cook vegetables to death."

Kay had once been overweight and worried about gaining it back. She avoided rice and potatoes as if they were poison.

"Pasta and bread have no nutritional value," she added. "White bread isn't good either. Whole wheat would be better."

John Fay aimed an icy glare at Kay. He loved white bread, eating it in prodigious quantities mounded with peanut butter.

"Macaroni is good for you," I protested. "So is bread...in moderation."

Kay ignored me.

"All right," said John Blazo. "I'll see what I can do. Betty *does* try." Even behind his glasses, I saw his reproachful look. "She needs the job."

Fern took a bottle of mineral water from the refrigerator, then made himself two sandwiches, smothering the bread with thick margarine and heaping it with slices of onions.

"We should get a stove," I said, warming my hands on my

hot cup. "Cooking for nine people on a hot plate is ridiculous. We could teach Betty to make bread. I have a recipe for some good whole wheat bread. Just think, we could bake cookies and cakes, even meat loaf."

"We *could* look into buying a stove," said Mo. "But then we'd have to buy gas. It'd be more expensive." He crossed and uncrossed his long legs as he did when he was nervous.

Everyone started arguing then. Some thought we'd begun to spend too much money. John Blazo reminded us that before we women came, the men had gotten along fine without napkins. Kay suggested we cut paper napkins in half to cut expenses.

"I'll look at stove prices next time we go to the city," Mo said.

"Are we done with the kitchen? Because I want to talk about community prayer," said Kay. In her measured, calm voice, she asked, "What do you think about having prayer every day, just among ourselves?"

"I would *love* it," I said, smiling at her. Kay and I had talked about this subject earlier in my room, and decided today was a good time to bring it up. We thought praying together would help us grow closer. I was very fond of Kay, missing her when she was gone frequently on trips with Mo and Maria Dolores.

"What do the rest of you think?" Kay asked.

"It's a *good* idea," Fay said. "We could take turns preparing reflections."

"Why do we need to prepare prayer? Couldn't it be spontaneous?" John Blazo wanted to know. No one answered him. "When would we meet? We all have schedules."

"Before dinner, like 5:30," suggested Kay.

Mo agreed with us women. None of the others showed interest. Nevertheless, we plowed ahead, assigning a different person to lead the meetings each day.

Fern remained quiet, as he often was in big groups. Once,

the doorbell rang and he was gone for twenty minutes. We had set aside this time especially for our community. I felt annoyed. Why couldn't he tell people we were in a meeting?

Instead of sensing the atmosphere within the community, which seemed resistant to change, I plunged ahead with my own agenda. Maybe now would be a good time to tell them about the paint, I thought.

"Fay and I bought paint in the city to clean this joint up. We need volunteers to help us." I looked around. They all stared back.

"You bought *paint*," repeated John Blazo, "without consulting *us*?"

"What's wrong with how things are?" John Fay asked.

Fern nodded, between bites of onion sandwich.

"Well," I began, feeling defensive, "those marks are ugly." I pointed to the rust on the dining room walls.

Everyone stared, as if noticing the stains for the first time.

"Did you buy paint with your own money?" John Blazo asked.

Ohhh, I thought, he makes me mad! I'd been on my own for years, and resented John's control of house finances.

"No, we used house money," Fay said, her voice getting that edge to it as when she was angry.

Their response amazed me. It never occurred to me that I was being the typical newcomer, trying to change everything and alienating people in the process.

Mo cleared his throat and crossed his legs again. "How much did you buy?" he wanted to know.

"Well," I turned to Fay for support, "it was 16 gallons, wasn't it, Fay?"

"My God!" Mo said. He adjusted his glasses back and forth on his nose, his other nervous habit.

So far, Leon had been silent. Usually he sided with me.

"Come on Leon, isn't the bathroom a mess with all those stains on the walls?" I asked.

He pulled his head against his chest like a frightened bird. "I never noticed," he muttered.

John Fay said softly, "We're here to be an example to the people." He smiled gently, his eyes kind, but I felt ashamed.

"It wouldn't seem right to the people if we painted," **John Blazo** said. (left) "They live a heck of a lot worse than we do. Besides, I don't think it's so bad."

Fay and I exchanged wide-eyed disbelief.

"What should we do with all that paint?"

"Take it back," said John Blazo.

Everyone nodded. They agreed with him!

"Let's vote," said Mo. "All those against painting raise their hands."

The vote was seven to two. Mo sided with the others. Even Kay was opposed.

John Blazo added, "We should be helping the people instead of

thinking of ourselves."

I felt judged to be selfish. But we had to acquiesce to the majority opinion.

Fay and I hauled the 16 gallons to the *bodega*, storage shed. We never got around to returning them to the city, because fortunately, things would change in our community. (That's also **John**, below left, being goofy, playing nurse.)

Later that week, we met to pray. Fern was absent and didn't tell us why. Leon didn't come because we spoke Spanish. Maria Dolores was upset with Mo, so she stayed in her room. John Blazo and John Fay pleaded excuses. I was very disappointed. Where was this wonderful community I'd expected? Being a missionary wasn't so great. Maybe I'd made a mistake coming to Guatemala.

One day, I walked to the hospital to check on the baby whom Fay and I'd fought to have admitted. In the two weeks that had passed, she'd lost more weight. Healthy babies her age should look like their pictures could be on a Gerber jar.

But this little scrap of humanity would have a coffin for her next bed. Her hair, fine as silk thread, what little there was, had the reddish tint of the severely malnourished. Flies nested in her half-open eyes. Flies knew when someone was dying and sought moist cavities on any defenseless person.

The hospital room reeked of garbage and urine. Her parents fanned her, slapping at flies. The mother kept rubbing the baby's head, as Guatemalan women did with their sick children. The parents were out of place, ignored by everyone.

Suddenly, the baby stopped breathing. Instinctively, I gave her CPR, trying to ignore the white curdled patches of thrush on her tongue, a yeast infection. I forced myself to blow, determined to bring her back to life.

With a few breaths, once again her chest rose and fell against her bony ribs. Her parents regarded my efforts in silence, their eyes dark with pain.

"*Queremos llevarla a la casa...*We want to take her home," the mother finally said.

I understood why they didn't want her to die in this friendless place. I found the doctor and told him. When I removed her IV, the baby barely moved.

"Do you have a way home?" I asked.

"*No se preocupa,* don't worry, we can hitch a ride. We live nearby."

The father wrapped the baby in a rag and placed her gently in his wife's arms.

"*Esparan aqui,* wait here!" I said. "I'm going to get you a ride." I ran all the way home.

No one was there except Mo, doing paperwork in the office.

"Mo," I panted, "would you drive this family? Their baby is very sick. They want her to die at home."

"Sorry. I have mass in a few minutes."

"Can I use your car? It's only a short way from here."

He hesitated. He'd just gotten rid of his beat-up truck and bought a new Toyota land cruiser of which he was immensely proud.

"Do you know how to drive it?"

"Sure, I learned to drive a stick-shift in high school." I didn't add that had been 20 years before and I hadn't touched a stick-shift since.

"OK. Be careful." He handed me the keys.

"Thanks, Mo." What a generous person he was. I ran to the *bodega* where Mo parked. I was grateful he'd already gone to church and couldn't see me fumbling to start the thing. Finally, I got it going and jerked slowly to the hospital.

The family was waiting. The mother climbed in next to me, holding the baby. I ground the gears as we started off. Once we left Poptún, I felt safer on the road to San Luís, where there wasn't much traffic.

"*Donde viven...*where do you live?"

"*Aqui no mas*," said the mother, pointing ahead.

We drove on. I kept asking where their house was. The mother repeated, "*Muy cerca*...very close."

The baby lay quiet. Her parents stared ahead. I swallowed against the tightness in my chest and forced myself not to cry.

I couldn't quite remember how to shift, which I had to do often, as the road alternately rose and leveled off. A couple of times I killed the motor by not depressing the clutch to the floor. I am so short I had to stretch to reach the clutch. We bumped slowly over the rocks. I clutched the steering wheel, afraid we would tip over. Mo's vehicle felt top-heavy, as if the frame was too big for the tires.

"Where exactly do you live?" I asked for the fifth time.

The father spoke from the back seat, "Just a tiny way from San Luís."

My God! An hour away, at this rate. I'd better not tell Mo. We continued on. No one spoke. Luckily, no other vehicles were on the road. It was that quiet time of the late afternoon, when the hills took on shadows and the temperature was no longer boiling hot.

I glanced at the baby. Her skin had a bluish cast. I stopped in the empty road and lifted the rag. Her chest no longer moved.

I started the engine again. The parents had tears streaming down their cheeks. I couldn't speak. Just before San Luís, the father tapped me on the shoulder and signaled me to stop.

"Where is your house?"

"*Alla*." He pointed to the steep hill planted haphazardly in green corn, person-high.

"Can I drive up there?" I hated to leave them.

"No. Cars cannot go there."

They climbed out. "*Gracias, señorita, muy agradable,* you are very kind. *Dios se lo page*...God will repay you. *Que le vaya bien*...may you go well," said the father. He touched my arms gently. The mother embraced me, her baby between us.

The woman's smooth cheek touched mine, and she smiled as if I was the one who needed comfort. They climbed slowly up the hill on a trail through the corn, then disappeared from sight.

I longed to drive them all the way home. But it was probably further than he said. Soon dusk would fall and today was the first time I'd driven on this road. Too risky, even for my adventuresome tendencies.

I returned crushed by tremendous sadness and rage. There was no good reason for that baby to die. I wanted to scream at the doctor who seemed not to care, at the terrible system in this country, where the poor didn't have enough food and couldn't get medical care. That a baby should die from worms in her stomach was unspeakable. How could Fay and I make a difference with so many things stacked against us?

When I arrived home, I searched for Kay. She would understand. She might even cry with me. But she was teaching with Mo and Maria Dolores.

I slumped on the mahogany bench outside the kitchen. Fern was working on his motorcycle. Now and then he glanced at me.

I felt so sad, but unable to express it. No one seemed interested. The ache in my chest wouldn't go away.

Fern disappeared into his room, then came back carrying his guitar. He sat on the Adirondack wood chair, humming and singing mournful country ballads. I tried to enjoy his deep voice, but my feelings stayed stuck inside. Then slowly, tears came. Some of the tightness eased. Words weren't necessary after all. In this community where nothing seemed easy, someone understood. (That's the whole gang at left, sharing birthday smiles.)

After a while, Fern sang a faster song. "Two old maids sitting in the sand, each one wishing the other was a man." That made me laugh. Now I didn't feel so alone.

A year after that community meeting, with everyone in accord, Julio, our maintenance man, painted the rectory, convent offices and bathrooms, using every drop of the 16 gallons. Everyone agreed the paint made the compound a new place. There was no difference in our cockroach population though. Leon still captured them by the hundreds.

•

CHAPTER 6

THE JOYS OF
RURAL TRAVEL...
AN EXERCISE IN
FRUSTRATION
NOVEMBER 1977

Early one morning, I packed my suitcase and walked to the bus stop in front of the gas station. I was on my way to observe health classes in Las Cruces, a much smaller town about two hours by dirt road north of Poptún. My trip would take me through the strange terrain of the Petén, above. This was prior to starting our own clinic in the aldeas. Fay and I wanted ideas from experienced people before launching our own health program. The setup was taking us longer than anticipated, because in the aldeas, no system was in place.

Several people sat waiting on their bags and belongings. We chatted to pass the time.

Fay chose not to go, saying, "I've been to Las Cruces and it wasn't that great! Besides," she added, "Mo and I had a big fight when I was there." Mo had bawled her out when she gave some sick people money for medicines.

"I had to do *some*thing!" said Fay.

I couldn't blame her. In those early months, we didn't have medications. Mo had a point, too. We all agreed it shouldn't be a give-away program, because we wanted to encourage them to take responsibility for their own healthcare. Even though we received grants from German charity organizations and Maryknoll, there wasn't enough money for a free program.

After an hour, I crossed the street to the Hilltown for a cup of coffee. The atmosphere reminded me of dingy diners near bus stations. I gulped my coffee, but could have taken my time. For the next hour, I sat on my suitcase in the sweltering heat, fanned myself and shielded my eyes from the dust of vehicles churning up the road.

"*Que paso con el bus*...What's happened to the bus?" I asked a man waiting with his wife and four kids.

"*Saber*," he said.

This word meant "to know." The saying was peculiar to the Petén. People said *saber* when they didn't know *why* something happened.

"It could be in the ditch," he said.

Oh, dear. I might wind up there, too. I'd heard stories about the bus traversing the Petén, whose drivers had a reputation for drunk driving.

We'd nicknamed the bus: *El Famoso, peligroso, Fuente del Norte*, meaning the famous, dangerous, Fountain of the North. More than once, we rounded a curve to find a Fuente del Norte in a *barranca*, a ravine. The top-heavy buses on small wheels seemed destined to capsize. Miraculously, usually no one was hurt. Then people waited patiently at some lonely spot. Buses in Guatemala were packed to the last seat. Crowds stood in the aisles. Often, those stranded waited in vain; there would be no room for them on the next bus.

Often the driver and his helper sang with the mariachi music on the radio—static and all. The conductor collected tickets, hoisted people's cargo to the top and threw it down afterwards. Drivers were called *chofers,* and he and his helper often flirted with pretty girls sitting near the front.

Drivers always swung the steering wheel side to side to avoid the potholes. Amazingly, no one protested this crazy driving; they just accepted it as they did everything else. Often, seats had come loose from the platform so that as the bus pitched down the road, I had to clutch the rail to keep myself from sliding to the floor. People stashed chickens and turkeys under seats, and I never suspected the birds were there until they squawked, flapped their wings and tried to escape on their tied-together legs.

Once I sat next to a woman with two kids. She clutched a little pink pig that squealed as loudly as her two children. I can nap anywhere, but I never could on those buses.

Those drivers were probably the best mechanics in the world. In the early months, Fay and I took a trip to Flores. On our way back to Poptún, the bus broke down outside of San Benito, near Flores. The empty road and thick jungle growth pressed around us.

"*Que paso?*" I asked a man sitting in front of us.

"The axle is broken," he replied.

Even I, with my incompetence in mechanics, knew this problem might mean we'd have to hitch a ride or wait for the next bus. Instead, the driver crawled underneath and banged away for several hours. Then we hurtled on our way again. The driver had improvised a new axle on the road!

"How did he do that?" I asked the same man.

"*Saber*," he said.

Another incident happened one Sunday when only John Blazo and I were home. I stood at the kitchen window cleaning onions for spaghetti sauce. A sparkling yellow and red Fuente del Norte bus screeched to a halt in front of the rectory. The driver jumped out and banged on our door. I heard the conversation. Then Blazo dashed into the kitchen, the ever-present circle of keys jangling from his back pocket. He pushed his glasses up on his nose. "That's a new bus," he said. "The driver wants me to bless it."

He stuck a bottle under the faucet and filled it with tap water.

"What's *that* for?" I asked.

"To bless the bus."

"But I thought it had to be *holy* water," I protested.

"Where do you think holy water comes from?" John grinned.

While I watched from the window, he ceremoniously sprinkled water up and down the aisle. The driver folded his hands as if he were in church. Then he grinned at Blazo and sped off, leaving a screen of dust. That bus was going to need all the blessings it could get to survive the killer roads and crazy drivers of the Petén. Blazo whistled cheerfully from the rectory office. I smiled. Another myth down the drain. So much for "holy water."

At the bus stop in Poptún, I was so sweaty my jeans stuck to my legs. The family waited patiently. Children played games in the dust. They didn't complain. Finally, the gas station attendant told me the bus probably wouldn't come that day. We had waited two hours.

"*Mañana, talvez*, maybe," he said.

When I told the family, the father said, with a shrug and a smile, "*Asi es la vida*...that's life." We went our separate ways. I reminded myself these people experienced setbacks all the time, but I was still angry.

The next day, I waited two hours in the rain. The bus had broken down on the road to Poptún. The third morning, I tried again. Once I decide something, it takes a lot to make me change my mind.

Several hours later, I sat dejected outside the kitchen, my suitcase on the floor, wondering what I should do next. No one knew what had happened to the bus.

"Where's the bus?" asked John Blazo.

"*Saber*," I said.

Amidst greasy rags and motorcycle parts on the bench outside his room, **Fern** (below) was, as usual, relaxing by tinkering with a machine, this time a broken tape recorder.

"I could run you up to Las Cruces on the cycle if you don't mind a little mud," he said quietly.

"Really? That'd be great!"

We took off on his Honda with me gingerly hanging onto Fern's blue windbreaker. I was hesitant to hug his waist. After all, he was a priest.

Before long, the road outside Poptún roughened. Morning rain had made the surface slippery as oil.

Though Fern maneuvered deftly around the puddles, I was nervous. Soon I was clutching his waist, afraid of falling. We dipped through a mud hole and I instinctively put my foot out. That made us tip and we almost crashed. Fern managed to keep the cycle upright and said not a word of reproach. It had stopped raining. A warm wind whistled past us. Before long I got the hang of the rhythm and enjoyed the ride, surprised how

smoothly the cycle sped along the road. (That's exactly the sort of "road" we were on, above.) In a couple of hours, we roared into Las Cruces. Mud splattered the only pair of jeans I'd brought. Awkwardly, I climbed off the cycle to meet Del Marie, the Franciscan nun giving classes. Right then, I vowed never to travel without an extra pair of pants.

But Las Cruces was worth the trip. I saw muslin flip charts and the *Carlos Campesino*, Charlie the farmer, film strips. These were slides of people or cartoons produced by Maryknoll Father Ed McClear to teach everything from church doctrine to why it was a good idea to cover food from flies. Fay and I later made our own muslin flip charts and showed the filmstrips in the aldeas. They were immensely popular. In fact, one night, we played filmstrips to over 300 spellbound people in Chacté.

In Las Cruces, I received my first lesson on the animosity between the Catholics and the Evangelicals.

The imported religions were mostly Catholicism and

Protestant Fundamentalism or the Evangelicals in the Petén. Other religions didn't exist in Guatemala in significant numbers. The Indians practiced religion dating back hundreds of years. Their beliefs mixed Catholicism or Protestantism in a harmonious whole, but never forsook their Mayan culture for any one faith.

Rumor had it among us Catholics that the Evangelicals were fanatics funded by groups in the States. Once converted, people had to attend daily prayer meetings and were encouraged to renounce anyone in the family who hadn't been saved. Some pastors said taking medicines was a sin. A person must be saved by faith alone. Everything was God's will, even the premature deaths of babies from bronchitis or intestinal parasites. Fay and I later found some of these beliefs hindered our work in the aldeas.

On the first afternoon in Lac Cruces, a voice suddenly boomed from a loud speaker in the building next to us. It turned out to be the pastor of the Evangelical church announcing a little girl's death. She had died of worms. He sounded as though he was bawling us out, becoming louder until he was shouting. Before long, I was groaning when he started in again after a few minutes of blessed silence. Between yells, the congregation sang sweet evangelical hymns like *Alabare,* Praise, a hymn at distinct odds with the preacher's exhortations.

I tried to concentrate on Del Marie's class, but couldn't. In those early days I barely understood Petén Spanish. Someone screaming in the background didn't help. Now I knew why the Catholics and Evangelicals didn't get along.

Once I sneaked over and peaked in the window of the church. I was surprised to see the pastor haranguing only two or three people seated dully before him.

That pastor yelled all day and every night. I thought he might be a little crazy. The only thing I understood was "*Alleluia*" and "*Jesu Cristo*!"

I tend to be slightly paranoid, and wondered if he wanted to distract us so we couldn't hear the classes. From then on, I was prejudiced against the Evangelicals.

When I got back to Poptún, I told Fay about the noise in Las Cruces and she said, "The same thing happened when I went, only there wasn't a funeral."

I didn't know it then, but the issue of the Evangelicals and the Catholics would crop up over and over again while I lived in the Petén.

The bus didn't break down on the way back, and I only had to wait two extra hours. I was so exhausted from my sleepless nights in Las Cruces that I dozed with my head knocking against the window as we plunged down the road.

CHAPTER 7

OUR FIRST TRIP OUT...
TO THE OTHER
LOS ANGELES

APRIL 1978

   One morning in April of 1978, I awakened before 5 o'clock to the gush of rain from the gutter. The consoling thought was so much rain would clear the pila of bugs so I could wash my hair in it. I dressed in a hurry, grabbed my poncho and ran to the rectory. Shadows from the kerosene lamp flickered on the dining room wall. Mo had finished his yoga and was heating water for coffee.
   "What a morning! We can't go in this stuff, can we, Mo?"

Rain dripped from my nose and poncho. My rubber thongs left muddy tracks on the floor.

Mo stirred Nescafe into his cup. "Don't see why not," he said with absolute cheer. "It'll take a little longer, but take it easy and you'll do fine."

"Oh, ****!" I muttered. I wished we didn't have to go on this first working trip to the aldeas by ourselves, but I didn't say that to Mo. Fay and I had to prove ourselves, and braving all kinds of weather was part of the deal.

I made myself coffee and shivered. On the way to the convent, half my coffee sloshed out and rain fell in.

"Wake up, Fay! It's pouring, but Mo says we gotta go anyhow."

From Fay's room came a loud, "PISS!"

Luckily, we'd loaded the truck the night before. At 5:30 a.m. **Tox** (left) arrived. Salvador Tzi Bác, or Tox as we called him, was a seventeen-year-old Kek'chi boy from Chacté. Fern hired Tox, pronounced Tosh, as translator for our clinics. Tox became much more; our friend and reliable co-worker. As I started the motor, John Fay and Mo rounded the corner of the rectory. Fern held open the big wooden gate. Kay hugged me. "I'll miss you, Lizzie," she said with a fond smile.

Even John Blazo, rarely up before 7:00, wandered out in

his bathrobe, restraining a yawn. It felt good to be wished well on our way by these people I was slowly coming to love. Christmas, the saddest one of my life, had been disappointing. We had huge fights in our community about the food, how much money to spend, whether to have a cat around the place, and worst of all, we didn't communicate. During one fateful meeting with other Maryknollers, our jobs changed, too. Father John Breen, a veteran Maryknoller, thought we shouldn't start a Promoter program. He said we hadn't been in the country long enough to start such an ambitious program. Mo had wanted us to train promoters, villagers who could care for their village's health needs. This change in our job descriptions was disheartening and frustrating. Christmas was a lonely day. Some did not even show up for dinner. Fay, Kay, Mo and I had even thought of splitting off from the community. I had felt ready to give up. Now that meeting was a faint memory, because we were finally going to be doing something important.

After Christmas, Fay and I had spent two months in Jacaltenango, where Maryknoll sisters ran an excellent hospital. Jacaltenango was a beautiful town high in the mountains. We learned to run a clinic, how to identify every sort of worm under the microscope and became proficient in diagnosing tuberculosis and malaria. After Jacaltenango, thanks to Mo's efforts at acquiring funds, we spent two weeks in Guatemala City, buying thousands of dollars worth of medications and equipment, including our little Chevy Luv truck, in which we intended to visit the aldeas with our mobile clinic. We spent the last week back in Poptún, packaging medicines, sterilizing equipment and buying food.

Now the streets of Poptún were deserted except for a few trucks throwing mud on our windshield as we headed south.

By dawn, we neared San Luís, a town of several thousand. I loved this part of the drive. Green cornstalks rose man-high among the weeds (right). I couldn't help comparing these fields

to U.S. farm land stripped clean by tractors. From the winding road, lush valleys and low mountains rose and fell.

Sheets of rain swept the windshield. We crept along, being careful as Mo had told us. I was anxious, but excited to be traveling under such conditions. Freeways back home put me to sleep on long drives: There I sometimes had to stop for a nap, but I couldn't sleep on this road. Nothing but potholes, mud and rain.

Five hours later, we finally arrived in Los Angeles. We didn't measure distance by miles, only the hours it took to get somewhere. No one waited for us, unless you counted a single chicken scratching the dirt. The church, merely branches between two houses, was empty except for someone's wash hanging on a rope. When we stepped from the truck, the rain stopped.

"Gee, Fay, I thought someone would be waiting for us."

"Me, too."

"Maybe they don't want to come to our classes," I said.

Tox said nothing, but hung his head as if dejected.

Some villagers arrived, and I asked them what to do.

"*Esperan un poco...*Wait a while...*Ya mero vienen*...someone will come soon," a man said. They regarded us as if we had stepped from a UFO.

Finally, the catechist, Don Miguel, showed up. After the usual polite greetings and hand shakes, he asked, "What took you so long?"

"*El camino fue muy mal*," I said.

His question shouldn't have surprised me. Aldea people had no idea of the hazards of driving in bad weather as none of them drove.

I parked the truck by the school (above), whose roof and walls were tin. The floor was dirt. Walls sort of floated above the ground and gusts of wind set them rattling. There were a few benches, a table and blackboard in front.

Doña Maria, Don Miguel's wife, and a young Ladina lady were there waiting.

"*Bienvenidos*! Welcome!" Doña Maria exclaimed.

I felt better after Doña Maria gave me a gap-toothed smile and a hug. She and the other woman and Don Miguel helped unload the truck.

"*Si tocan el timbre*," Doña Maria said. If we rang the bell, people would come.

Tox found the hammer and clanged away on an iron triangle. After three sets of clanging, we had 12 ladies, an equal number of little girls and a few boys. Don Miguel was the only man attending. This whole process took about an hour. The pace was leisurely in these little towns.

We set up our stage props for the skit we'd planned: a *palangana*, a basin, and a red jug. I played Señora Ramirez, who meets Señora Tzi, played by Fay, at the river. I attempt to balance the water jug on my head like the aldea women. Fay pretends to scoop up water. A little boy wearing a T-shirt that covered only half his bloated stomach agreed to be Fay's "pretend child."

The dialogue began like this:

"Buenas dias, Señora Ramirez."

"Buenas dias, Señora Tzi."

"Como esta?...How are you?"

"Muy triste...very sad, and worried about my little Miguel," says Señora Tzi, pointing to her little "son."

"He's tired and his stomach hurts. And he has diarrhea. He even eats dirt."

"I bet your kid has *parasitos*...worms," says Señora Ramirez, balancing the jug on her head and nodding wisely.

"Really? How can you tell?" says Señora Tzi.

"By that *panzón*, big stomach. *Y la diarrea*. And the diarrhea. He's pale too."

"Hmmm," says Señora Tzi, looking thoughtfully at her son. "Señora, why are *your* six kids so healthy?"

"Because I boil my water for 20 minutes to kill *los parasitos y germenes*, the parasites and germs," replies Señora Ramirez.

During the dialogue, the jug wobbled. Had it held water, it would have been easier to balance. It teetered, then tumbled to the ground, provoking giggles from our audience.

The drama continued with Señora Ramirez telling where worms come from, how to make boiled water palatable and about worm medicine.

Fay, a natural ham, enjoyed herself all along. Once we swung into things, I found myself throwing in new lines for more laughs. People chuckled and at the end they applauded. I should have been an actress! What a painless way to teach.

In high spirits, we set up clinic in the school. The teacher hadn't shown up. We were lucky to have a place, but I pitied the kids who missed school. What a system this government had. It made me angry. No wonder people were illiterate.

We moved seating outside, then arranged bottles of antibiotics, packages of worm and malaria medicine on benches inside. We set up the microscope outdoors, and kept our otoscope and stethoscopes nearby on the children's desks.

By this time, a mob of people had gathered, milling around like restless shoppers. They eyed the bottles and bags of medicines with something like hunger, and squeezed into the school, watching our every move. It made me nervous to be observed because this was the first time we'd held a clinic.

Tox unfolded a gray metal table we'd bought in the city. He set it outside to fill out charts. We recorded each person's name, birthdate, if known, diagnosis and medications. We also kept a tally of charges.

The *consulta* was 25¢ Guatemalan currency, (at that time equal in value to American money) plus whatever the medications cost. Fay and I were opposed to free programs. They weren't as successful as those that expected people to pay a small fee. Besides, even though we received funds from the German charity organizations, Adveniat and Miserior, there wasn't enough money for free clinics. Later on, trained health promoters would run the clinics. They needed to charge for their services. People would be used to this minimal fee.

Getting names was confusing. Women kept their maiden name and the Ladino women added *de* at the end. The husband's name was different, and the children were named after both. On later visits, we had trouble finding charts. No one remembered what names had been used, not even the patient. The one saving grace was that Tox, who'd grown up in nearby Chacté, knew many of the families.

Birthdates posed another problem.

*"Cuantos años tiene?...*How old are you?"

"*Pues*, about 30 years old."

"When were you born?"

"*Quien sabe...solo Dios*...who knows...only God," came the philosophical reply.

I never figured out Tox's system for recording birthdates, but he didn't mix up anyone.

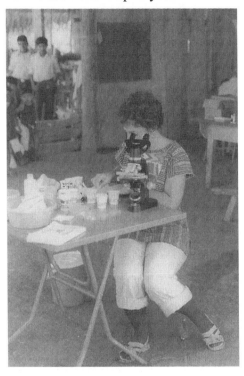

Fay and I took turns at the microscope, a sorry piece of equipment we had borrowed from the hospital in Poptún.(That's me at the left with a newer one.) It had only one eyepiece and no matter how I tried to focus it, the lens was like looking through scratched glasses. Nearly 100 people watched, parking themselves in front of the microscope and blocking the light.

Where had everyone come from? They seemed to have materialized from the jungle. Every few minutes I lifted my head.

"*Por favor*...please. I can't see. Would you move to the side?" I asked.

They moved. At least that group did, but they were mystified. No one had ever seen a microscope.

Inside the school, another mass of people ogled us. This was hard to accept, as I was used to privacy when I dealt with patients. These villagers had no privacy anywhere in their

lives, a luxury I had never appreciated until now. They crushed
next to me. Hands brushed my arms. Children fingered my
hair. I hadn't understood that our American way is a no-touch
system. Later on, I loved this difference in personal space and
basked in the free affection I received. It was a marvelously
healthy quality of these very poor people, but in the first
months, one more adjustment.

Tox collected stool samples. The table was crammed with
every kind of container imaginable.

"*Mirra*, look," he announced in his quiet voice. "Seventy-
four samples!"

Some specimens were folded in bits of cardboard, scraps
of paper or wrapped in banana leaves. Others looked like
they'd been expelled in the last century. And some were the
semi-digested masses of ascaris, or roundworm, which smelled
like a plugged toilet.

As I took my turn at the microscope, Tox called in a low
voice, "Liz!" He had a big grin on his face and an eight-ounce
jar of feces in one hand. We both began to giggle, but then
stopped. We didn't want to offend the owner of that jar. From

then on, we learned to say, "Just a *small* specimen," and
"*fresh.*"

As the afternoon wore on, people gave us mildly pained
looks. Every now and then I apologized.

"*Lo siento,* I'm sorry, we'll see you as soon as we can."
The interviews often sounded the same.

"*Que es lo que tiene?* What symptoms do you have?"

"*Dolor del estomago. Diarrea. Tos. Muy palido.* Everyone
had a stomach ache, diarrhea, a cough and was anemic. If I had
the parasites in my stomach that we saw in these stool
specimens, I'd have a hell of a stomach ache, too. When we
told them they had *parasitos*, patients regarded us blankly. In
this aldea, they called worms *lombrices*.

Tox stayed busy filling out charts, his table submerged in
papers. "How much longer do we have to wait?" patients asked
him. Poor Tox, he didn't know *what* to say.

"*Es que hay tanta gente…*so many people," he said,
distressed.

"We weren't
expecting such a
crowd," I explained to
them. "We're not
prepared to handle you
all. We'll do better next
time."

I rushed through
each examination, that
familiar frenzy I'd
experienced in
hospitals at home, too
much work, people
waiting and not enough
time.

Mothers shushed
their babies. Starving

dogs slouched under the microscope table and scratched at fleas. Numbness enveloped me.

"Fay," I said, "I saw another woman with abdominal pain and couldn't do a pelvic exam. I should make curtains to screen part of the room. I can buy some cheap fabric in Poptún."

"Yeah. You could use the cots for people to lie down," Fay said.

We didn't even take time for lunch. The rainy day had turned into a scorcher. In spite of the T-shirt I wore, sweat trickled down my back. The intense heat made breathing difficult. Flies zoomed around my head, diving onto the stool specimens, while I peered through the microscope. The odor of feces was pervasive.

I've always had a strong stomach. Odors and blood rarely bothered me. Even so, this was too much. I never had headaches, but that day my head throbbed at my temples, making me move with care. My eyes burned and watered. I strained to see the fuzzy shapes of parasitic eggs we'd identified easily in Jacaltenango. I adjusted the mirror, but it was getting impossible to see. By dusk, patients still waited, their faces enduring.

"Get the lantern, Tox," Fay said.

The Coleman lantern sat so close, it felt like it was burning my face. Insects circled our heads, then popped when they hit the lantern's hot glass.

We finally finished when ours was the only light that shone along that dark road. As the last patient departed, carrying his bag of medicines, we heaved sighs of relief. I'd never spoken Spanish for so many hours. Thinking in another language was exhausting. I longed to revert to my mother tongue, but we couldn't, since Tox was there.

"That was awful," I sighed. "I didn't have time to teach, did you?" We'd intended each consultation to be a teaching session, but with all those patients, it'd been impossible.

Fay shook her head and yawned loudly. "We'll have to limit how many people we see," she said. "I'm so hungry I could die."

"I just want a cup of coffee," I said, "more than anything."

Tox lit the kerosene stove and I fried canned Vienna sausages with fresh eggs and potatoes while Fay cut up cucumbers, carrots, tomatoes and onions for a salad. We never had lettuce because, although it grew beautifully, insects devoured it in the Petén.

I had to admit cooking beat looking at poop under the microscope. Tox and Fay and I sat down finally at 9:00 to eat our dinner at the same gray metal table where Tox had received all the stool specimens.

"From now on we have to keep one table clean," I said.

Our kerosene lamp sat on the teacher's desk, circled by a zillion bugs. Dinner was very tasty, and I marveled at how fresh the vegetables were, even though they weren't as blemish free as in the States.

"Let's make a rule. Have people attend classes first in order to come through the clinic. Otherwise they won't bother," I said.

"Yeah." Fay yawned again, her fork suspended in mid-air. "God, I'm tired. Aaaaaaahhhh. We need our own microscope," she continued. "That one was ridiculous. I faked half the stuff cause I couldn't see."

"Me, too." We grinned. We were two of a kind, Fay and I.

"Don't you like carrots, Tox?" I asked.

He was shifting them around on his plate. "*Si pero*...I've

never eaten them this way. I don't think I like them raw." He looked up to check if it was permissible to dislike what we'd cooked.

"That's okay. I love carrots. I'll eat yours," I told him.

He smiled and scraped the carrots off his plate and onto mine.

How heavenly to be away from the crowd. The only sounds were crickets and an occasional truck. I was exhausted, but satisfied. We'd learned how to conduct the clinic and helped people who hadn't been helped in a long time, if ever. No one had told us what to do and I loved that freedom.

"Tox, you did super with the paperwork," I said. Only a teenager, he had performed remarkably well.

"We'll teach you to look at poop, too," Fay told him.

Under any other circumstances this would have been an unattractive offer. But Tox was eager to learn. He seemed well-suited to medical work: calm, gentle and unaffected by the sound and smell of sickness. He ducked his head in that shy way of his and smiled. You could tell he was pleased.

That night, Fay and I slept in the school, while Tox curled up in his new sleeping bag in the truck. He slept there all the nights we stayed in the aldeas to prevent theft as well as any gossip that he was sleeping with us. Tox didn't mind the truck. He claimed it was more comfortable than sleeping at home in Chacté.

I awakened with many bites from the little red bugs prolific in Los Angeles. They bit fiercely and caused stinging and intense itching. I scratched myself all night long.

Wind rattled the tin roof and walls. I feared the roof would blow off, and had the feeling the school was barely standing up. On a later trip to Los Angeles, the wind did, in fact, blow off all but one slab of tin roofing.

The evening before we left for Chacalté, the next aldea, Don Miguel stepped in the door, and removing his straw cowboy hat, gave us a reminder of the stark reality of aldea life. "The men can't come to classes tonight," he said. "We must make coffins. We will be gathering at the home of a man whose two sons drowned in the river today."

CHAPTER 8

MASSACRE AT PANZÓS

MAY 1978

Sadly, death was a common occurrence in the Petén. I listened to the radio broadcast in stunned disbelief. More than a hundred Kek'chi had been massacred in the town of Panzós, in Alta Verapáz, the department west of the Petén.

The soldiers who killed them were from the post in Poptún. I'd seen those men drunk and staggering through town, brandishing their guns recklessly. People were afraid, but no one questioned the military, which had the power of the

government. Later, people said Colonel Benedicto Lucas
Garcia ordered the massacre.

A group of us from different missions were in the tourist
town of Panajachél, on beautiful Lake Atitlán (below),
attending a theology meeting when the news came. We
clustered around the radio and listened for details. For that day
and the next, all anyone could talk about was the massacre. I
thought of the Kek'chi people I knew, almost childlike in their
simplicity, the most graceful, whole people I'd ever met.

"I could murder an army man myself if he were here," I
said to Fay. How could anyone do this to them? With the
military, it was one outrage after another. They got away with
whatever they wanted because no one could stop them.

Already there were conflicting reports. The radio and
newspapers—government controlled— said the Kek'chi were
to blame, that a Kek'chi man had started everything when he
cut off a soldier's ear. The government told its version of lies to
the international press. Then the Justice and Peace Committee

of the Catholic Church in Guatemala, which investigated human rights violations, issued its report: the army had ordered and staged the killings.

At Panajachél, we met with all the missionaries attending the theology conference. One priest said, "We should do something."

"True," another agreed. "How about a public denouncement?"

"We could get kicked out," replied someone else. "Then what good would we be?"

A priest said, "I'm going to tell what happened next Sunday at mass."

"Liz and I can cover the aldeas," Fay suggested.

"You women shouldn't get involved. It's too dangerous," someone objected.

Fay shot to her feet. "What do you mean? We're missionaries, too. This is a moral obligation."

We argued back and forth. "If condemning the massacre is something we believe, then speaking out doesn't make any difference who tells the truth, men or women," Fay said.

Silence. The men stared at us. They could see Fay and I weren't about to back down. I agreed we should take some action, but the thought of arousing the ire of the commandant or anyone else in the government scared me. Fay's tendencies to say whatever she thought worried me. We had to proceed calmly and think before we acted.

"We could take up a collection for the families of the victims," John Blazo suggested.

Gradually, tension eased. I knew the men were trying to be protective. They were well aware from experience how dangerous speaking up could be in this society.

A Belgian priest helping people establish cooperatives had been forced to leave the country when he denounced the massacre. Cooperatives were a threat to the wealthy. They were owned by the people to store and sell corn and beans, giving them control over prices and distribution.

In 1976, Maryknoll priest Father Bill Woods, who helped a group of Mayans build cooperatives in a jungle area called the Ixcán, died in a plane crash. At first, it seemed an accident, but later, most experts believed government forces shot down his plane.

What happened in Panzós felt like a friend had been killed. The Kek'chi had become more to me than people wearing colorful costumes. We felt pain when their children died and shared their joy at something good. We laughed and cried together. In our hearts, we were bonded. Even now, all these years later, the link remains unbreakable.

I loved the Kek'chi because they were dignified and hard-working people with great faith. Others looked down upon them, but I thought the Kek'chi *more* civilized than the upper classes.

Fay and I knew we must be diplomatic or we would find ourselves booted out of the country or dead. We had to be careful not to display any political alliances. Our promoters needed licenses to practice, which required government approval. If we weren't careful, all we were working toward could be destroyed by one careless move. We had good reason to fear government retaliation.

I remembered what had happened earlier that May, 1978 in Poptún. One day, a knock came at the rectory door. John Blazo opened it and saw two soldiers standing there, an army vehicle pulled up in front.

"*¿Se encuentra una mujer que se llama Elizabeth aqui*? Is there a woman named Elizabeth living here?"

"Yes, there is," said John slowly. "Why do you ask?"

"*Queremos pregunatarle algo*. We want to ask her some questions."

John came to get me. Then he fetched John Fay. My heart began pounding. What had I done? I couldn't think of anything requiring soldiers.

John Fay and Blazo came with me to the reception area where the men waited. Blazo whispered, "Calm down. Nothing's gonna happen. You haven't done anything wrong. We'll stay right here."

We went in and the soldiers rose to their feet. Their expressions were cold. I was shaking.

"*¿Se llama Elizabeth?*" one said.

"Yes, my name is Elizabeth Desimone."

They exchanged looks. One frowned at the paper in his hand, then inspected me closely.

"Your name is not Elizabeth...?" He gave a French last name.

"No."

"Do you visit the aldeas?"

"Yes, every week. We have a mobile clinic."

"Are you from France?"

"No, the United States."

"Were you in Machaquilaíto last week?" Machaquilaíto lay deep in the jungle, an aldea that could only be reached during the dry season.

"No, I've never been there."

John Fay spoke up. "I can vouch for Liz. She was in the aldeas close to San Luís all last week. You must have her confused with someone else."

The soldiers again consulted their paper, then me.

"*Bueno, gracias. Perdóne la molestia, señorita.*" They nodded like robots and left.

I took a while to calm down, having felt terror in their presence. Here was power. They could have dragged me off and neither John Fay nor Blazo could have done a thing. In this country, you could be accused, tortured and killed, even if you were innocent. The government wouldn't worry about having made a mistake. It didn't care.

"I wonder what *that* was about," muttered Blazo.

No one knew. Later, I heard rumors that a French woman also named Elizabeth had been involved with the guerillas.

After the meeting in Panajachél, we decided each mission should plan some action. Our Poptún team distributed copies of the Justice-and-Peace report at all the masses in town. Through this church report, people would hear the truth.

Fay and I would give a talk in the aldeas. Hardly anyone there could read. As usual, Fay was more ready to take a stand than I.

The first town we visited was Los Angeles, where the people gathered in the school.

Fay stood. "Today we're shortening the health class to tell you what happened to our friends, the Kek'chi." Fay gestured with her hands, her delicately featured face bright with the expression I had come to know. When she believed in something deeply, her voice developed fervor and her eyes glowed. Fay had been born to fight for a cause.

The familiar faces of the aldea people listened without moving a muscle. In these isolated towns, no newspapers could be found, but many families had battery-operated radios and listened to them constantly.

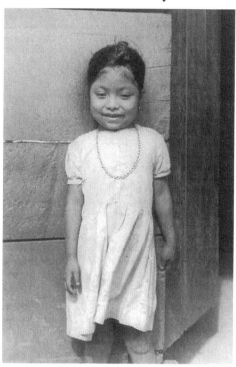

"On May 29th, 1978, in the town of Panzós, in the department of Alta Verapáz, a group of Kek'chi met with the authorities to discuss what was happening to their property. For years, they'd farmed beautiful land alongside a river. They worked hard and made the soil very productive. That land was taken from them without explanation. The people complained, but no one listened.

"Finally, the mayor promised their voices would be heard if they attended a public meeting. So hundreds of them went to town. When they'd gathered in the square, all of a sudden soldiers and wealthy landowners opened fire with automatic weapons. More than one hundred men, women and children were killed.

"Even before the massacre, tractors dug a big grave and trucks were waiting to haul away the bodies. The executions had been planned beforehand. The radio and newspapers say the Kek'chi were at fault, that they deserved to die because they were protesting. We want you to know the truth."

Spellbound, the people listened to Fay. I admired her

whole-heartedly, but I could never have spoken up like that. I was too afraid.

Some men I hadn't seen before stood at the back of the room. I shifted uneasily. Could they be *confidenciales*, informants, local men hired by the military, all too willing to report someone critical of the government?

After Fay spoke, there was silence. Never before had we experienced such absorbed attention. No one, however, asked any questions or commented other than a *"Que horible!"* Maybe they were as fearful as I.

"We're collecting donations for the families of the victims," Fay added. "Anything you can give. We'll take them to Panzós, where they'll be distributed by the Benedictine Fathers who've worked with the Kek'chi for years."

Don Miguel, the lead catechist, rose. "Señorita Fay, we feel sad at what happened to our brothers and sisters in Panzós. I will personally go to the people here one by one and collect donations."

Someone took off his hat and passed it. Many people put in a few centavos and apologized it wasn't more.

Later that night, Don Miguel returned, bent over by a huge plastic bag on his shoulders. *"Mira,"* he beamed. "Even the Protestants gave me donations!"

He pulled sacks of corn and beans from the bag, each carefully wrapped in paper or plastic. One person gave a cup of salt. Another, a pound of sugar. One even gave a package of soap powder. Don Miguel carefully counted out $7.42. I swallowed the lump in my throat and thanked him. On the average, these people earned less than $300 a year.

And so it went, in village after village. People listened transfixed. No one said one word against the government. In the Kek'chi aldeas, as Fay recounted the story, the women covered their faces or whispered among themselves. We didn't know their thoughts. But when we passed the collection basket, they donated their precious centavos.

In Chacté, a town with many Kek'chi, they gave us $14. When we returned to Poptún, our little truck was loaded down with gunny sacks of corn, beans, salt and sugar, and the people had given us almost $50.

By that time, Fay had given several talks. Her example inspired me. I figured if trouble resulted, at least I'd be speaking up about something important. I began speaking out about Panzós as well. But I never lost my fear.

Nothing ever happened. But shortly after the massacre, a nun in Panzós who denounced the massacre was expelled from the country by the government and never returned.

First came the death of Maryknoll Father Bill Woods in a suspicious plane crash in 1976. Then came the killings at Panzós, and a storm of army violence began against the people that had not been equaled since the late '60s, when the guerilla movements started. Twelve priests were murdered. The Catholic church was recognized as the only institution speaking out for the poor. Its mission was to be aligned with the poor. For that, it endured persecution.

I'd already left Guatemala in 1980. Then in late 1981, both Fern and Fay departed from Guatemala. They were advised to leave by the Maryknoll superior, who feared for their safety. Fern spoke Kek'chi and was so trusted by them that the military concluded he must be helping the guerillas. The commandant appeared on TV and accused Fay and others on our team of being communists. Those were the years when the word communist excused the army's atrocious acts.

It took a while to understand the reason for Panzós. Oil and nickel had been discovered near Kek'chi regions, making them immensely valuable. Army officers had seized control of much Kek'chi property. In fact, it was called the "land of the generals." The army and rich landowners were determined that the rights of the poor campesinos would not interfere with the goals of economic growth and development of exports. The massacre had been planned by the landowners and the army. In the end, the murders were motivated by greed.

News in the international press was distinctly the government version. In fact, *The New York Times* in a brief item, on May 31, 1978, reported that 38 people had been killed, but that number has been disputed and may be as high as 100. The victims were squatters fighting the landowners, the article claimed, portraying them as disgruntled peasants who'd attacked a military post after being stirred up by guerillas. Neither the government nor the army ever admitted its role in the massacre.

In later years, we marveled that more hadn't happened after we denounced Panzós. Priests, lay workers, teachers and thousands of campesinos had been tortured and killed for less.

According to news sources, in Guatemala in 2009, even with the peace accords, people are still tortured and murdered—as many as 4,000 women in the last five years.

CHAPTER 9

THE GIFT...
WINNING
THE PEOPLE

MAY 1978

A few weeks after the massacre we ventured on a trip to La Cumbre, another village about two hours beyond Poptún. (The people of the village are pictured with me above.) By the end of our day in La Cumbre, where we were teaching classes and holding a clinic, I was exhausted. One more mother carrying an infant wrapped in a shabby blanket caught my attention—except this mother clutched her baby and paced. She didn't speak, but her expression said, "I know we didn't get here in time for clinic, but my baby...*por favor,* please, *señorita.*" How could we refuse? I sighed, knowing I'd have to take the time to screen her, to see what the baby had. Thank God, this was the last patient.

Fay, Tox and I regularly visited La Cumbre for clinic and health classes. Ladinos and the Kek'chi Indians populated this small town. They didn't quite trust us yet, two foreign missionary nurses. Some utilized our clinic and attended classes, but the majority stayed away. They believed the Guatemalan pastor of the Evangelical church, who said we gave out dangerous medicine. He accused us of being mixed up with the devil. Sometimes we heard him shouting these remarks through a megaphone.

Even the Catholics were leery and made us set up our clinic in a three-sided shelter (above), poor cover from the hard winds and sudden bursts of rain. At night, however, they let us sleep inside the church. Like the shelter, it was built of vertical branches, with a dirt floor, covered by a thatched roof. On hot days, after morning clinic, we took naps on homemade benches in the cool, quiet church. For clinic, we moved the benches outside to the shelter, using some to line up the bottles of antibiotics, cough syrup, iron and vitamin pills, and others for people to sit on while they waited their turn.

La Cumbre consisted of a few *tiendas*, small stores stocked with meager supplies of plastic bags of sugar, soap powder, rubber sandals and—no surprise to anyone who's traveled to remote places—good old Coca Cola. A scattering of thatched-roof houses seemed to be plopped at random in the hills. The church perched on the highest point overlooking the sleepy little town.

Sometimes at dusk, I sat outside on logs and watched the gorgeous red sunset. Carrying our equipment up that steep slope made me sweat and complain—but the view was prettier up there, surrounded by the dense greenery of the jungle. In La Cumbre, I wrote my first poem about missionary life. I had some time on my hands, because people didn't use our clinic much.

Now I quickly finished with another child I was examining and rose to question the last mother, whose worried face made me uneasy. I unwrapped the blanket. Inside, a baby boy gasped for breath; his face was dusky blue. Mucus gurgled with each labored breath.

For a second, I couldn't move. Then I snatched him from his mother's arms and rushed to our make-shift table.

"*Porque no* me *dijo que era tan enfermo*...Why didn't you tell me he was so sick?" I yelled over my shoulder.

With one hand, I swept instruments aside and laid him down. I lifted his chin to extend his neck. When I opened his mouth, I saw his throat drowning in thick yellow mucus. I reached in with my fingers and tried to pull out the ropes of stringy phlegm, but it was so thick, it couldn't be moved.

"Fay. Hurry. Get the bulb syringe! Tox! The emergency box!"

Tox froze momentarily. Then he jumped into action, assembling the IV equipment. He hammered a nail into the shelter wall from which to hang the IV bottle, while I hollered instructions.

Fay bent over the little form. She tried to suction his mouth with the bulb syringe, but no mucus came through—it was too gluey. We used bulb syringes in the States to clear the noses of newborn babies—they weren't meant to cope with such a horribly obstructed airway.

"God, oh God." Fay's words ended in a sob.

The baby's feather heart beat so fast I couldn't count. His breathing sounded like someone gargling. Fay placed her lips over his nose and mouth and blew. Over and over she tried. She straightened up. "Nothing. I can't get any breaths through." My despair was reflected in her face.

"Keep breathing. We have to keep trying!" I could hardly get the words out.

Tox stood by helplessly, his normally stoic expression pinched in concern. I looked up once. The shelter was crowded with people too curious to leave.

I couldn't stop trying. Before Guatemala, I'd worked in an emergency department for years. There, everything conceivable was done to save a life. If only we had better equipment here! This would never have happened in the States. We continued to work over the baby.

After what seemed like an hour, but was only a few minutes, his chest stopped moving, and he lay lifeless before us. Fay and I, and many of the men, women and children stood together with tears running down our faces. I smoothed back the soft dark hair from the child's forehead, then wrapped the blanket around him. Such a beautiful baby. I hugged his mother as she sobbed in my arms.

"*Lo llevo al doctor en San Luís...*I took him to the doctor in San Luís. I gave him cough syrup four times a day, just like he told me...but it didn't help. The doctor said come back if he wasn't better, but the trip costs so much. Every day he got sicker." She buried her face in the blanket.

Today, she went on, he'd gotten worse. She brought him to us, praying we might help.

"I didn't think he was going to die. He was so healthy looking, wasn't he señorita?"

It was true. His clothes were patched, but clean. He was chubby, as an eight-month old should be, with velvety chestnut skin.

I thought of so many things as she told her story. Why hadn't an antibiotic been prescribed? The likelihood of complications was great in this disease-prone population. Why had the mother stood by while Fay and I examined patients suffering nothing worse than worms? Couldn't this woman have come earlier? I blamed myself, too. Why didn't I look up sooner? With a few extra minutes, could we have saved him?

Slowly, people drifted away. Neighbors led the mother home as Fay and I began to clean up the mess. Someone said there'd be a prayer service later that night in the baby's home.

"Maybe we should cancel our classes," I suggested to Don Julian, the catechist. "It doesn't seem right to teach nutrition now."

But Don Julian told us to go on as planned.

We fixed a simple dinner. No one said much while we waited for class to start, each of us locked in our private sadness. I kept seeing the baby's face, and I felt like crying again. The disgust I was beginning to feel for those running this government, the ones who should do something to provide better health care, grew even stronger. I thought perhaps a few villagers might come to class, but that most would stay with the baby's family.

As 7:00 p.m. approached, people began arriving. Soon the shelter was full of men, women and children, both Ladino and Kek'chi, and a crowd stood at the back. We never had such a turnout in this aldea. Fay and Tox and I glanced at each other, amazed. The people of La Cumbre were giving us the gift of their presence. I felt as if comforting arms were embracing me;

my depression lifted.

While Fay and I expounded on the merits of breast milk and Tox translated, I looked out at the people listening with total attention and courtesy, their expressions the most humble I had ever seen. My fatigue melted away.

After class, we walked down the hill single file along a dark path lit only by our bobbing flashlights. Tox seemed to know the way. We arrived at the house where everyone had gathered.

Inside, we were welcomed as if we were royalty. A man rose and motioned me to sit on his stool, and a woman insisted that Fay take the only other seat in the house. Their dead baby, dressed now in finer clothes, lay on a rough wooden table in the center of the room. The surface was covered with a white cloth, and white flowers wound in a crown through his dark

curls. White candles burned on each corner of the table, flickering shadows on the stick walls and straw roof. On a bed next to the child, lay his brother and sister, asleep.

Don Julian stood. *"Hermanos en Cristo, vamos a rezar*, Brothers and Sisters in Christ, let us pray." He made the sign of the cross, then sank to his knees and began to pray. *"Padre nuestro*...Our Father..."

People knelt around me and I

followed them. The grainy dirt bit into my knees. Instead of praying, I thought about how these people accepted whatever life brought to them. In that simple house, peace surrounded me.

Afterward we wound our way back to the church, a black silhouette at the top of the hill. "I wonder where the mother got the money for that cloth and the new clothes?" I asked Tox.

"*Los vecinos,* the neighbors. Someone else paid for the candles. *Asi se hace.* That's how it's done."

That day marked the beginning of change in La Cumbre. We no longer heard a word about bad medicine. From then on, we had so many patients, we couldn't see them all.

CHAPTER 10

A BIRTHDAY
LIKE NO OTHER

JUNE 1978

**On June 29, 1978, I spent the day working with Fay
and Tox in the aldea of Chacté.** A stupefying depression
settled on me. I tried talking to myself. "Snap out of it! You're
the one who didn't remember your birthday when you and Fay
planned this trip. It's your own fault you're in this god-
forsaken place." I'd mentioned my birthday to Fay earlier that
day, when I began feeling sorry for myself.

It was muggy-hot and I hadn't bathed or washed my hair

in three days. The mosquito bites on my legs stung, tempting me to give them a good raking, but I was afraid I'd get a new case of impetigo from scratching with filthy hands and dirt-encrusted fingernails.

Clinic was hectic as usual. Helping us in his eager but rather bumbling way was Tox's good friend, Francisco (below, right, helping with patient records).

Francisco was full of high spirits and a talker. It was "*Seño*," this and "*Seño*" that, short for senorita. He asked questions all day. I was less than cordial towards him.

We closed clinic a little early. "Lizzie, honey," Fay said, "take some time for yourself. I'm gonna fix a yummy dinner. I'll call you when it's done."

"OK, Fay. Thanks, dear."

I went for a walk alone, pondering. The moist air of late afternoon was pleasant and more breathable. On the road below, trucks and occasional cars stirred the dust. Kek'chi women, red clay jugs mounted on their heads, headed for the river. Although I prayed I might accept the day, my black mood lingered.

Finally, Fay called me. She'd taken pains to make the table especially nice. There were candles and a plastic glass filled with yellow and red flowers.

"Gee, Fay, where'd you get those?"

She grinned mischievously. "From the graveyard over there."

"Oh, Fay." I shook my head. What would I do without Fay? God bless her. She'd spent one and a-half-hours cooking our favorite dinner—potatoes, sausages and eggs—which took a while, because she had to boil the potatoes first, then fry the sausages on our one-burner stove.

Tox and Francisco joked during dinner but I only felt overwhelmingly sad and guilty for not responding to their efforts. Tox observed me with that serious look of his. He was a perceptive kid, sensing whenever I felt blue. I forced myself to smile back.

After dinner, Fay passed around *Nucitas*, my favorite Guatemalan candy. It came in square plastic containers, like miniature puddings. We used tiny scoops to dig out the creamy chocolate.

Afterward, Fay, Tox and Francisco cleaned up while I sat on a log to read. Tox and Francisco flicked the dishtowel at each other, goofing off as only teenagers can do.

"In my house, only women do the dishes," Francisco announced. "This is the first time I have helped."

"That's what Tox told us too, but we all eat, so we all can help clean up," Fay informed him. At dusk, Tox and Francisco disappeared. Fay and I sat talking until time for night class.

Then, from down the hill, a burst of explosions shattered the evening. The booms rose toward the church.

"What's that?" I asked. "Firecrackers!"

"It's Tox. He wanted to celebrate your birthday."

"Oh, Fay, I hate them! Firecrackers at weddings drive me nuts!"

"I know," said Fay.

The blasts continued. I jumped with each one. Bam! Crack! Crack! Crack!

Then I saw Tox climbing toward us. He stooped to light another firecracker, unable to hide his excitement. Sometimes I worried about him, for he loved gadgets and other things like cameras and tape recorders of the Ladino culture. He even seemed at times ashamed of his Kek'chi origins.

I knew he'd spent a precious amount of his own money. Didn't he know I loathed firecrackers? They scared me. When I was four, a little girl I played with nearly had her thumb blown off by a firecracker on the Fourth of July.

The blasts made me cringe as Tox and Francisco climbed the hill. Gun-like reports reminded me of the first time I'd heard firecrackers here.

One Saturday in the early months after I arrived in Poptún, I happened to be at mass during a wedding. At the consecration, I knelt looking toward the altar. John Fay lifted his hands over the bread and wine. *"Santifica, Señor, estos dones..."*

The bride and groom knelt, she in the traditional white gown and he in a dark suit. They were flanked by six bridesmaids, whose dresses billowed in a profusion of pink taffeta.

Suddenly, what sounded like guns exploded on the church steps! Rat tat tat, bam! Crack!

I whipped around, afraid I'd see soldiers, but it was only teen-age boys lighting firecrackers on the church steps. Firecrackers were traditional for almost any celebration such as birthdays, baptisms and every fiesta.

Now I recalled that wedding, thinking how I might not like the gifts people gave me, but they were precious nonetheless.

On that melancholy day in 1978, Tox and Francisco

walked toward me smiling. "They are for you," Tox said, "for your birthday." His smile wanted to please. A burnt paper smell wafted closer. I'd never known Tox to buy anyone a gift. I felt a faint lifting of my depression.

Before I could thank him, I heard a guitar softly strumming and someone singing, "*Feliz cumpleaños a ti*...Happy Birthday to you."

I recognized that deep contralto voice! Mimi, Teresa's sixteen-year-old sister. Teresa owned the store where we'd stayed that first night in the aldeas. Mimi was a lovely Ladino girl with large dark eyes and flowing brown hair.

Mimi sang, guitar in her arms, accompanied by Teresa, her kids and several neighbors. Their voices blended in harmony, as they approached.

We relaxed on a log by the church in the cool night, the sky lit by thousands of stars, while Mimi played song after song, her voice so stirring, I wanted to cry. She sang the joyous melodies of the campesinos, some from church, like "*Te Ofrecemos Padre Nuestro*" and "*Que Alegria Cuando me Dijeron.*"

Then Teresa handed me a package. I unwrapped it to find three bars of men's soap, the scent so pungent I sneezed, and a can of oatmeal. I tried not to smile.

My mood was definitely on the upswing, for I was being shown that I was loved and appreciated.

Then through the dark a familiar figure emerged from the jungle growth. Fern! He walked with a weary step, his mud-splattered clothes matching our own bedraggled appearances.

"Fern! What are you doing here?" I asked.

"Happy Birthday." He mopped his matted hair with a dirty handkerchief.

"Thank you! Where did you come from?"

"One of the aldeas."

"How far is that?"

"About six hours."

"My God! Did you *walk?*" He nodded, looking away in embarrassment. He'd walked six hours from a remote aldea, then rode his motorcycle to Chacté. This time I did cry. I was happier than I'd ever been at any birthday.

We taught a health class that night, but I could hardly concentrate, thinking of all the gifts I'd received. Fern sat with the people listening attentively. Afterwards he said, "I wish people listened to my sermons as closely they do to you ladies. I'm gonna have to try your drama techniques."

After class, Fern walked back to where he'd left his motorcycle, Tox went home to his parents' house to sleep. Fay and I were alone in the church, so she pulled out a bottle of martinis she'd brought from home and we downed them, giggling on our folding cots in the dark.

When we returned to Poptún, there was no time to think of birthdays. We had to attend a meeting in Flores for all the diocesan teams working in the Petén. On the last night, the Poptún group went out to dinner to celebrate my birthday. Flores was fun because there were some decent restaurants. We ate at *La Paloma Blanca*, The White Dove, where I feasted on fresh shrimp.

Riding home, I sat in back with John Fay and Fern. We

were in a great mood. This birthday had been the best of my life, without any of the things I used to consider important in the States. A flood of happiness rushed over me. I reached out to hold Fern's and then John Fay's hands.

At first I thought John would be too shy, but he smiled at me in the dark and tightened his grip, grasping my hand warmly all the way home.

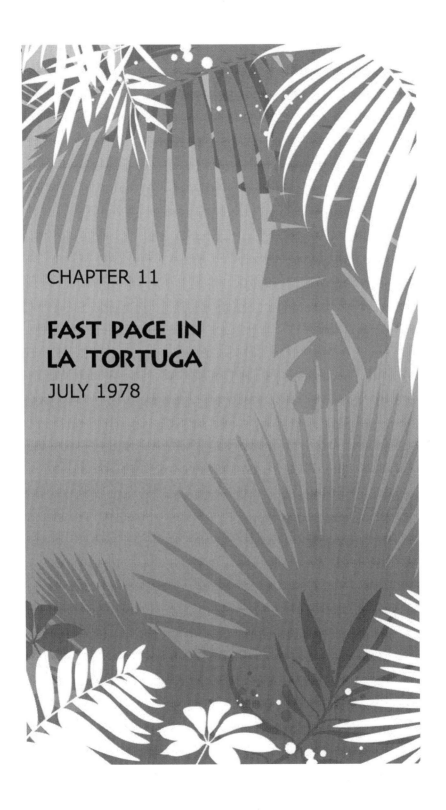

CHAPTER 11

FAST PACE IN
LA TORTUGA
JULY 1978

The next month found us in yet another tiny jungle village. Throwing on grass-stained jeans and yesterday's T-shirt, I quietly opened the back door of the church where Fay and I slept when we visited La Tortuga for clinic and health classes.

The Guatemalan morning was gorgeous, with pinkish-white clouds like flowers in the sky. No one was around this early, allowing me the privacy for a quick trip down the muddy trail to the bushes. Like most of the villages we visited, there were no outhouses here. Nevertheless, I liked La Tortuga, meaning turtle, a village of congenial people.

A young woman blocked my path.

"*Buenos dias*," I said. My interior dialogue was not so polite.

"*Buenos dias.*" She looked down shyly, shifting the baby in her arms. Her polyester dress was poorly mended; her toes poked through the cracks in her shoes.

"Did you want something?"

"*Si, quiero pasar por la clinica.*"

"Oh, clinic doesn't start for two more hours. We'll be glad to see you at 8:00. *Con permiso.*"

Irritated at the interruption, I headed for the bushes. Suddenly, I stopped. What if...darn! I turned around.

"*Que es el problema?*"

"The baby. He's had diarrhea and vomiting. *Esta muy grave*, he is very sick."

As I pulled off the blanket, the baby's head flopped back. At once, the familiar adrenalin surge of an emergency made my heart race. "How long?"

"Three days."

Though he needed treatment immediately, I wasn't sure he'd survive the two-hour trip to the Poptún hospital.

"Let us drive you."

"No! We have no money!"

"The church will pay. Don't worry."

"NO!"

In life or death cases we couldn't let lack of money stand in the way of getting treatment. Frustrated by her stubbornness, I directed her inside.

"Fay, get up! This baby is really sick. The mother refuses the hospital."

Fay sat up on her folding cot. Her hair was matted to her head on one side and stuck out on the other. She groaned and started dressing.

The baby lay still as I touched him. His skin stayed wrinkled when I pinched it, a sign of dehydration, and the fontanel, the soft spot on the infant's head was sunken. I'd never seen a baby so dehydrated who was still alive.

"*¿Como se llama?*"

"He is called Manuel," the mother said softly. She watched him with that look of hopelessness I'd often seen before, stroking his forehead over and over.

"When did he last urinate?" I asked.

"*Quien sabe*," she said. "He's had constant green diarrhea. *Pura agua*...like water."

My eyes met Fay's. We had to do something.

"Lizzie, is there anything we could do here?" asked Fay.

"I could give him an injection for vomiting. We could try some *suero*," I said, referring to our home-made electrolyte fluid. "I don't know how good I am starting IVs on babies."

Again we tried to persuade the mother to go to the hospital. She just shook her head. Finally, she rose, disgusted.

I thought, she's probably terrified of the hospital, too often a death sentence where villagers were mistreated or ignored.

"Please wait! We'll try, but we can't promise he'll make it. You must help."

She nodded, regarding me with dark eyes revealing fright.

Fay made the *suero*, while I injected him with *Nauseol* to stop the vomiting.

Like a baby bird, he swallowed the spoonful of fluid I held to his dry lips, not opening his eyes.

Watching intently, his mother smiled as I started the IV. Expecting flat veins from dehydration, I was surprised the needle slipped in easily. For the first time, the mother seemed pleased. People thought only shots had power. Since Fay and I had come to the aldeas, we battled daily over shots. People begged for injections. They thought vitamin injections were the answer to their exhaustion from malnutrition. They didn't believe us when we said oral medications were often more effective. Sometimes we yielded and administered *Complejo B*, Vitamin B, simply because we hadn't the energy to argue.

"Even with the IV, he needs liquids by mouth," I explained. "*Suero* has sugar and salt, the things he's lost."

Eight o'clock brought the usual gathering of patients for the clinic. Quickly, I escaped for a now urgent trip to the bushes.

Every few minutes throughout the long day, I left the patients I was seeing to check on Manuel. "Did you give him the suero?" I repeatedly asked the mother. She would shake her head no. This mother's passivity was getting on my nerves. I couldn't seem to make her understand. She was a lovely young woman with big eyes like a frightened deer, but she must not be very bright.

Late in the afternoon, Manuel whimpered. Then wet his diaper! I felt like shouting, "Hooray!" We had all but won.

That night the mother stayed for our classes. Manuel was a potent example of what we were trying to teach: how quickly one can die of dehydration, how simple home-made fluids can result in a miraculous recovery.

By the time classes were over, Manuel had perked up enough to go home. The mother nodded as we instructed her to give him suero plus sulfa for his intestinal infection.

On the way to Poptún, Fay and I discussed, as we always did, our day's work in the clinic.

"I feel guilty that I almost made that woman wait to be seen. Manuel might have died." I reflected on how I needed to be more flexible.

"I wonder if the mother will remember how to make the suero," Fay worried.

"Or how important it is to have him take it," I added.

"I think we should have a class on diarrhea. So many parents don't know what to do."

"Good idea, Lizzie. Let's plan that for next time."

While we visited other villages during the following two months, we thought of Manuel often. When we returned to La Tortuga, there sat his mother in our class on dehydration. Neither Fay nor I was artistically inclined and our diarrhea drawings proved it (below). Even so, people got a big bang out of our "green poop and brown poop" illustrations.

At the end of class, I asked for someone to review the preparation of *suero*, as I always did.

Manuel's mother smiled shyly, looked at her baby and explained, "First boil water for twenty minutes. Add the juice of an orange, a tablespoon of sugar, a quarter teaspoon of salt and a pinch of soda. Give the baby a teaspoon at a time. Babies get dehydrated if you don't give them fluids."

Manuel regarded us through eyes that shone like black marbles. Now we didn't have to worry; the mother I'd thought couldn't learn had memorized the formula and kept her baby alive. We were grateful for every victory we won.

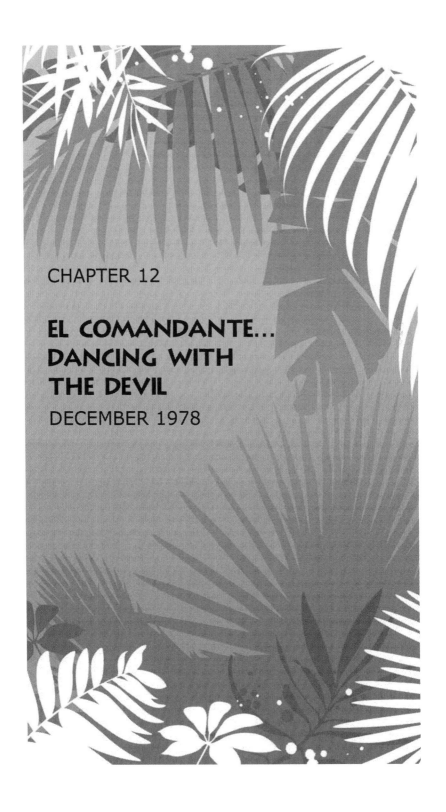

CHAPTER 12

EL COMANDANTE...
DANCING WITH
THE DEVIL

DECEMBER 1978

This jungle had a dark side, for sure, and the black heart of it was undoubtedly Colonel Benedicto Lucas. With his suave, dark good looks, he exuded mystery. He was known as *El Comandante* and ran the thousand-man army base in Poptún. (Those are his soldiers, above, checking ID.) People considered him intelligent, in contrast to his brother, Romeo Lucas Garcia, the President of Guatemala. Everyone joked about the stupidity of President Lucas.

Half the women in Poptún were ready to throw themselves at Colonel Lucas. Plenty already had, if one believed the numerous young ladies who claimed he was the father of their children.

He was *padrino* to many families in Poptún. In Guatemala, being the godfather didn't necessarily mean that person was a spiritual mentor. It usually meant the family was less well off. Padrinos paid a baby's baptism expenses and provided gifts, which parents couldn't afford. Many people around Poptún were indebted to the comandante, as to a mafioso, because he sided with them in land disputes or protected them when someone gave them a hard time. Recipients of his "gifts" were expected to keep quiet about his abuses of power.

Lucas was asked to be the witness at a marriage. Fern refused to perform the wedding because Lucas set such a bad moral example in the community. We constantly heard of new girls he was getting pregnant. Lucas sent a substitute to the rehearsal as witness. At the actual ceremony, Lucas stepped forward. An awkward moment for Fern. Confrontation might cause problems. Fern chose to let the clash go, but he was unhappy. This showdown was one way the comandante proved he was the wily conniver everyone said.

Another time, Lucas asked both John Fay and Fern if he could be padrino for ten babies. Lucas claimed he "didn't have time" for the pre-baptismal talks. John reminded Lucas he was a married man, yet lived with prostitutes, and that Lucas had ordered the murders of some campesinos in San Luís.

Both Fern and John denied Lucas's request to be godfather. While drinking heavily in San Luís, the comandante vowed that Fern's and John's days in Poptún and San Luís were numbered. He would *never* help the church in Poptún, he said, because it was communistic.

Lucas drove a white Toyota Land Cruiser, a replica of Mo's. "With my luck," Mo said, "they'll mistake me for him and assassinate me for driving the same friggin' car!"

The comandante had grown up in Cobán, in the *departmento* or state of Altaverapáz, where the majority of Kek'chi lived. People said the reason Lucas spoke the language so well was that he himself was part Kek'chi. He also trained in counter-insurgency in the School of the Americas in Panama, completing three courses, two while an army captain in combat intelligence in 1965 and the other in 1970, as lieutenant colonel. He served in the French foreign legion, spoke French fluently and passable English. Gossip had it that he had been married at least twice.

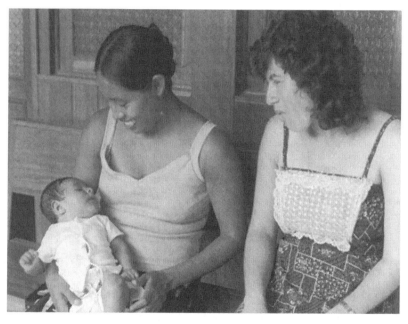

In 1978, the church in Poptún sponsored a Christmas dance. Fay and I attended with **Mecca**, (above left) our cook, and **Marina**, (above right) who washed our clothes. The *salón* of the church was packed with young people, kids running around and older folks sitting along the walls watching. Every available space was crowded with dancers. I leaned against the wall and enjoyed the rock beat pounding through to my feet. I

loved watching the Guatemalans' uninhibited rhythm. Hardly anyone was a wallflower at Latin dances. I was hoping someone would ask me, when Lico approached and asked to dance. I liked **Lico**, (left) the teacher in our literacy program, a young man of charm and a come-hither smile. I felt happy, caught up in the lively atmosphere.

Then, across the room, I spied Lucas. What was *he* doing here? Mocking the church or paying his respects? Who knew?

Half the women followed him with their eyes, looks seething with invitation. He danced with several, while surveying the hall as if he commanded this crowd, too. Those dark eyes riveted me from across the hall, and I sensed his intention.

"How can I keep him from asking me?" I whispered to Mecca.

"You can't. Just don't talk. That's how we discourage those whom we don't care to dance with a second time," she whispered back.

Suddenly, he stood at my side. "*¿Quiere bailar?*" he murmured.

Before I could summon the courage to refuse, he guided me smoothly into the crowd. I felt both attracted and repelled, ashamed to be seen dancing with him and afraid I had done

something to provoke his interest. I knew I had a tendency to
flirt. What a hypocrite I was! Hadn't I criticized him with all
the rest? And now, when my moment came to take a stand, I let
it slip by. I couldn't respect such an evil man, yet here I was
dancing with him.

Earlier in May of that year, after the massacre of the
Kek'chi people in Panzós, many said Lucas was responsible.
Missionaries who protested the massacre were forced to leave
the country. He was the most powerful man in all the Petén.
The comandante could kick us out or have us killed. I
determined not to talk. I held myself stiff, and my insides
churned.

Finally, the dance ended. He bowed slightly, barely
holding my elbow with smooth familiarity. Up close, I saw the
Rudolf Valentino curve to his nostril. His smile didn't quite
reach his unreadable eyes. I congratulated myself on keeping
my mouth shut, as I like nothing better than talking with
people.

He propelled me over to Mecca, Marina and Fay, his hand
on my back. They gave me knowing looks. Then he asked Fay
to dance and I watched them sweep into the crowd. I surmised
he was paying his "respects" to the church, because in a way,
we represented the church in that town. I was relieved when he
left the salón.

Fay must have felt as I did. "God, he's sexy," she sighed,
"and what a dancer!"

In the next year, 1979, John Blazo, Fay Hauer and I were
invited to the wedding of an employee, with a sit-down dinner,
liquor and a live band. After the ceremony and reception, the
father of the bride invited us home. Only on our arrival did we
realize the party was on the comandante's property.

A marimba band was playing and couples danced. Young,
pretty women giggled, and there were cases of Johnny Walker
Black Label whisky. Half the people were drunk. I couldn't
help thinking how Lucas had gotten rich by stealing the poor

campesinos' land. I was disgusted with myself for being there.

Afterwards when John Blazo, Fay and I talked, they said they felt guilty, too. Lucas had paid for the wedding. Now that family owed him favors. After my own reluctance to refuse to dance with Lucas and attending the party on his property, I understood better the complexity of corruption in Guatemala. Making changes was difficult.

Before I left Guatemala in February 1980, union members were tortured and killed. Lawyers, teachers and university students trying to change the corrupt political structures disappeared. Opposition to the government was labeled communistic. Wealthy landowners and the military wanted things kept as they were.

In the highlands, guerillas gained the trust of many Indian groups, sometimes taking over entire towns. Who were these mysterious guerillas? I had never seen any, at least not that I was aware.

Bodies were found along the road in the Petén. Guerillas, claimed the army. Sometimes the dead were soldiers ambushed by guerillas. But while I was there, from 1977 to 1980, I was mostly ignorant of what was going on and why. (Left, a murdered man lies in his coffin.)

After I left Guatemala, I continued to follow the fate of the country in the news, and I was saddened to

see it explode in hate. President Romeo Lucas Garcia turned to
his brother, Benedicto Lucas, to quash the unrest. The
comandante bombed the highlands, destroying villages and
killing thousands. It made no difference if the people resisted
the guerillas; the army terrorized villagers after contact had
been made with them. The comandante used tactics he had
learned in Algiers, fighting for the French. People were forced
to move into model villages so their activities could be
controlled. Civil patrols began to monitor guerilla movement in
and out of town.

Ditches became cemeteries of the maimed and mutilated,
streets became the sites of drive-by killings. Men in
plainclothes drove late-model cars with tinted windows and no
license plates. The army snatched individuals suspected of
guerilla activity from their homes in the middle of the night or
even in broad daylight. Victims, if their bodies were ever
found, were discovered with eyes gouged out, tongues cut out,
breasts hacked off and a bullet to the back of the head. People
trembled in terror of who would be murdered next.

Fay Hauer and Dr. Evelyn St. Onge, who taught the health
promoters after I left, and Fern Gosselin from our team,
attended the dedication of a church in Tanjóc, hiking into the
small community. The comandante was invited too.
Afterwards, he appeared on TV, and accused our team of being
communists. He said Fay was posing as a nun and deceiving
the people. Lucas mentioned he had seen two good-looking
women from Poptún in Tanjóc. They carried backpacks, he
said, used false names and trained guerillas deep in the jungle.
Everyone knew he was referring to Fay Hauer and Dr. Evelyn
St.Onge.

On television Lucas said, "The Marxist priests grieve me
because I am a Catholic." He said they were enemies of the
Guatemaltecos, the Guatemalans, and should be thrown out of
the country.

Twelve priests, hundreds of catechists, teachers,

promoters, and thousands of campesinos had already been murdered. Fay Hauer and Fern Gosselin left Poptún in 1981. Fay returned only after she knew Lucas had retired from the army. Fern Gosselin waited until 1988 to visit the Petén.

The comandante became the mayor of Poptún. He lost an election to be the president of Guatemala. I heard he is no longer svelte. The military base still dominates Poptún. The kaibiles, similar to our special forces, expert at fighting the guerillas, are stationed there (pictured on the following page).

Because I am an American, I feel responsible for the comandante. After I returned to the U.S. I kept track of goings on there and became more politically active. Through those activities I learned that American interference in Guatemala has a long history, rooted in greed. The United Fruit Company of the U.S. owned more than 550 million acres of land, and didn't want any of its holdings to be redistributed as Arbenz, the reformist president intended. After Arbenz's ouster in 1954, instigated by the CIA, the government relied on the army to maintain order. Any attempt by reform-minded groups was smashed by the army. The United States has funneled aid to the Guatemalan military to maintain the status quo, while

mouthing words that supported democracy.

The U.S. Army School of the Americas in Panama was founded in 1946, supposedly to promote stability in the region. But it soon earned the nickname, School of Assassins. In 1984, the school was kicked out of Panama and relocated at Fort Benning, Georgia.

There, Latin American soldiers learn counterinsurgency, military intelligence and psychological operations. Most of the officers cited for the rape and murder of Maryknoll sisters Ita Ford and Maura Clark, Ursuline nun Dorothy Kazel, and lay missioner Jean Donovan, were graduates of the school. The assassination of Archbishop Romero and the murder of the six priests in El Salvador were also credited to this group. There is a move in the U.S. to close the school, and hopefully it may eventually happen.

Rigoberta Menchú, a Guatemalan Indian woman who won the Nobel Peace prize and others mounted a campaign in Spain in 1995 to convict former President Lucas Garcia and his brother, Benedicto Lucas Garcia and other high ranking army men of thousands of deaths of innocent Guatemalans during the 1980s. Between January 1980 and Lucas's overthrow two years later, human rights groups cited no fewer than 344 massacres. The brothers were able to retire without hindrance to their large estates in northern Guatemala, whence Benedicto, at least, continued to dabble in politics until civilian rule began gradually to increase the risk of prosecution. Unfortunately, trial and punishment never came to pass. In later years the ex-president fled to Venezuela, where he was safe from extradition to Spain, and he died in Venezuela in 2006. Unfortunately, the constitutional court in Guatemala blocked several initiatives of the Spanish courts demanding information and testimony from Guatemala. There is no outcome, yet. Benedcito Lucas still visits Poptún but now lives in Antigua, Guatemala with his third wife.

I wonder if the massacre of Panzós would have happened

if Lucas had not been trained at the School of the Americas. He and others like him are partly products of our own sick policies in Central America.

CHAPTER 13

THE GOOD
CHRISTMAS...
THE TENDER TURKEY
DECEMBER 1978

My mood lifted that December with preparations for Christmas. Leon and I sat on the patio one night and made our plans. Rain poured a water curtain. I wore my Bolivian sweater of soft alpaca wool. At night, I often went to bed in my flannel nightgown and wool socks. Even under six blankets, I shivered. I'd never dreamed the jungle could be so cold.

I handed Leon a bowl of popcorn. "Sorry, Leon, it got a little over done." I had a tendency to burn things on our quirky gas stove.

"I don't mind," he said. "It's nice and crunchy." He was packaging bugs to mail to the States. On the broad arms of the Adirondack chair were string, rubber bands, small bottles, plastic containers and tiny envelopes he made of scraps of paper. Long before it was the "in" thing, Leon recycled more junk than anyone I'd ever seen. His lap was piled with plastic bags holding various bugs. One bag contained about 100 cockroaches of all sizes.

He munched on unpopped and charred kernels from the bottom of the bowl. Now and then, he lifted his balding head and smiled shyly. Leon never complained about the food, although he had the most peculiar eating habits of anyone I'd ever known, such as honey on his mashed potatoes.

Just the fact I was talking with him made him happy. Sitting there at peace, last year's Christmas was forgotten. I'd been miserable, lonely, feeling unaccepted and as though I would never fit in. But between then and now, Fay and I had started our work. It made a huge difference in my adjustment to be doing something worthwhile.

"Let's get our tree soon. I love to decorate the Christmas tree, Leon."

"We can't have a tree this year," he said. "Blazo says it's against the law. The town is making an effort at conservation."

"What! Making a fuss about a few trees when Lucas cuts down acres to pasture his cows? That's a bunch of baloney."

Colonel Lucas commanded the military base in Poptún. His brother was president of Guatemala. They owned thousands of acres in the Petén, which people said they had acquired illegally.

"I'll get one myself. Christmas isn't Christmas without a tree. I don't *care* if I'm arrested."

Leon regarded me, apparently amazed by my indignant tirade. "Maybe I could find you one." His tone was reluctant.

"That would be wonderful, Leon." I ignored his doubts,

determined to get my tree.

The next day I sat in the sala, cursing the treadle sewing machine. The dumb thing refused to wind the bobbin. Leon shuffled in bearing what looked like a dead plant.

"Here's your Christmas tree, Liz." His broad lips curved into a smile as he propped it against the wall. How could I tell him this spindly stick simply wouldn't do?

Fern poked his head in the door, frowned at the bush, then at me. "Hmmmm," he said with a smile, and resumed fooling with his motorcycle on the patio.

"Leon...thank you...but, well...I just don't think a cactus looks like a *Christmas* tree," I burst out.

Leon must have felt hurt, for he kept his head down. But I was determined to get what I wanted.

"Fern," I called, "Could you *please*, puulllease get us a *real* tree?"

Fern said nothing. After a few minutes, he called to Leon. "Come on, Leon. Let's get a tree or we'll never hear the end of it."

They drove off in the parish vehicle, returning with a lush pine of sweeping branches and two-inch needles. The pungent aroma filled the sala. Even back home I had never seen such a crisp tree. We were lucky that Poptún was at an elevation where pine trees grew.

"It's beautiful," I breathed. Oh, this was going to be a *good* Christmas, I could tell.

"You should have seen Fern," Leon said, beaming. "Drove right up to Lucas's property. Fern climbed one of the tallest trees and sawed off the top." Leon's hurt feelings must be over, for he looked as pleased as I felt.

"Oh, dear, I hope nobody saw you," I said.

To take a tree from the commandant's land was risky. At least Fern had chopped just the top half.

Leon propped the tree in a bucket of dirt and stood it in the sala, while I found the decorations from last year, a few red, green and gold glass balls.

The mildewed walls didn't matter when I looked at the tree.

On our way back from Jacal the previous year, where we'd learned tropical medicine at the hospital run by the Maryknoll sisters, Fay and I rode the bus into the city. We stopped to rest where the cliffs fell away below the road in steep plunges. We sat on a rock, gazing at the terraced rows of corn. Indian children approached us selling **Quetzal birds** (left) they had made from dyed red- and-green chicken feathers, hung from a loop of red embroidery thread.

The national bird, the Quetzal, lived in remote areas of the highlands or jungle. I loved its symbolism: a graceful being of brilliant feathers and a curving long tail, reputed to die in captivity. To me, the bird mirrored the plight of the Guatemalans. I bought two-dozen birds for *diez centavos*, ten cents each, thinking they would make lovely Christmas decorations some day.

Now I climbed a chair and hung the ornaments that Pastora Lira, a young woman from Nicaragua, and John Blazo handed me, enjoying the needles pricking my hands. Colorful

feathers of the Quetzal birds stood out against the dark green branches.

Every year since I returned home to Seattle, I decorate my Christmas tree with those same birds. I remember as I loop them over the branches that beautiful place where I bought them, the children who made them and that special Christmas.

John Fay watched from the door.

"Hi John. Wanna help? Isn't this a gorgeous tree?" I asked.

He shook his head. "No thanks, Liz. Let me know when you're ready to shop."

Later that day, John and I planned to buy gifts for our cook Mecca, Marina the laundress, Julio the maintenance man,

Tox and Hermelindo, our translators, and Doña Hortensia's kids—**Mario** (above) and **Maria Edna** (left, with **Fay**)—who helped us clean up and prepare for aldea trips

"Look what I've got," Mo said, handing me a box. Carefully he removed a ceramic nativity group in primary colors, placing the crib on the table and a row of figurines with grotesquely painted faces on each side.

"There." Mo admired his work, hands on his skinny hips. "Doesn't that look good?"

I remembered the manger scene from last year, only now its garishness didn't bother me.

Fay stopped by, licking her fingers and murmuring, "Mmmmm, yummy." She'd been making her specialty; chocolate peanut butter fudge. (That's **Fay** on the right, with **Kay** baking for Chirstmas.) Fay took one look at Mo's contribution and swooped in to rearrange it.

"You can't just put them in a row like that. It's not artistic!" She shifted the pieces around, and put half the figurines back in the box. "We don't need all these."

"Now just a minute, Fay. I happen to like this manger scene. It only cost me five dollars for all these pieces," Mo said.

They argued for a few minutes. Finally, they put out every piece again, but arranged each to Fay's satisfaction.

"There. That looks better." After Mo left, Fay added, "Even if it is a cheap little set."

I breathed the pine scent and smiled. We were a real family after all. This Christmas promised to be a vast improvement over our first.

Months earlier, Fern had carried home a young turkey someone gave him. The tom roamed freely in our fenced yard. Marina, our laundress, and Fay spoiled him by feeding him corn by hand. Fay had always loved animals. I often heard her crooning when she fed him a special treat, "That's a good turkey." By Christmas he stalked the grounds plump and healthy.

Long before Christmas, I began my secret project, making signs for everyone's door. The same carpenter who had built our chairs and wardrobe closets cut mahogany rectangles with holes in each end. I threaded leather ties in the openings to hang the signs. Mo's logo was easy: "Another biggee!" I painted names and a logo for each person, and could hardly wait to see their reactions.

We drew names for a gift exchange. Unlike last year's heated arguments, our community meetings now were congenial. Before, we'd disagreed on theology, our jobs, food, and spending money. I could barely remember the details of what I'd been upset about then. Now John Blazo volunteered to be Santa and to emcee our employee party. We would celebrate mass just for us. We were drawing closer as a group. A feeling of good will filled the air with fun.

I went shopping with **Pastora Lira**, (below) who lived in the room adjoining mine. She had come to Poptún when it

 became dangerous for her in Nicaragua. Pastora had helped feed people, even some revolutionaries, because she didn't discriminate about whom she fed. She knew John Blazo and Fern when they worked in Nicaragua, so she sought refuge in Poptún. Recently, she'd helped John Blazo prepare children for First Communion and other parish activities. When Pastora came, it was

wonderful for John, because he had someone to work with.

Pastora and I stepped carefully down the muddy road through town. I wore my green rain poncho. Like many Seattleites used to drizzly rain, I rarely used an umbrella or covered my head. But if I didn't wear a poncho in the Petén, I'd be drenched.

The mercado was a collection of flimsy wood buildings surrounding a concrete structure. Vendors offered fruits and vegetables, slaughtered beef and chicken, and sold everything from shoes to saddles. When one entered, it was to be met by the aroma of fresh bread and flowers, the bloody smell of raw meat and the moist odors of mud and rain.

I walked gingerly, my sandals slipping in the mud. We filled our plastic shopping bags with carrots, radishes, potatoes and *guiskil*, the Guatemalan zucchini. A hand of bananas cost 15¢ and a bag of apples grown in the highlands 25¢. Eggs were expensive at seven cents each. I loved the fruits and vegetables, not so perfect looking as in the States, but they tasted better.

"Pastora, do you think there's any pumpkin?" I wanted to make pies.

"I've never heard of that," she said. "Maybe it's only something you have *en los Estados Unidos*."

Instead, we bought several large squash and *panella*, a sweet like brown sugar or molasses. It came in square blocks.

We stopped at Doña Mincha's, considered the best store in town. One could buy fabric, thread and boxed chocolates, although I'd eaten some candy from there that was moldy. Small boxes of Tampax for $3.50, triple the U.S. price, were stuffed behind glass cases with Oil of Olay and Camay soap. Washington state Delicious apples, wrapped in green tissue paper, sold for $2.50 apiece. I'd never seen such huge apples, even at home.

On one wall, Doña Mincha stocked liquors and wines. "I'd love some wine," I said.

"Get some," said Pastora, agreeable as always. The two

bottles on the shelf were labeled *Made in Guatemala.* Mo had warned me, "Don't buy wine made in Guatemala. It's disgusting."

I purchased two bottles because I love wine and it was Christmas. Surely it couldn't be as bad as Mo claimed.

When we arrived home, Pastora and I cut the squash into chunks and boiled it. Then we grated the hard blocks of panella. The whole process took hours. Out of the oven and golden brown, the pies smelled of cinnamon and molasses.

The day before Christmas, Leon and Fern went off with a hatchet and slaughtered the turkey. Both men had grown up on farms and knew how to kill birds, everyone said. Fay didn't object; maybe she was resigned to our turkey's fate.

On Christmas Day, Kay got up early to stuff the turkey.

"Look how plump it is, Lizzie. I'm going to baste it with butter and it'll be soooo good."

I suddenly had an idea. "Wait a minute, Kay." I ran across to the convent *bodega,* storeroom, where Fay and I kept our medical equipment and found a syringe with a three-inch needle attached.

"Oh, my God," Kay said, when I handed it to her. "What's that for?"

"To inject the butter on the inside and the meat will be even more tender. I hear these turkeys can be really tough, especially if you let them roam."

Kay accepted the syringe as if she might have to endure a shot from the thick needle herself. But later I peeked in and saw her bending over the oven door, expertly shooting butter into the meat.

"This is kinda fun." She grinned.

Fay was in her element. She hummed off-key as she set the table with the cloths we saved for special occasions (right). Both were Guatemalan fabric, one a pale yellow and the other a deep forest green. Each had Mayan symbols, birds and ducks and variegated stripes. She placed candles at either end and

arranged a centerpiece of red and green Christmas balls in the middle.

Later, she boiled potatoes. "I make gooood mashed potatoes!" she said while she mashed, adding milk and butter, then tasted a forkful. "Uuuummmmm yummy, that's good."

Fern tinkered with someone's radio on the patio. He liked fiddling with mechanical things in his leisure time. From his room wailed Freddy Fender. Freddy Fender was popular in Poptún. In fact, there was a little restaurant that always played his music. Now Freddy crooned mournfully, "Roses are red, my love, violets are blue, ooh whoo, whoo, whoo."

"I hate Freddy Fender," Fay hollered out. "Play something else, Fern."

Fern switched tapes. Next we heard a Nicaraguan group singing "Son tus perfumeres, mujer." Literally translated it meant, "It is your perfume, woman." Now and then Fern wandered into the kitchen and injected communion wine into the turkey.

"Wine will make it tender," he said.

At dinnertime, we sat down in the *champa*, our outdoor gazebo, to fresh-squeezed orange juice from our backyard trees, lima beans from Leon's garden, and bread from the Devine farm outside Poptún. Carol and Mike Devine, a couple from the U.S., baked homemade bread at their farm, the Finca Ixobel. Leon drove to their place every Saturday for bread and fresh eggs. All the food except the turkey was on the table, steaming and sending out rich aromas.

Blazo ceremoniously opened the wine, one arm draped with a towel. Enough wine for an inch for each person. Kay and Fern were still carving the turkey. We waited five minutes. Occasionally, someone hollered toward the kitchen, "Hey, what's going on out there?" We waited another five minutes. Still they didn't come.

Finally, Fay stomped off to look into the delay. "The vegetables are getting cold!" I heard her say. She came back in a moment. "Let's go ahead. They'll be out in a minute."

We held hands around the table while Mo prayed. We clinked glasses and said the traditional Guatemalan toast, "*Salud, dinero, y amor, y tiempo para gozarles.*" Health, money and love, and time to enjoy them. I sipped the wine and screwed up my face at the sickly sweet taste, but drank it down. After all, it was wine.

We began to eat. I felt nervous. Where *were* Kay and Fern? After a while, they finally appeared; Fern carried a large platter heaped with turkey. The only thing missing at our dinner was cranberry sauce, but it didn't matter.

I relaxed. Jokes and happy conversation floated around me. The food was good. The warmth was palpable. Somehow, we had become a community, without elaborate plans to make it happen, and probably most important, without expectations. (That's **Kay** cutting **Leon**'s hair, right, in another of her many roles.)

What a strange group we were. Surely God had a greater sense of humor than anyone, bringing us together in one

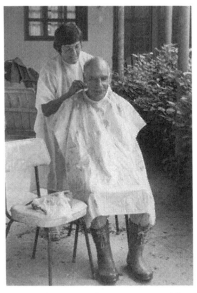

purpose. Sitting at that table and feeling so completely happy, I knew that coming to Guatemala had been one of the best things I'd ever done.

After dinner, John Blazo washed dishes, singing cheerfully as he worked. John Fay dried and put away, his blue eyes sparkling.

We brought out the pies. They were especially rich and spicy with the panella. No one mentioned they were squash instead of pumpkin.

Next, we began our gift exchange. Kay received a plant from Leon in a beautiful clay pot from the mercado. It was about as ugly as the Christmas tree he'd brought me, but Kay

received it graciously as she always did. Leon tried so hard to please.

Everyone unwrapped the door signs I'd made. Leon promptly hung his. "Leon's Room," the logo said. A butterfly was painted on the side. When I visited the Petén years later in 1989, Leon still had his sign up.

Kay had drawn my name. She gave me her own favorite tape of Judy Collins, "Colors." She smiled when she saw her door sign: Studer's Tea Shoppe & Counseling Service (left).

The drawing was by Maria Dolores. Kay loved tea and was a great listener—our informal in house-psychiatrist.

Then when everyone had settled down and finished opening gifts, Kay cleared her throat. "Quiet everybody. I have an announcement."

The buzz of conversation stopped.

"I have a confession to make. Our *farm boys* forgot to take the gizzard out of the turkey!"

A moment of stunned silence, then everyone jabbered at once.

Kay went on. "You should have seen when I took the turkey from the oven. A pouch stuck out, green...and shiny. Ready to burst. I called Fern right away. He said it was the gizzard. Oh...it was awful cutting into that thing. It smelled rotten and the meat was gray. We cut all around until there was no bad meat. It tasted fine, so we served it anyhow and decided not tell you guys until after. That's what took us so long in the kitchen." She grinned.

We all groaned and made disgusted noises. Fern and Leon avoided looking at anybody, but I noticed they had slight grins. After the uproar died down, I told Kay, "It tasted good to me."

No one got sick. The turkey had been delicious and most of all, tender. Laughter was one of the best gifts we received that Christmas.

CHAPTER 14

LIVING IN THE ALDEAS... O PIONEERS

1978-1979

On our many trips into the jungle to educate and treat patients, we experienced a roller coaster of emotions. At five o'clock one morning, I awakened with a start. A man stood rock silent by my cot in the shelter where we slept. "Fay, wake up!" I whispered.

She bolted up as if we were being attacked. We stared at the man and he stared back. Finally, he said, *"Tengo mi muestra,* I have my specimen," and handed Fay a small match box emitting a poopy smell.

"*Muchas gracias*," Fay said groggily and pulled her sleeping bag around her nightgown. "Clinic isn't until eight. *Nos vemos*, we'll see you later."

The man remained several minutes before slipping away without a noise. This was their way. In their culture, it's impolite to leave abruptly. The Kek'chi people I knew passed the time first, considering it rude to launch into what they wanted without inquiring how everything was in your life first. After he left, we burst out laughing.

"It's still warm!" hooted Fay.

"Oh, God, Fay can you believe it?" I snuggled into my sleeping bag, but it was a long time before I drifted off because I couldn't stop giggling.

The man had been so obedient to our request for a "fresh" specimen. I loved how people responded so sincerely to us, but sometimes the circumstances were *too* hilarious.

We'd learned that examining dry stool resulted in an unrecognizable mess under the microscope. Now we knew Tox was getting the point across to bring a "warm" sample when he translated our classes into the Kek'chi language.

Maybe we hadn't explained clearly what time clinic started. If we had, the man would have been there at 8:00, as if he wore a Timex on his wrist. Without watches or clocks, the people of the aldeas were invariably on time.

Almost every trip had such amusing incidents. Looking back on those days, I know the funny moments helped me survive mission life.

We visited two or three aldeas a week, working from 8:00 in the morning until 9:00 at night, with evening classes for the men and boys who worked in the fields during the day (left). Women and girls came then too, as we were the only diversion from the tedium of their lives.

After six days, it was back to Poptún. On Saturdays we cleaned slides and thermometers, sterilized equipment, packaged medicines, then bought fruits and vegetables for our next trip. Sometimes we even worked on Sundays.

At first we didn't know how exhausting such a schedule could be. We saw the desperate needs of the people and wanted to help. (That's me taking a medical history, left.) Too, we hoped to prove lay women could survive the rigors of mission life and "do" something. After all, we were the first lay women these people had ever met, and we were pioneering this program in this area.

Each aldea had its own particular character, which made the repetition of our routine bearable. Chacalté was nearly all Kek'chi. The first time we went there, the villagers eyed us suspiciously. Women went around bare breasted. They refused to share the dwelling where they cooked beans and tortillas over a fire on the ground. There, women prepared the big community meal when John Fay visited for mass. Instead, they made us set up clinic and sleep in the shelter next to the church.

The church overlooked the road and was indistinguishable from the other huts, until one went inside. A poor wooden altar was decorated with pink and blue plastic and a bloody statue of Christ. But I loved that place, for it stayed cool even during the hottest part of the day. Within its shadows, a spirit of prayer emanated, as if many had meditated there.

The only ones in Chacalté who paid any attention to us were a pack of rowdy boys (right). Maybe their teacher played hooky because school was never in session when we were there.

The moment they saw us drive up, the boys ran down the hill shouting, "Fay! Elizabeth!" They helped us unload our truck and carried everything with an endearing spirit of fun. I resented the fact that no adults ever greeted us. Fay didn't have such high expectations.

One day when we arrived in Chacalté, our boys were playing soccer with rags held together with twine and shreds of an old ball. They had to stop every few minutes to lash it together again.

"We *gotta* get a decent ball for them," Fay said.

"Next time we go to the city. We can use our sponsor money," I agreed.

Fay and I had people who sent us donations, which we used for the $20 treatment for leischmaniasis, caused by a protozoal-bearing sand fly, the *mosca chiclera*, which burrows into the skin and causes ugly ulcers that won't heal.

"I wonder if these boys go to school?" said Fay. "Maybe we can get them books."

The next time we went to the city, we bought children's picture books and a soccer ball. They were a huge hit. Most

people had seen only a Bible. I wished we could have bought a new ball for every aldea.

When Fay and I arrived in the next town, we'd tell Tox, first thing, "Get the book box, please."

Everyone loved looking at pictures, even though they couldn't read (left). During succeeding visits I took tons of photos, put them in albums and we brought them to the aldeas from then on. People loved seeing their pictures (below). The books and album enthralled them while they waited for hours for their turns in the clinic.

The amazing thing was that not one item of all the hundreds of things we carried with us was ever stolen. And these were a very deprived people.

One hot day in Chacalté, no one signed up for clinic or came to the classes. We decided to stay the night anyhow as going to the next aldea meant packing up the truck again. Our favorite gang of boys swung exuberantly from our lean-to roof.

One little boy, Sebastian, ran around nude except for an open shirt, his stomach swelled with parasites. (That's a malnourished aldea boy, left, happy to get Incaparina, a powdered protein supplement.)

Fay and I tried teaching them English while they taught us Kek'chi. "*Chaquil ac a cuib*," I said. This meant "that you go well." The little boys giggled. "Haa waar yuu tuudaay?" Sebastian said.

That night we fixed chocolate pudding to cheer us up. I mixed it with powdered milk, and Tox patiently beat the lumps out with a wooden spoon. The kids, who had grown up on tortillas and beans, watched, fascinated, and jabbered to each other in Kek'chi, the aroma of chocolate filling the lean-to.

Sebastian gingerly licked the first spoonful. He broke into a face-splitting smile smudged with chocolate and devoured his portion, then held out his spoon for more.

Fay and Tox and I and the five little boys shared the treat, the most fun I'd ever had eating chocolate pudding. Afterward the kids licked the pan and fought over the mixing spoon.

The Chacalté people refused to come to classes, but wanted to be seen in the clinic anyhow. They were outraged at the 25¢ consultation fee, expecting a free exam and free medication. I examined a little boy, who cried as if he was being killed when I checked his ear. His mother snatched him away, muttering sharp Kek'chi words, and aimed me a caustic look. At first, Fay and I kept hoping to win them over. We even asked John Fay to put in a plug for us on his trips to say mass. Nothing worked. Eventually, we stopped going there.

I asked Tox why they didn't accept us.

"They're a funny lot," he said. In 1989, when I again visited Poptún, I learned some young men from Chacalté were studying to be health promoters. The people of Chacalté had needed time to accept something new.

Fay and I worried when no one came to classes. Did it mean they didn't trust us? Gradually, we stopped asking questions and welcomed the rest.

By noon one warm day in Chacté, Tox's hometown, no one had showed up for morning classes. **Tox** went to his parents' house (below left with his family).

We'd been in the aldeas several days. When I ran my fingers through my hair, it felt stiff with dust.

"Let's go to the river and take a bath," said Fay.

We walked downhill to an open spot with dense foliage shielding it. We carried our wash basins, towels, shampoo and

clean clothes. No one was in sight. Normally, the river was a popular place. I put my clothes on the rocks. The sky darkened, then opened and poured, soaking us within seconds.

"It's lunch time," I said. "I bet no one will come. Let's just bathe in the nude."

Fay raised her eyebrows, her brown eyes gleaming. "OK," she said, and pulled off her T-shirt.

We stripped off our muddy clothes and let the warm rain be our shower while thick bushes screened us. I felt deliciously daring. Great fun, until we had to don soaked clothes over wet skin and slosh back to the church. Another time, **Fay** managed to wash her hair in the tiniest of creeks, (above).

We treasured such times. In most villages, crowds attended our clinics. We felt grateful to John Fay and Fern, who helped us be accepted.

Sometimes we bathed in other rivers, and saw women and girls doing laundry and bathing in their clothes. They sudsed their hair and lathered their skin. But they were so discreet that no one glimpsed even a breast. The only sign that they had bathed was wet hair and the clinging damp dresses they changed to clean ones before anyone got a look.

They scrubbed clothes with the same harsh soap they used to bathe themselves. No one could afford shampoo. After pounding, the dirtiest fabrics were amazingly clean, the "whites," a brilliant white. They laid them to dry by the river or carried them in basins on their heads, spreading everything out to dry on grass by their homes.

Most aldeas had a school consisting of stick buildings with dirt floors, homemade benches and desks and a blackboard with a rippling green surface hard to write on. Schools were usually staffed by young teachers fulfilling their year in the *campo,* the countryside, to become certified and to get the posts they wanted in bigger towns later. Some showed up only two days a week or missed entire weeks because no one supervised them.

Many girls never went to school. People thought an education was more important for boys, and since parents could afford to send only one child, boys went.

I asked, "Does school cost so much?"

"No," said one mother, "it's free, but we can't buy the paper and pencils."

Notebooks cost 29¢ and pencils were a nickel. At that time, Guatemalan money was equal to U.S. money. Children had no texts. They had to copy what the teacher wrote on the board into their notebooks. At first, I thought this a poor way to teach, but when I saw how the children remembered facts, I realized drills were excellent.

Because people lacked mental stimulation and educational materials of any kind, our books were immensely popular. I often said to Fay, "I think people come to classes and clinic so they can look at the books and album, not because they're sick."

There certainly was a thirst to learn. People remembered everything we said, long after we'd forgotten.

Sometimes though, during our classes, especially when we'd been congratulating ourselves on our popularity, I would see an old Kek'chi woman dozing on a church bench.

Las Cañas was a favorite village where Ruben, a young teacher, taught school. When we held classes there, he brought the children, making them sit quietly in back.

One day, I sneaked out for a breath of air and wandered over to the school. There was **Ruben**, (with **Fay** in the center of the photo, below) repeating word for word our lesson on boiling water. He encouraged children to memorize the content. "Why do you boil the water?" he asked.

"To kill the worm eggs," the kids said in unison.

"For how many minutes do you boil it?"

"*Viente minutos!*" they shouted. Twenty minutes.

People watched everything we did as though we were the local circus. After months of canned hot dogs, Spam, and tuna, I loathed the sight of those tins, but villagers thought what we ate was luxurious. They waited for us to open a can, then asked humbly for the empty and ran off thoroughly delighted. Sometimes they argued over who would get the containers. I felt ashamed to be tired of tuna.

At every turn, we were reminded of the differences between our two cultures. While driving to the aldeas one trip, Tox threw a piece of paper out the window. Fay spoke sharply to him.

"Tox, don't do that. We can't litter the countryside. Pretty soon it will look like a garbage dump. Please, put all the waste in this litter bag."

Tox stared at Fay as if she were insane. This concept was completely new to him. Contrary to what Fay said though, we never noticed waste. Every scrap of paper or empty bottle was used. Edible waste was devoured by roaming pigs and chickens. There was no such thing as waste paper. The majority of people didn't have any kind of paper in their homes, other than a curling-edged calendar on the wall from another year. If someone wanted to write a letter, they bought one piece of paper and one envelope at a time.

One Christmas I received cards and was writing letters in the aldeas to my friends and family. Several children gathered around and touched the cards. I gave one to a little girl who ran off with it clutched to her chest. She plopped down against the church wall and fingered the paper as if it was pure gold. After that, I gave out all the rest, too.

One job Tox hated was disposing of the garbage. We'd bought a shovel for that purpose. At the end of the day, Tox dug a hole and buried the stool specimens from clinic as well as matchboxes, bottles and corn leaves brimming with dried or runny feces, covered by flies and exuding a nauseating stench.

"Did you take care of the garbage?" Fay would remind him.

"Yes, Fay," he replied in disgust.

Always, people were nearby. I tried to finish with my patients first so I could begin dinner. Cooking was a good outlet for me. No interacting with anyone was involved. Being surrounded by people from early morning until bedtime was driving me crazy.

Fay was a recent nursing graduate so for her, the clinic was a brand new experience. Though I'd been a nurse for years and a nurse practitioner for about a year, I still found the clinic tedious. I recognized the tremendous need for medical care, could hardly wait until our promoters would handle clinics. On the other hand, I looked forward to classes, something Fay found old hat. I enjoyed teaching and was pleased at how people listened to me. (Here I'm teaching dental health while **Tox** translates. Those are my pathetic tooth drawings.)

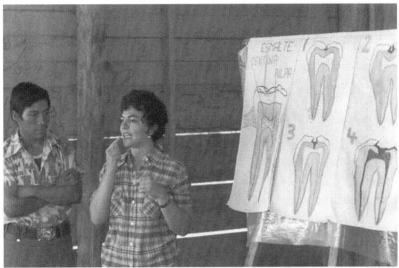

One afternoon, after the usual exhausting day, I hurried to finish with my patients. By the time Fay completed clinic, I had supper well under way.

"*Why* did you finish so early? I like to cook once in a while too!" She was furious.

Then she saw the Spam sizzling in the frying pan.

"I can't stand it! I hate Spam! I'm never going to eat Spam again!" With that she stomped off.

"Poor Fay," I said to Tox. "She's so tired."

He nodded and looked at me with understanding. I knew what she meant. I often felt the same myself, almost overwhelmed by fatigue.

She returned a few minutes later, strained and pale. Her eyes were red and puffy.

"Fay," I said, "You don't have to eat any more Spam. Here, I fixed you a sandwich. Tox will eat your share."

Tox loved whatever we cooked. We sat down at the table. I covered the Spam with a plate so Fay wouldn't even have to look at it.

One or the other of us would often have a fit about something, but thank God, it wasn't both at the same time. I often said to Fay, "This is just one glorified camping trip! When I get back to the States and suggest going camping, remind me of this!" Even though we were both still in our 30s, sometimes the hardships did get to us.

Tox had a calm nature. He showed distress only when Fay and I erupted into arguments. Fortunately, she and I talked out our differences. Soon we'd be friends again.

I'd never lived so intimately with anyone. Some of Fay's habits I found irritating. She misplaced the otoscope and moved the medicines around in the clinic while seeing patients. When I reached for something that wasn't there, I got angry. Fay couldn't see why little things like those could upset me so.

Once we cut down aldea visits to four days a week instead of six, each of us was much easier to live with.

I was grateful Fay and I were working together because I couldn't have done it alone. Usually when I was at my absolute end, Fay would rescue me saying, "Why don't you go cook? I'll finish up here."

One thing neither of us could hardly stand were the *Fijase* ladies. We called them that because when we asked what brought them to clinic they answered, "*Fijase*, I have a headache," and "*Fijase*, I have a backache," and "*Fijase*, I have *terrible* shoulder pain." *Fijase* meant "would you believe" or "imagine that."

They dramatized pain in all parts of the body, voices an irritating whine. They begged for vitamin shots and iron pills, convinced they were anemic.

We learned to spot the Fijase ladies by their needy look. I felt sorry for them, but found them difficult to deal with. I was thankful there weren't more. Thinking back, I realize they needed the attention their family or community couldn't give. These women might have been depressed and thought any medicine would make them feel better. The Fijase ladies loved coming to clinic to talk about their aches and pains.

"I'll take the Fijase ladies today," I said when I was feeling more energetic.

"Oh, good, Lizzie." Fay had a tough time tolerating them, too.

Tox was a blessing, although he annoyed me occasionally. Some days he didn't want to work. He was especially obstinate when I pointed this out to him. I complained to Fay, "It's hard enough with all the stuff we have to put up with without having a pouting teenager, too."

Yet Tox knew our moods and did thoughtful things when one of us felt down.

Fay loved teaching him English, especially swear words. He learned quickly and his pronunciation was excellent. While we sat at the table one night after supper, Fay asked, "Tox, say the words you learned today."

Tox mimicked Fay, "****head. Bull****. Horse****. How are you today?" Then he gave us one of his wide, beautiful smiles. We all laughed.

I loved asking Tox about the Kek'chi culture. One day, I asked, "Do men like men?"

"Of course," said Tox, puzzled.

I tried again. "Do men have sex with men or women with other women?"

Tox's jaw dropped. "No." He shook his head. "I have never heard of such a thing." It was common to see young boys lounging against each other, unembarrassed by touching. Girls held hands or strolled arm in arm to church. But there was something asexual about all of this behavior.

Tox was the youngest in his family. When we drove past his mother's home in Chacté, she often ran out for a little visit. She spoke no Spanish and we spoke no Kek'chi, but it didn't matter. We were friends of her son.

One day, we stopped to see her. She wore the Kek'chi *traje*, a loose white blouse with the sleeves and neck

embroidered in brilliant hues of red, blue and purple. A full,
gathered, black-plaid skirt circled her waist. Silver earrings
swung from her ears, and silvery beads glittered around her
neck. Gray-black hair wound neatly in a braid down her back.
She was magnificent for having raised a dozen children. (She is
pictured below.)

"*Mamá*," she said, and pointed to Fay. Then she pointed at
me, "*Mamá.*" She poked her chest. "*Mamá*," she repeated, then
pulled Tox against her in a fierce hug and grinned.

She was right! We were old enough to be Tox's mothers
and sometimes, we acted as though we were. And sometimes
Tox acted like our rebellious teenaged son.

Tox was a bit of a flirt. In every aldea, young girls eyed
him. I loved watching their subtle under-lashes looks. Tox
played the field. I'm sure all the girls felt they were his *novia*,
his special girlfriend.

Tox was a true gentleman. He carried our heaviest
equipment: the microscope box, the metal tool boxes filled
with medicines and the wood cots, three at a time on his
shoulders.

I struggled up the hills. Why, I wondered, were churches always on top of the highest point? Perhaps because it was more beautiful up there, with a view of the countryside. I invariably wound up with mud on my jeans, hands and rear end. Tox hiked along holding my hand, while I slipped and skidded backwards.

The local people practically ran everywhere, carrying heavy loads, never falling or looking as though they traveled through mud except for dirty feet and a few splatters on their lower legs.

Guatemalan women (left) balanced impossible loads on their heads, a baby on their backs, a toddler clutching their skirts, yet walked gracefully and proud, as if dancing a primitive ballet.

The hikes up and down were excellent exercise. I shed my excess weight and began feeling healthier than ever in my life. But after a morning in the aldeas, Fay and I looked like we'd been rolling in mud.

No matter how dirty my hair, it curled in the intense humidity. Fay's hair was straight. She rolled it in curlers. It fluffed prettily for one day in light brown waves around her face. The rest of the time she wore a scarf gypsy style to hide her hair.

After class in the evening, Fay and I took sponge baths. Because we used only three cups, the water resembled bathtub scum. When we ran out of water, we had to truck to the river to refill our gallon jugs, and by the time we returned, were sweaty enough to need another bath. There were no village wells. Fay and I hauled boiled water and *agua potable,* usable but not drinkable, in big plastic containers from Poptún. That way, we wouldn't have to use contaminated river water unless we ran out.

We never divined why, but Fay and I were the ones in the Poptún community always bitten by insects. Amazingly, we never contracted malaria, though mosquitoes stung us by the hundreds. We did not take anti-malarial medication, nor did we recommend it to others in our community, because of the side effects, which included blindness. We later regretted that decision when Kay, who worked with Mo on the leadership team, suffered debilitating malaria. I did acquire impetigo three times, a skin infection caused by scratching with filthy nails.

We tried repellant. It didn't work. Fay took Vitamin B. It didn't work, either. I bought long cotton socks on the advice of people who told me nothing could bite through the fabric. They had never met the bugs of the Petén! Bites were one of the most miserable parts of our aldea trips. When we returned to Poptún, my backside and various other parts of my anatomy would be covered with red itchy welts. Mosquitoes attacked while we were doing our business in the bushes.

After dinner, which we cooked in the village church or lean to, we took turns cleaning up. Tox helped too, though he informed us Kek'chi men didn't do housework. We were stingy with the water we used to wash dishes, too. Half-way through, it turned black, but we kept washing anyhow. We didn't want to hike down to the river for more.

In the evenings, I liked time alone before classes began. One night, I took a walk in Las Cañas. The day was turning cool, but still as thick with moisture as a greenhouse. Crickets and frogs sang a noisy symphony in the twilight. No one was around. My mind was a million miles away. The road rose in a slight incline. At the top, perhaps ten feet away, a log stretched across the way. I kept strolling, not even wondering where such a long, skinny log had come from. As I got closer, the log slithered away.

That was no log! It was a snake! I let out a screech, and ran back to the church.

We had another scary experience one night in the same place, Las Cañas. Tox had been goofing off with his friend, Miguel. When they were together, we couldn't get much work out of either one. During classes, Miguel and Tox's cousins teased him unmercifully while he translated, making comments that kept them all giggling. More teenagers lounged outside the church door, hips jutting at lazy angles, offering smart remarks. All we saw were their eyes peering through the slats.

After dinner, Tox took off to Miguel's house. We waited for him, but at 9:30, he still hadn't showed up.

"Where *is* that Tox?" said Fay. "I'm gonna see what he's up to."

She strode like a righteous mother to Miguel's house, then came back looking mollified. "I expected mischief, but when I peeked in, they were sitting by the fire, playing guitars and singing hymns in Kek'chi." Tox later came back and slept in his sleeping bag in the truck, as always.

Fay and I prepared for bed in the shelter. In Las Cañas the villagers didn't want us to sleep in the church. I rolled my sleeping bag onto the folding cot.

Suddenly, Fay screeched and pointed under the cot. "A snake!"

We fled from the lean-to. There is only one thing I hate worse than rats, and that's snakes.

Fay pounded on the truck door, yelling, "Tox! *Levantete! Una culebra!*

He sat up, grumbling a little, as if he didn't believe Fay,

but he did grab the machete from under the seat.

Creeping slowly into the shelter, Tox peered under the cot, removed the leather machete sheath and struck the blade several times against a pile of rocks. A tiny snake with diamond markings on its back and yellow at the jaw slithered out. Tox smashed the snake with a rock again and again, then threw the remains into the brush. He came back looking sobered.

"*Fue una Barba Amarilla*," he said. The Barba Amarilla, yellow beard, was notorious as one of the most deadly of snakes. Even though this one had been a baby, it could have killed.

After that, Fay and I didn't care if people got mad. We just grabbed our cots and sleeping bags and slept in the church.

Another time in Chacté, we were screening for the tenth time a Carlos Campesino filmstrip called *Juanita y la Mosca*, about the need to cover food from flies. Fay and I took turns because showing the same film in fifteen aldeas felt like high-school, enduring a lecture on *Beowulf*. I presented the movie that night while Fay relaxed in back of the church.

Suddenly, there was a commotion and Fay's voice rose in protest. "*Dejalo!*" she shouted. "Leave it be!" People rushed to her. The unmistakable stink of skunk spread through the darkened room. The men took out their machetes to kill it.

"No!" Fay screamed. "It's just a poor animal! Let him go."

They stared at her as if she was crazy, but let the skunk go.

The stench was almost unbearable. It penetrated my nose and throat and clung to my clothes. People drifted back to where I sat in front of the battery-run projector, holding my queasy stomach.

"What should we do?" I asked them.

"*Terminemus*," came the reply. "Let's finish."

That's funny, I thought. Afterward, I asked one of the

ladies why they'd wanted to continue and she said, "*Terminemus* means stop. We thought it was *you* who wanted to finish the film!"

After dinner, I often went for a walk alone. I prayed that I might stick out my time in Guatemala and asked God to forgive my crabbiness. I prayed for the aldea people, too, because, by then, their sufferings were tunneling like highways into my heart.

In the mornings, I was the first one up. While Fay slept, I heated water for coffee. Then I snuggled in my sleeping bag with *Streams in the Desert*, first written in 1925 by Mrs. Charles Cowan, a missionary in China. Even though she wrote in flowery language, I related to her feelings. She, like me, had difficulty serving others when she had her own failings.

In the aldeas, little things I'd coped with at home became major character flaws. I wasn't as well adjusted as I'd thought. The missionary experience revealed faults I never knew existed, nor could I hide behind constant activities, going to dinner and the movies and the consumerism of life in the States.

Morning was my favorite part of the day. The churches often held a view of the surrounding valleys. I loved surveying the greenery below me. There was a peacefulness in the isolation and simple life of the aldeas that I'd never found in any other place. During those times, I gathered strength to endure one more day at the clinic. In my nightgown, I sipped coffee and read the Bible or wrote letters home, such as this one to my friend in Edmonds, Washington.

Parroquia San Pedro Martir
Poptún, Petén
Dear Kathy,
  This life is certainly interesting. I'm not bored. At first, I thought I'd have to give up and come back home. Everything seemed so strange. I thought I'd never get

used to all the dirt, bugs, cold showers, humidity, the whole *ambiente* of the place, atmosphere.

We are giving classes...Can you imagine that? Me who was so afraid before a group? Now I'm turning into a...blabbermouth. I actually enjoy being up there teaching...It's not easy here...The people make it worthwhile. They are a pleasure to be around. I can't believe their simplicity, their humility, their gentleness. I think I'm falling in love with them. They are so responsive to us. We could say the dumbest thing in the whole world and they'd still accept us. They have much in intangibles and so very little in worldly things.

The community is slowly beginning to gel. Of course, there are difficulties trying to adjust to so many people. One of the problems is being far from any entertainment or going to a nice restaurant or doing things I took for granted in the States...I never thought it would be hard living with celibates. In fact, I never thought of it, period, but it sure is...They're not available, so it's damn frustrating. I wonder if they're frustrated too. They must be if they're human.

It is really a blessing...to live with such a large group...but the group isn't nearly large enough in other ways...Our circle is much smaller here, so we become more dependent on each other...Oh, Kathy, pray for me that I will...not be overwhelmed.

It also helped to write my feelings in poems:

Images
Faces so brown
Eyes bright and shining
I just need to smile once and it's returned.

So warm, so sweet, so gentle are your smiles
Touching, you have no fear of this
So tender are your touches, with respect for me as me.
You all respond so to me, how gifted I feel
Me who's never taught, and doesn't know how,
somehow it's easy with you.
You inspire me to do my best for you.
I ask myself, how can you be how you are with so little,
and Why aren't I more with all that I have?

In spite of the difficulties, I wanted to continue and sensed God calling me on. I felt moved by the people, always the people, by their silent suffering and spirit of joy. And even with all the sadness of their lives, woven through everything was their humor.

They helped us laugh. We shared a basic sameness, in spite of our differences. Some of the most hilarious experiences happened when we translated from one language to another.

Bananas grew in wide variety in the Petén. There were the small and sugar sweet red bananas. *Platanos* had the consistency of wood. I loved them sliced in spears and fried soft and golden brown. Cooking brought out their flavor. And there were the same yellow bananas we have in the States, but those in the Petén were picked when ripe and had a sweeter flavor than any banana I'd ever tasted.

One day, we stood in front of the church in Actilá, where the people were all Kek'chi, expounding on nutrition. Tox was on my right, translating.

"Bananas are very good for you," I said.

Tox muttered something in Kek'chi, then bent over and covered his face. Little snorts escaped his mouth.

Everyone laughed until tears glistened on their cheeks. Pretty soon we were all holding our sides in helpless laughter even though Fay and I didn't know what was so funny.

Afterward Tox explained. "In Kek'chi, banana means penis."

Knowing this didn't stop us from talking about bananas. Now that we knew the meaning, we tried to get as much mileage out of the joke as possible.

Tox told us that *masa le mol* in Kek'chi meant "how delicious are the eggs." In Kek'chi, as in other cultures, eggs were a euphemism for a man's testicles. Sometimes we used the Kek' chi expression deliberately, rolling our eyes. People were delighted.

Another nutrition class was for parents of infants under one year of age. Mothers breastfed until babies were 12 or 14 months old, and sometimes until age two or three or four. Breast milk was perfect until children were about six months old, but after that, they needed supplemental foods. It was not unusual to see six-month-old babies develop anemia and become underweight.

We performed a skit to teach that class. Behind the church, or crouched behind the altar, Fay and I stuffed pillows under our blouses. Fay would plead, "Lizzie, wait a minute. I can't get everything under here right."

I tugged and stuffed the pillow up her blouse, and we would be giggling like crazy when we walked out on "stage." People held their sides, laughing while tears rolled down their faces when they saw us looking "pregnant." We pretended to meet while washing clothes and discovered we might have our babies on the same day. Of course we do.

The drama continued with Fay and me meeting again when our babies were eight months old.

"But, señora," Fay said to me, "why is it that Rosa Elena is bigger than my baby, Dominga?"

Fay looked with dissatisfaction at "Dominga," a rag doll with red yarn hair. The people howled at these names. Why, I don't know.

I gave Fay a superior look (above). "My baby is bigger because I give her bananas, oatmeal, orange juice and egg yolks." I stroked Rosa Elena's orange yarn hair.

"I only give Dominga *el pecho*." Fay patted her modest breast.

The villagers loved that skit, hooting especially when Fay held her "baby" away from her as Dominga started to wet, just like the Kek'chi women did. I complained, with one hand on my pillow stomach, holding my back and making a face. We got another laugh when Fay announced, "It's time to go. *Es tiempo para alimentar*, to feed my man." In Spanish, you only *alimenta* animals.

We drew a chart picturing different foods. Only half these items were available, since people didn't have gardens. Fay and I frequently discussed how to get people to raise more vegetables and fruits. People didn't know how to plant vegetables, they didn't understand why vegetables and fruits were important for health because they were uneducated.

Eventually, Leon began a garden and sold seedlings to the villagers. But in the beginning, people ate only corn tortillas and beans in quantity, and maybe an occasional egg.

When John Fay visited, women cooked giant black cauldrons of *caldo de pollo*, chicken soup with *guiskil*, Guatemalan zucchini, and rice, reserved for special occasions, as chicken was the lobster of the aldeas. That delicacy appeared only four or five times a year in the larger towns. Smaller towns served hard-boiled eggs with beans and chiles when the priest came.

In season, there were oranges, mangos, pineapple and papaya, the most delicious fruit I'd ever tasted. A truck occasionally passed through with vegetables and fruit. We taught people to share all food with the baby, even if it was available only once a year.

One of my greatest failings was lack of patience. People often wanted us to attend to more patients than we had time for. They had no idea how taxing it was for us to see sick people every day.

Sometimes they insisted, "Couldn't one more family come through the clinic?" (An aldea man and his daughter waiting to see us, below.)

I would snap, "No! We've already seen 18 this afternoon.

You'll have to wait till tomorrow." Then I'd feel guilty. A man in Cansís, where we always had a busy clinic, claimed his wife was *muy grave*, so ill she couldn't possibly get to our clinic. He insisted we come to his home. (Right, I'm doing a home visit in a different aldea). Fay and I reluctantly closed for the day, even though we had many more patients scheduled. We followed him to his home in the jungle where we found his

wife slapping tortillas, no sicker than our other patients. She did complain of stomach pains, probably from parasites, but we regretted we'd made others wait because of her.

In spite of our grouchiness, people knew we cared for them. They kept coming to classes and the clinic. I'd never felt so needed in nursing, ever.

Sometimes our bathroom experiences were hilarious.

One dark night in La Tortuga, where the church sat in a clearing, there were no bushes close by. Fay and I were always at a loss knowing where to relieve ourselves in that village. She said, "Oh, no, La Tortuga again. No place to pee."

That night, rain drummed on the tin roof. Suddenly, a pain tore through my stomach, whereupon I grabbed my poncho and boots and rushed out. Rain fell in sheets, lightning streaked the sky and thunder cracked only a few feet away. My boots stuck in mud and I had to wrench them out.

The pain was so intense I couldn't wait. By a clump of brush, I crouched. Hopefully, no one would be around in this downpour, but I couldn't be sure. Aldea people went out in amazingly horrible weather.

While I huddled there feeling sharp cramps that left me gasping, voices came from inside a shack, no more than five feet away, but I didn't care. I was grateful for the thunder, and

hoped the lightning wouldn't strike where I squatted. Then I
giggled. Tomorrow someone might find the evidence, but
maybe the rain would clean up after me. I'd learned to shed
some modesty about bodily functions, because one couldn't
possibly be modest or private here in the aldeas.

I dashed back to the church. When I told Fay, we were in
hysterics.

A couple of months later, we visited La Tortuga again.
The rain pounded the tin roof as though thousands of feet were
running overhead. We shouted to make ourselves heard over
the downpour.

"This makes me wanna pee." Fay wet her pants
sometimes when it rained so loudly.

"I'm not going out *there*," she said. At the back of the
church she called out, "I found a hole." She'd found a crack in
the cement wall, which funneled to the outside.

When we got home to Poptún, Fay told the community
and some were embarrassed. But others understood and could
tell similar stories.

Fern said people were constantly asking for advice or
wanting to talk. No matter where he was, someone was always
hanging around when he visited the aldeas.

One morning he rose at 4:00 a.m. to avoid running into
anyone on his way to the bushes. He'd just squatted when a
voice came from a few feet away.

"*Buenas dias, Padre*," said a campesino, tipping his hat
politely.

While Fern hunched there, acutely embarrassed, the man
continued talking at length about a problem. When Fern stood,
the man accompanied him back to the church, talking all the
way.

Fay and I learned to travel with a swatch of toilet paper in
a pocket. You never knew where there might be an available
spot and you could never count on toilet paper.

I used to get mad at her, because she always wanted some

of mine. "You never remember to bring your own," I scolded her.

On one trip to Guatemala City by bus, before we bought our Chevy Luv, the bus stopped at the Rio Dulce to wait for the ferry to cross the river. Suddenly, I developed stomach cramps and knew diarrhea was imminent. We searched for an outhouse or bathroom, but found none in that river place. There were only ramshackle lean-tos where the proprietors sold mercado items. I was getting desperate. With Fay leading, I held my stomach and stumbled down a path to a fenced enclosure. Inside, were about 10 enormous filthy pigs rooting around in the dirt. Fay and I climbed the fence and while I squatted, Fay shooed the pigs away with a stick. "Back you lousy pigs!" She hollered. "Back."

When I was done and feeling greatly relieved, I looked back. The pigs were poking around right where I had just been.

I remember Santo Domingo, an all-Kek'chi aldea. One night, we were performing our puppet show on the importance

of wearing shoes. The stage, an easel frame, was made of flimsy wood, which tottered on thin legs. From it hung a muslin flip chart.

I had sewn hand puppets named Juanito and Mario (with **Tox**, left). Juanito wore shoes and Mario did not. We stood behind the easel, waving Juanito and Mario over the edge, talking in little boy voices in

Spanish.

Suddenly, the easel crashed to the ground. We stood there with puppets on our hands, looking surprised. People laughed uproariously. We did, too. Children fell off the church benches and rolled on the dirt floor, clutching their sides. They thought this was a part of the show. Ten minutes passed before order was restored. We wondered if anyone had caught the point of the class, the importance of wearing shoes.

In Santo Domingo, it was especially important because that aldea had an unusually high incidence of hookworm. Hookworm larvae entered through the soles of the feet or through contaminated drinking water.

That morning, I'd examined a whole family's stool specimens; each had wall-to-wall hookworm larvae. One little girl of five was pale as clay, her gums and even her inner eyelid almost white. I heard a loud heart murmur, too, all signs of acute anemia. (That's **Fay** with an aldea baby, below.)

When Tox checked her blood count, he looked alarmed. "Liz, the hemoglobin is three."

Normal hemoglobin for children that age is eleven. We poked her finger again to make sure we hadn't made a mistake. Had this child been in the States, she would have been transfused with blood. But there she was, still walking and probably still helping her mother make tortillas. And we were not in the States, so there was no blood and no blood donors.

I gave her and the other children worm medicine, iron tablets, vitamins and Incaparina, a powdered protein supplement, along with plenty of dietary advice and my usual lecture about boiling water, wearing shoes and covering the food.

Two months later, I checked the children again. Their stool specimens were relatively free of parasites, and their color had improved. The little girl's heart murmur diminished. Her hemoglobin had jumped to six, and her skin was now a rich brown. Best of all, her eyes sparkled with life. Those were the moments that kept me going.

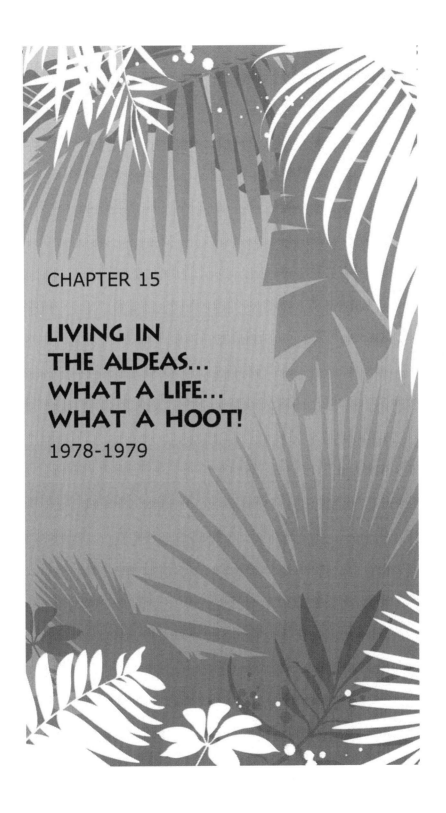

CHAPTER 15

LIVING IN THE ALDEAS... WHAT A LIFE... WHAT A HOOT!

1978-1979

**We did have fun with the people in the aldeas, which
made the daily grind bearable.** But I had a hard time
accepting the lack of privacy. Once, Fay and I were behind the
church brushing our teeth (that's what Fay's doing, above). My
canteen of boiled water swung from my neck. I spat a mouthful
of toothpaste into the bushes, then looked up when I felt
someone staring. About ten kids stood there, wondering, no
doubt, what the white foam was dripping from my mouth, since

they couldn't afford toothpaste. They'd hardly ever used toothbrushes, either, until we came along. They cleaned their teeth with an index finger or picked at their reddened gums with pieces of sugar cane.

People couldn't comprehend how we could stand being by ourselves. I would have loved it if they'd left us alone sometimes. Many months passed before I realized the need for privacy was mine, not theirs.

"¿No tiene esposo...o hijos?...you don't have a husband or children?" Pity saddened their faces on hearing this fact. For them, happiness was being with others.

A lady in El Crucero brought in her little daughter, who held her head to one side because of a boil on her neck.

"¿Pueden curarla? Can you cure her?" the mother asked.

Fay turned to me. Her eyebrows rose in a question.

"Well, I never have, but I've seen it done a hundred times. I'll try," I ventured.

There were perhaps fifteen people gathered in the church. Everyone jabbered when they heard I was going to lance it.

"We have to clear the church," I said. I wasn't about to incise a boil for the first time with people watching me. They would bunch close, I imagined, while I developed clumsy hands.

Everyone groaned in disappointment when Fay and Tox shooed them out of the church (above).

The little girl lay on a bench. The humid air closed around us once the door shut. The tin roof absorbed heat and reflected it down like a broiler oven. She didn't move while I covered her neck in sterile towels, nor did she flinch when I injected the area with a local anesthetic.

Firmly, I cut into the mound with the pointed tip scalpel. Pus shot across the towels and just missed my eyes. The putrid stench wafted through the church. At that same moment, voices at the window said collectively, "*Ay Dios!*"

I looked up. The same people who'd been inside now gawked through the open window. They'd pulled up benches and were standing on them outside.

"Can you believe it, Fay?" I shook my head. "I'm their entertainment for the day."

I continued cleansing the boil. Now that the worst was over, it didn't bother me to be observed.

"*La doctora le curó,*" someone said. "The doctor cured her." Though I kept reminding people I was a nurse practitioner, they still called me doctor. When I finished, everyone filed back into the church, regarding me as if were the Petén's answer to the famous heart surgeon, Michael De

Bakey.

After I discovered the need for a screen during private exams, I bought pink cotton, hemmed it into sheets and fastened ties on the corners. Thereafter, we screened a portion of the church for our "exam room."

One day in Chinchilá, a girl complained of abdominal pain. After eliciting a history, I led her behind the pink curtains and directed her to lie down. Just as I was ready to lift the sheet, I sensed someone watching. It turned out to be eyes peering through the slats of the building.

"Honestly!" I muttered. "Fay, make those people go away." After a long time, the eyes finally left.

This frank curiosity drove us nuts. In Boca del Monte one day, the mothers crowded around the microscope to see the worm eggs in their kids' feces. (In another aldea a Kek'chi woman looks into the microscope, left.) We encouraged this, so people could learn that worm eggs were real. The idea that things existed that they couldn't see continued to amaze them.

But those ladies hardly gave Fay breathing space. She glared at them. "*Me hacen nervioso!*...you're making me nervous!"

The ladies' mouths sagged in surprise.

I stepped in. "She can't see under the microscope when

you crowd around. Please, stand back."

They moved away—for about ten minutes. Then they bunched up around the table again, giggling, until Fay sighed and rolled her eyes at me and I asked them to move once more.

This fascination to observe everything we did was the case in all the aldeas. People stood closer, sat closer, than I was used to. I hadn't realized there was an unspoken taboo in the U.S., where everyone maintained an invisible bubble of several feet around each person. Children were fascinated by Fay's light hair, caressing her fair-skinned arms, marveling at the blond hair on them.

Sometimes people stayed after the clinic and classes. They didn't want us to feel alone.

Nearly always, they brought gifts. Once it was two brown eggs nestled in corn leaves. Another time, a whole hand of bananas, fresh off the tree, or a juicy pineapple. And my favorite: homemade corn tortillas (being made, left).

Before Guatemala, I hardly knew tortillas. The

ones in the aldeas were hearty and thick as pancakes. We liked to buy fresh ones from women in the villages. Though I looked for them when I returned to the States, I never found the excellent tortillas of the aldeas.

Sometimes the only sounds I heard besides dogs barking, chickens and crickets, was the click-clack-clack of the *molino* motor, where women ground corn. If there was no molino, women substituted a meat grinder apparatus. It took hours. Women arose at four to make two dozen to send with their men to the fields for lunch.

I thought watching women making tortillas was like observing expert potters. They patted the soft dough gently, rapidly, clapping, stretching the dough into perfect rounds. Once or twice I tried to shape one myself, ending up with uneven dough with holes. The other ladies laughed kindly at my efforts. In their families, even ten year-old girls made perfect tortillas.

The other dietary staple was black beans boiled with garlic and salt in huge pots. The legumes were served like soup or the water was drained off and the beans were mashed and refried with oil. Either way, they were filling and delicious. People insisted on eating them with chile peppers, for they considered a meal incomplete without hot chile. Forks were uncommon. With a tortilla in one hand, a chile in the other, villagers used this flatbread like shovels to scoop the beans.

In La Tortuga, a woman brought us a plucked chicken. Chickens ran loose to scavenge food, making them tough. People steamed chicken slowly for hours to tenderize it.

"I know," said Fay, "let's cook fried chicken!"

"That thing is old. It's gonna be tough."

"I don't care! It'll be good for a change. Don't worry," she said. "I'll do the cooking!"

"Fine. I don't wanna have anything to do with that bird. Besides, it'll probably burn before it gets cooked."

Fay paid no attention. "****," she muttered as she cut up

the chicken with our dull knife. Finally, she succeeded in hacking it to pieces.

Meanwhile, I tended patients. Before long I smelled something burning.

When I finished with clinic, I walked to where Fay had set up our stove on a church bench. She looked up from the frying pan and gave me a triumphant smile.

"It did kinda burn," she confessed sheepishly. "But it's better than Spam!"

We sat down. Tox and I restrained smiles as we chewed doggedly at the charred chicken, which was half-raw on the inside.

"This *is* more interesting than hot dogs," I admitted.

Cooking with our kerosene stove was always an adventure. **Fay** was afraid of the stove (above). She asked Tox to light it if he were available. Once flames leaped high, almost touching the dry straw and I feared the roof would catch fire. Fay screamed and threw the stove to the ground. That finished the second stove she'd bought when she was home on vacation.

After lunch, we napped. At two, people would begin arriving for clinic. They set my nerves on edge because many came early and chattered. Fay, on the other hand, could immediately conk out.

Can I ever forget those hard church benches? The heat of the afternoon suffocated me, as I tossed carefully from side to side, trying not to fall off, nagged by the thought that our patients would soon be there.

One pure pleasure was finally turning in for the night. When we had begun visiting the aldeas, Mo gave us three wood-and-canvas cots, which folded up like a bundle of sticks.

I thought they might be difficult to sleep on. I never, however, slept so well as I did on those cots.

After night class, I made sure never to take the bed reserved for patients because I didn't want another case of scabies. Tox would say goodnight and head down the hill to sleep in the truck.

One of us turned off the Coleman lantern and we crawled into our sleeping bags. Almost as soon as my head hit the pillow, I'd fall asleep. This sound rest at night restored me for the next day's work.

I was continually inspired by how the people's faith harmonized with their way of life. When the harvest was plentiful, it was: *Gracias a Dios*...Thanks be to God. Whenever calamity or sickness struck, they prayed first.

They rarely complained, but accepted misfortunes without a protest. This trait had its drawbacks because their passivity encouraged the military and the rich to take advantage of them. Mistreated for centuries, villagers assumed they were helpless to make changes. I didn't realize how much I complained—and how little I had to complain about—until I met the people of the aldeas.

After only a few visits, Fay and I began to experience the

rancor between the churches, which at first seriously hampered our work. We received a potent example of this animosity in La Cumbre. The first time we visited with John Fay, we were warmly received. People had such trust in the priest, they accepted anything in connection with the Catholic faith. As visitors, we were welcome, but when we returned alone for our health clinic, it was another story.

The Evangelical pastor in La Cumbre begged the people to repent, using battery-run megaphones to blast his message all over town. Townsfolk liked the new songs and the excitement of these church services, which lasted until late in the evenings, after the men had come home from the fields. The program filled a void in their lives.

In the Catholic church, priests were regarded as the center of religious services. Few in number and spread mighty thin, they visited the aldeas rarely, especially those far in the interior. People were hungry for a spiritual presence. Priests had time only for confessions, mass, baptisms, and weddings, not so much for people's problems.

The Evangelical pastor lived right in their village. He was present when children sickened or someone died. He prayed with them and collected money for the coffin. Alcohol was forbidden, so alcoholism decreased. This reform was a success that Catholics couldn't claim. No wonder Evangelicals were winning converts.

Aldea Catholics were largely unschooled in their faith. There were no church-run schools except in larger cities, and no religious-preparation classes. Children hadn't made their First Communion because no one taught them. Rituals had been handed down through the years, like lighting candles, and incense or praying for intercession to a saint, but few townsfolk knew what such symbols meant. Catechists—religious leaders in the community—sometimes attended courses in the fundamentals of the faith, but often, they too, were misinformed. When John Blazo and Pastora taught catechism classes for children in Poptún, parents by the hundreds signed up their kids.

Into this void sprouted the Evangelical churches like weeds in a neglected garden. Every time we turned around, a new church had been built, with names like *Iglesia de Dios de Cristianidad,* The Christian Church of God, or *Capilla Evangelica*, Evangelical Chapel.

Competition and antagonism between the churches continues even today. After I left Guatemala and became a political activist, I learned that some people thought that Evangelical churches were in Guatemala to keep people compliant, believing their horrible conditions in life were *la voluntad de Dios*, God's will. In most Evangelical churches, there was little social awareness or sermons examining the roots of poverty. During the presidency of Rios Montt, parishes funded by Evangelical churches in California, with connections to the Guatemalan military and U.S. businesses, mounted a campaign to recruit converts to the Evangelical church. A "keep them down on the farm and ignorant" motivation. Often, neither the pastor nor the people knew anything of this motive. Rural populations were starved for spiritual food. The Evangelical religion practiced in those forgotten towns helped them overlook, for a time, how deprived they really were.

The Catholics of La Cumbre competed with the Evangelical churches by holding their own prayer meetings. They, too, bought a megaphone and conducted the same boring services far into the evening.

Fay and I were surprised at our first clinic in La Cumbre when few people attended. For a large aldea, it was a poor showing. One lady who did come told me, "The Evangelicals preach against you. The pastors say you're from the devil because you're led by the Pope. People are afraid. *Los Evangelicos* say medicine isn't necessary. Faith alone can cure you."

On examining this woman's stool specimen, I found wall-

to-wall parasites on the slide: *ascaris, trichuria* and *uncinaria*. The tiny *uncinaria* larvae burrow through the soles of the feet, migrate to the intestines, where larvae grow into adult worms, suck blood from small arteries and cause anemia.

"As for me," she went on, "I've been sick with diarrhea too long. I want your medicine."

On our next visit, the same woman, Doña Maria, returned. She sat down at the gray metal table we used to interview patients. (Her daughters are pictured above.)

"*¿Como esta, señora?*" I asked.

Her face lit up with pure joy. "*Muy bien, Gracias a Dios.*"

"Did you pass any worms?"

"*Ay, Dios mio, si!*" she beamed. "Two hundred and fourteen! I've never passed so many. The diarrhea is gone. And look. My stomach is getting flatter." She smoothed her dress across her abdomen, immensely pleased.

I sat there with my mouth gaping. "And how do you know you passed so many?"

"I counted them. They were like this." She spread her thumb and index finger apart six inches. "Long and white and flat. Some no bigger than a thread. You have very good medicine," she said. "Those Evangelicals are foolish with their talk about devils."

Doña Maria's bragging about our *good* medicine helped us be accepted in La Cumbre. After a few months, both Catholics and Evangelicals attended our clinics.

Yaltutú, the farthest north aldea that we visited, gave us one more experience with the competition between the churches. **Carlos Bran**, (above center with **Fay** and **Tox**) a slim young man with sparkling eyes, was only 25, but he already had a wife and three children. He worked hard in the corn fields. At night, he conducted prayer services. Because the Evangelicals had a thriving community, he feared Catholics would leave if he didn't have entertaining prayer meetings.

The first time Fay, Tox and I visited Yaltutú, Carlos gathered the people in church. In the church, I read aloud from St. Paul's Epistle to the Corinthians, about the importance of gifts in the church, including the gift of healing. I wanted to counteract the Evangelical preaching that claimed only faith was necessary. After that, I began our class on wearing shoes to prevent parasites.

Carlos interrupted. *"Con permiso, Señorita Elizabeth, primero vamos a resar*...Excuse me, first we must pray."

Carlos knelt, hands folded and eyes closed. *"Ponganse de rodillas, hermanos y hermanas*, kneel, brothers and sisters."

We knelt on the rocky ground. I groaned under my breath while Carlos read the Bible with the fervor of Billy Graham. Next, we recited the rosary. Then, accompanied by a young man on guitar, we sang *"Yo Tengo un Amigo Que me Ama,* I Have a Friend Who Loves Me," and two hymns to the Virgin.

When I creaked up from kneeling, I had to pick out tiny rocks imbedded in my knees. After that, I felt foolish putting on a puppet show using the hand puppets Juanito and Mario, and screening the silly Carlos Campesino filmstrips on the importance of wearing shoes. But the people responded with equal verve to the prayer services and to our class.

Yaltutú became a favorite aldea. Carlos always made us feel appreciated and loved. Before class, he prayed: "We thank you Lord, for our dear friends, Fay and Elizabeth, who came from so far to help us." He prayed for our families too, for he felt they must miss us. In some villages, we had young, willing helpers.

But in Yaltutú one day, I realized we were still outsiders. A lady sat waiting for clinic, a baby in her arms. Two children played at her feet. The little boy began misbehaving, tired of doing nothing. She whispered, *"Cayate, o las gringas le dan una inyeccion*!...Quiet or the gringos will give you a shot!" The child was immediately silent and looked at us as if we were monsters.

When it was time to leave an aldea, we were recharged with new energy. People there helped us carry everything to the truck, (right) where we hurriedly threw our gear in back in a jumbled mess. We were anxious to drive home. Villagers watched from the hill, calling out,*"¿Cuando vengan otra vez*?...when are you coming again?"

They were happy to have had a bit of entertainment while we tried to purge them of worms. We were delighted that one more class was done, bringing us closer to a promoter program.

One night, on the way back from Boca del Monte, an aldea close to Poptún, I sang, "I'm soooo glad we're through. Next week we stay home. Yeah! Yeah." We would be planning another series of classes in Poptún.

Usually I drove at night because Fay's vision was poor. As we started off, people waved and children yelled, "*Adios! Que le vaya bien!*...Goodbye, go with God. May you go well!"

I honked the horn. We moved slowly down the lonely road with no light to point the way except our high beams, which probed the blackness like a train in a tunnel. Often, we passed no other vehicles on those late trips into Poptún.

The past week had gone well. We'd treated scores more children in Boca del Monte than the first time we visited.

"Did you notice how many ascaris this place had?" I said. "Wonder why some aldeas have more of some worms. Would be neat to do research."

"Yeah, to have the time." Fay yawned loudly. "It's just another wormy aldea."

"You're getting really good at identifying worm eggs under the microscope, Tox," she said.

"Gracias." He was pleased. We smiled at one another. What a relief there would be no sick people for a week, thank God.

"We have penicillin, but only a half gallon of cough syrup. Just about out of *ampicilina*," mused Fay. "I suppose we'll have to buy more."

"I don't wanna go. Let's ask Blazo. He's going to Guatemala City next week."

The drive to the city was dusty or muddy, depending on the season. We always came back exhausted, so we avoided it whenever we could.

As we approached town, few people were in the streets, except for prostitutes falling out of the bars, or soldiers, equally drunk.

Checking for mail was the highlight of our return. Sometimes it was eleven at night before we got back, with the lights out and everyone in bed. We occasionally sat up talking

with John Blazo or Mo. If Kay was home, we told each other our latest escapades. The three of us might share a shot of apricot brandy I kept in my closet. Kay claimed to dislike liquor. "This stuff tastes awful," she said. But then she made a face and gulped it down.

After a week in the aldeas, sitting on a real toilet, even with its rusty stains, and then falling into my damp bed felt incredibly cushy. That year and a half in the aldeas was the single most important thing Fay and I ever did, because we came to know the people and they began to trust us. As Fay trudges up yet another hill to set up our makeshift clinic (left) she is followed by a willing helper who carries our supplies.

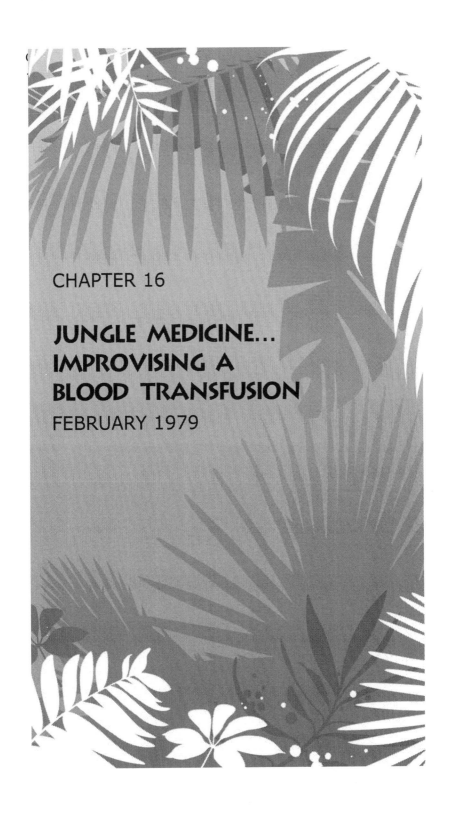

CHAPTER 16

JUNGLE MEDICINE... IMPROVISING A BLOOD TRANSFUSION

FEBRUARY 1979

**Señora Olga Garcia de Milian, a tall, extremely pale
Ladino woman, glided ghostlike into our clinic in La
Tortuga.** Tox, who stuck each patient's finger to test for
anemia, checked hers twice. Her hemoglobin was three and a
half. Stoic Tox was alarmed because normal for women was 12
to 16.

Fay and I decided to bring her back to Poptún for blood
transfusions. What amazed me was that she was still walking.

While I complained about being tired, Olga had reason to complain and didn't. She'd already been purged of parasites. Pregnancy and blood loss at the recent birth of her baby were the other causes of her anemia. It would take months for her body to produce enough new cells to get her blood count normal. Post-partum problems were common with rural women, such as this Kek'chi mom (left).

"I can give her blood," Fay said. "I've done it tons of times in the States."

"Not me. I had hepatitis," I said.

"We'll manage. How about you, Tox?" asked Fay.

"*Talvez no quiero*, maybe I don't want to," Tox said slowly. "I think I would become weak. *En mi gente*, among my people, I have never heard of anyone giving blood."

"You'll do fine," said Fay. "Your body will make new blood in a couple of months. Just think how you'd be helping the poor señora. I bet your blood is really strong. You would hardly miss a pint. We'll give you juice and cookies afterwards and you can lie down to rest."

Tox's eyes widened as if he'd glimpsed his own death when he heard "pint," and I wondered if even Fay's considerable powers of persuasion would do the trick this time. She explained that his body held five *quarts* of blood before he calmed down.

"Now, let's see. Who else could donate?" mused Fay. "Maybe the guys. Mo will."

"He's out with Kay in La Libertad," I reminded her. "And John Blazo had hepatitis too."

"We'll get somebody. Three units should be plenty. That'll get her up three points with each unit," Fay said, sure, as usual, of the solution.

I wasn't as confident, knowing how difficult things could be in that country. But this poor woman deserved our best shot. It was up to us to help her as much as we could.

Two nights later, after we ended class at 10 P.M, we

arrived home with Olga, her husband, Moises, and baby, Lorena, only forty days old.

Fay settled them in the room beside the pharmacy. The next morning, I went to the hospital. "*Lo siento*, I'm sorry," said Dr Zepeda, who was in charge that day. In contrast to the medical director, an incompetent alcoholic, Dr. Zepeda was a compassionate man and a good doctor. "There's no equipment to draw blood or administer it. But," he went on, "the hospital near Flores has bottles and tubing." As it happened, Mo and Kay were headed for Flores. We contacted them through Bishop Jorge Mario, who obtained what we needed and sent it to Poptún with Kay and Mo.

The next day, humble Don Asisclo, who taught in our *alfabetización,* or literacy, program, gave the first pint. Olga received it that afternoon. I was beginning to feel our efforts would work this time.

Fay tried to talk Tox into giving blood. Miguel, Tox's friend from Las Cañas happened to be visiting.

"No, Fay," Tox said. "I don't want to. "*Es estranjo*, it's strange to think my blood would be in someone else." He shook his head. By the look on both his and Miguel's face, I could tell a transfusion was a repugnant idea.

Fay was undeterred.

"Let's just see what your hemoglobin is." She stuck Tox's and Miguel's fingers. They giggled and acted silly as they always did when they were together.

"I have the strongest blood," said Tox.

"*Mi sangre es muy rico,*" boasted Miguel, making a muscle on his biceps.

Tox's hemoglobin was highest. Somehow, Fay appealed to his macho instincts of being the "strongest." He willingly provided the next unit that afternoon. Lorena, the lab tech, stored it in the refrigerator, to be given two days later. In all, four people who worked with us volunteered. All were universal donors with type O, which anyone can receive.

Everything appeared to be going smoothly, but not for long.

Sunday morning, Lorena sent for Fay and told her Dr. Zepeda and the doctor from the military base had used the blood and the special tubing for a 20-year-old victim of a machete wound who died. We were left with no suitable supplies. Particular tubing is necessary to administer blood. With one unit, Olga's hemoglobin climbed to five. Still, she was dangerously anemic.

We left for our scheduled trip to the aldeas on Monday. When we returned days later from Chinchilá, we found Olga, Moises and the baby still at the convent. Olga hadn't received her second unit of blood, so Fay went to the hospital to see why things were screwed up again. In the lab, she met Lorena, who explained she'd found the transfusion equipment in the hospital garbage and was re-sterilizing it. This was 1978, years before AIDS was discovered, and before the transmission of Hepatitis B was fully known, so it wasn't so outrageous to consider re-using blood tubing. If Lorena could get the other tubing from the military hospital, Olga could receive blood that afternoon.

Fay returned to the hospital with Olga, but Lorena didn't show up. Fay sat outside with the mamas waiting with their kids for the well-child clinic. Dr. Zepeda sat down next to her. In his soft, apologetic way, he told her, "We don't have the solution to prevent clotting. We thought there was some in the pharmacy, but no, our supplies are depleted." He sighed and looked away.

Fay held back tears and explained how exasperating it was for us to work like dogs in the aldeas, and then come home to more frustrations coping with the hospital.

Dr. Zepeda shrugged. "That's how it is for everyone in health care in the Petén." He wasn't unkind, only truthful.

"We'll probably get equipment in another 15 days," he added. One of the hospital's major problems was lack of basic

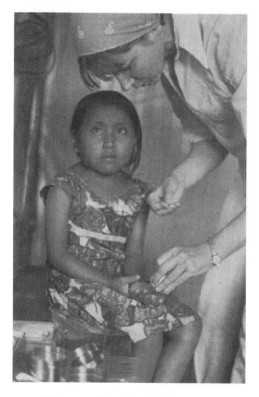

equipment: IVs, medications and plates.

By now, Fay had become skeptical of "probably." (That's **Fay** drawing blood for testing, left.) Nothing could be certain in this country. Fay appealed to Chepe, our parish administrator, a wheeler-dealer and former administrator of the military hospital. "The heck with that!" Chepe said. "My friend is going to the capital tomorrow. I'll ask him to bring tubing."

We sent Olga back to La Tortuga with sacks of vitamins, iron and Incaparina, a protein powder. She also supplemented breast feeding with Similac formula, so baby Lorena was fattening up.

Olga planned to return for Lorena's baptism and to receive another pint of blood if all went well. Fay would be Lorena's godmother.

When Fay and I went to the capital two weeks later, we bought several transfusion sets with health program money to have on hand, just in case.

Olga received two units the following month, which brought her hemoglobin to eight. It was a good thing we had our own supplies, because the hospital had run out of tubing again.

One of the most frustrating things about all of this was

that soldiers at the military base were getting whatever care and medicines they needed. The country's money poured into keeping the army in tip-top shape, while the poor had to buy their own IVs in the pharmacy.

After this experience, I wrote in my journal: "If anything can go wrong, it almost always does. These foul-ups underlined the injustice to the poor. If we who have so many other resources have such rotten luck, how can the poor help but get cheated?"

CHAPTER 17

LOVING
BABY MARIA
OF LAS CAÑAS
MARCH 1979

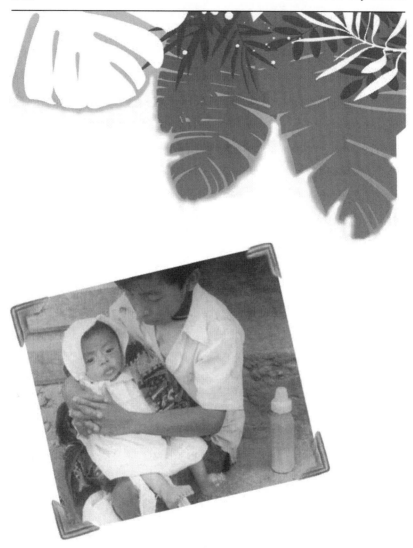

Fay dreamed of eventually adopting a Guatemalan child. She championed the cause of every starving youngster who came to her attention. Two-year-old Guadalupe had Fay running to the hospital daily with special food until Guadalupe began to eat normally. Fay helped so many children, I can't remember them all. But no one was quite like **baby Maria** (above with her brother, **Vicente**).

Tox's sister lived in Las Cañas, an aldea so tiny it didn't

have a store. Nevertheless, this village was one of our favorite places because we were well accepted there. We also loved it because Rubén, the school teacher, had convinced the people to build a latrine. What luxury to hurry there instead of squatting by a bush. Tox loved Las Cañas too because one of his best friends, Miguel, lived there. Miguel was devilish and charming, with bright button eyes. Every time he helped in our clinic, he signed up more patients than we could possibly see. Miguel would coax, "Just four more, seño. They came from so far away." How could we say no?

Las Cañas (above) consisted of Miguel's house, Tox's sister's house, the school, church and a trail through the jungle to aldeas where many Kek'chi made their homes.

After the birth of her last child, Maria, Tox's sister, died. She left behind the infant, a husband and 11 other children.

Rubén told us what happened. "I tried to take her to the hospital, but she wouldn't go. She didn't want any man to

"look at her." Before she died, she told us she had named
Teresa from Chacté to be *la madrina,* the godmother, and to
raise the baby. Barely 30 years old and Maria hemorrhaged to
death. There was nothing I could do," said Rubén.

I admired Rubén, who drove every day from Poptún to
teach in Las Cañas, a community few people cared about. Now
his eyebrows met in a frown.

"What happened to the baby?" I was almost afraid to ask,
fearful of more bad news.

"Doing well, *gracias a Dios.* But who knows how long
she'll stay that way."

"Lizzie," said Fay, "let's visit and see how she's doing."

"Yeah," I agreed, "let's do. Poor baby."

A few yards from the church was the home with kids of all
ages staring at us. This was a Kek'chi family, so the little girls
wore the same cotton blouse as the women, square-necked,
short-sleeved and tucked into a faded Kek'chi *traje,* skirt. The
boys wore ragged pants and patched shirts. All were barefoot.

Tox said something to the children in Kek'chi. A boy with
a thatch of black hair so thick it sprung from his head like

porcupine needles, led us through the yard where chickens and a bony dog scuttled out of the way. In a dark, thatched-roof hut (like the one at left) hunched Tox's brother-in-law, his face expressionless. On the hammock slung from the rafters, the oldest child, a thin girl of perhaps twelve, held the infant wrapped in rags.

We examined the baby and found her scrawny, but healthy. Even then, she had a responsive gaze I'd seen in few infants.

"She's beautiful," I told the father, expressing my condolences about his wife. "*Lo siento de su esposa.*" We touched him on the shoulders, the polite greeting among the Kek'chi. He nodded and averted his eyes. I couldn't read his feelings.

"What is she called?" I asked.

"Maria," he said. Just like her mother.

We sat in silence a while, then Fay asked, "What are you feeding her?"

The girl showed us the can of powdered milk, Nido. Fay and I exchanged glances. Whole milk wasn't good for new babies. Too high in protein, it often caused diarrhea.

"Are you boiling the water?" I asked.

The girl glanced at her father, then shook her head. I raised my eyebrows at Fay.

"Remember, in unboiled water there are probably *parasitos*. The baby will get sick if the water isn't boiled. It's really important." Fay smiled to soften the force of her words.

"Nido is good for adults, but not the baby," I added. "She needs formula. It's like a mother's milk."

As usual, Tox translated into Kek'chi. The process was tedious and we must have lost a little meaning in translating.

"Teresa has Similac. Let's go buy a bunch. We can use our sponsor money," I said.

Teresa, the designated godmother, owned a prosperous store in Chacté. Poorer families often asked her to be

godmother. We bought every can of Similac she had. "I would
be happy to take the baby," she said. "But I doubt it will
happen. *La familia no quiere.*" The baby's family was
opposed.

Back in Las Cañas, the oldest girl poured water from the
steaming black cauldron on the fire. We visited with them until
the water cooled. While we waited, a chicken pecked around
our feet, then flew to the table and stalked back and forth.
From there, with a squawk, it landed on the dirt floor. The girl
removed the nipple from baby Maria's bottle, placing it on the
table exactly where the chicken had been standing.

"No...no! Don't let the nipple touch anything dirty or the
baby will get sick from the germs," Fay admonished. She
asked for soap and washed the nipple, leaving it to soak in a
cup of hot water.

It was so frustrating with these families. The microscopic
world of germs was unknown to them. Before we came, they'd
never heard of bacteria. Even after looking under the
microscope, I'm not sure they made the connection. Because
they lacked basic education, disease was hard for them to
understand.

With Tox translating patiently into Kek'chi, we showed
the girl how to prepare formula. She hadn't attended school
and understood only a few words in Spanish. She, however,
was the only one who showed interest. The others were too
young and the father too withdrawn.

We told them to let us know when they ran out of formula.
Similac was far too expensive for them to manage.

That night, Fay and I attended a novena, a prayer service
for the nine days following the mother's death. The younger
children slept on sacks of corn. After the catechist led us in
prayers, Tox, Miguel and Luis, the oldest son, played guitars
and sang mournful songs in Kek'chi.

The next day we left Las Cañas, feeling we'd done all we
could, and thinking in our naiveté they would contact us when

they ran out of Similac.

Two months later, we returned to Las Cañas. The first thing we did was visit baby Maria. On entering the smoky hut, I noted disorder. Clothes were flung over the rafters. Children ran around half naked, snot-nosed and dirty faced. The mother's presence was clearly missing from this house. The infant swung gently in a hammock. Fay picked her up, exclaiming, "Oh Lizzie, *look* at her!" Fay's face crumpled and she blinked back tears. She held Maria in a fierce hug.

The baby whimpered. Only those suffering eyes were alert.

Fay rocked and crooned, "Maria, Maria, oh little baby, what's happened to you?"

"Why does she look *tan malo*, so bad?" she demanded. Tox translated into Kek'chi, but even with his probable diplomacy, the father couldn't miss Fay's disgust.

The father replied with stony indifference, "She has diarrhea and as soon as we give her milk it goes right through. We're doing everything we can."

"Are you boiling the water? Are you mixing the formula as we told you?" Fay demanded.

The family scurried around in response to our questions. We learned the oldest girl had been watering down the formula to make it last longer. They were not boiling the water. Something black was stuck in the nipple tip.

Anger boiled in me, but I tried not to show it. But my feelings paled in comparison to Fay's, for this baby had entered her heart. She paced with Maria in her arms. "Why didn't you come for more formula? We could have helped you!"

We should have given them more money to begin with, I thought, instead of expecting them to ask us. Maybe they were embarrassed to accept charity. I knew the extreme pride of the Kek'chi. Ladino families didn't mind owing a debt for medicines and clinic visits. But not the Kek'chi. They paid immediately, not coming to the clinic if they had no money.

"You're not doing anything like we told you! I'm taking her to Poptún. She's dehydrated and needs special care!" Fay announced.

The family was opposed. We argued at length. Fay finally said, "OK, where's the coffin? If you don't let us take her, that's where she'll be!"

With these words, the father reluctantly gave in.

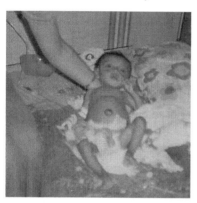

Back in Poptún, I started an IV and we gave her antibiotics (left). Mo, Kay and John Blazo came to see her. They looked in pity at the pathetic little form. Some in our community expressed concern that Fay couldn't both care for the child and continue working in the aldeas. And what would happen, someone asked, if the child died while under Fay's care? Might the family blame us?

By that time, Fay had her own rented house near the convent. After helping Maria over the immediate crisis, she took the baby home and cared for her as if she were her own child. Within days, Maria drank formula and gobbled down thinned oatmeal without having diarrhea. Fay was thrilled and took great pride in this progress. She grew more attached to Maria as each day passed.

"I'm going to talk to the family, Lizzie, and see if they'll let me keep her. After all, Teresa has her own family. She probably doesn't want her as much as I do. I could do so much for her."

"You're absolutely right, Fay. If she goes back to them, she'll wind up sick again." I took pictures of Maria, who resembled a big-eyed doll in the white bonnet Fay had bought her.

In a few weeks, baby Maria was well enough to travel back to Las Cañas. The family was happy to see her and the children crowded around, chattering in Kek'chi. They took turns holding her, examining Maria's new clothes.

But they vehemently opposed giving the baby to Teresa to raise, nor would they let Fay adopt her.

Fay cried. "She would be my only child. I could care for her if she got sick. Please..."

They were immovable. Fay shouted, with tears running down her cheeks. "Keep her! But take a good look because it'll be a long time till she looks like this again!"

She thrust Maria into the father's arms, then jumped in the truck and slammed the door. I turned from Fay to the family. I agreed with Fay and felt her anguish. But what could we do? The family stood by the roadside, staring coldly at us. The father grasped Maria tightly in his arms, as if he were afraid we would run back and snatch her.

"*Lo siento*, I'm sorry," I said, feeling a profound regret for what was happening to Fay and the baby. Had we made enemies with these people who'd been our friends? I admired Fay, but trying to change their minds was hopeless.

 The Kek'chi were attached to their children. To give up a child was unthinkable. I remember asking Fern why there were no orphans among the Kek'chi. He told me kids without parents were absorbed within the community. One never knew children lacked blood parents. They just melted into a family.

In their value system they *must* keep this baby. Even if

they realized the child might die, they were likely to ascribe it to the *voluntad de Dios*, the will of God, their way of accepting whatever happened in life.

I couldn't help thinking, once again, that if the whole system was different in Guatemala, Maria's mother wouldn't have died, nor would she have had so many children. Birth control and prenatal care were non-existent in these remote aldeas.

There were more practical reasons for keeping children. A child was another pair of hands working in the corn fields, and someone to care for parents in old age.

In that moment, with Fay driving furiously towards Poptún, I realized anew the chasm that separated our two cultures.

Soon after, Fay developed severe hepatitis and went to the States on leave. Afterward, I drove by Las Cañas with Tox. We stopped to see the baby. Fay's prediction had come true. Maria had diarrhea, a fever and congested cough. I gave her antibiotics, bought Similac and gave the family cash for more formula. I pleaded with them to boil the water, and washed the nipple, which was caked with dirt again. I believed she was doomed. Knowing Fay still cared, I wrote to her about visiting baby Maria.

A few weeks later, baby Maria did indeed die. Another senseless death. We all grieved—especially Fay.

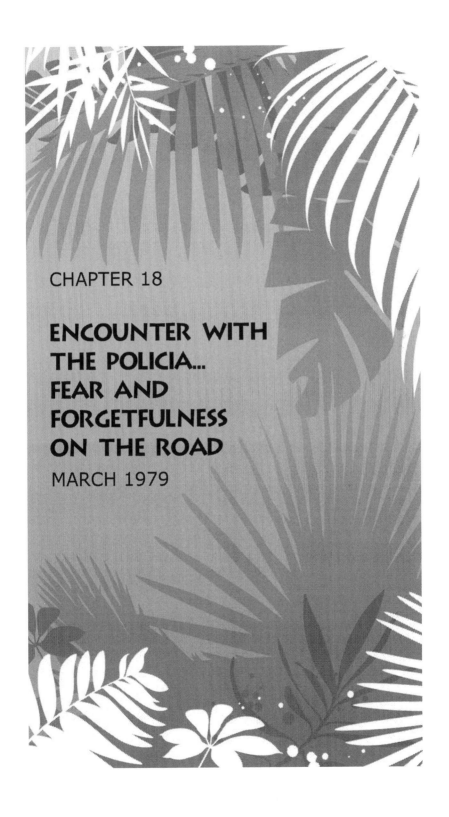

CHAPTER 18

ENCOUNTER WITH THE POLICIA... FEAR AND FORGETFULNESS ON THE ROAD

MARCH 1979

The next month Fay and I and Tox headed off to El Crucero, another aldea not too far from Poptún. With the road to ourselves, I couldn't figure out why Fay hugged the side as if there was a white line down the middle. (That's **Fay**, right, and I in front of our trusty Chevy Luv truck.) We lived and worked so closely together that I had a hard time accepting Fay's habits. She was more tolerant of me. With each bump, Tox and I smashed against each other sitting together on the front seat. One or two lonely houses broke the monotony of the dense foliage by the road. On these trips, I'd begun to feel oppressed by the utter sameness of each day.

Before long we'd have to buy new shocks. But if I said something to Fay, she'd be upset. That week she fought with Mo.

"You aim for the friggin' potholes," Mo had said. "At least avoid them or you'll ruin the springs."

"You should talk, Mo. What about those three you've replaced and your land cruiser isn't even two years old?"

Mo groaned and rolled his eyes. No one had the last word with Fay.

Shortly after San Luís, Fay turned the truck toward El Crucero. At the turn-off, two green-uniformed hacienda police watched us approach, hands on their American-made carbines.

"*Alla la policia*, there's the police," said Tox, as if we needed to be told.

I shared his unspoken dread. They waved us over, jabbing with their nightsticks. Fay slowed to a stop.

"Now what!" I said.

They swaggered toward us. One nearly tripped on the uneven road.

Tox whispered, "*Estan borachos. Cuidado.*" He didn't have to warn me they were drunk.

The heavier one leaned in through Fay's partly open window. His stomach flattened against the glass. The other one balanced on my side against the door. He regarded Tox and me as if we were scum off his shoes. His bloodshot eyes lingered on the word "Petén," on my yellow T-shirt, then moved slowly up to my face. I stared right back. I hate it when men are so obvious.

"*¿Donde van?*" he demanded. I smelled liquor. I forced myself to be calm, though I wanted to scream and run. Immediately, I sensed a menace in their presence. Fear pumped my heart faster.

Tox, his voice shaking, explained we were on our way to the aldeas for a clinic. He had every reason to be afraid, for those local police were infamous in the Petén for brutality. They broke laws it was their job to enforce. We'd been warned to be very careful in our dealings with them. It frightened me to see Tox's reaction. He'd never before shown fear of anything.

The policeman leered at Fay. Fay hated drunks. She abhorred leering men even more.

"Why did you stop us?" she challenged him. She made no attempt to hide her anger.

He straightened, pulled down his hat and adjusted his gun. His dough belly rolled over his belt.

"It's our job to patrol this road. We've never seen you before!"

"We've been driving back and forth for over a year," I said, wishing I could pull back the words, as I immediately knew I was provoking them more.

"*¿Donde esta su cédula?*" the one at Tox's window demanded. He stuck his arm in the window. Tox removed his identification from his wallet, a card no Guatemalan dared travel without. The policeman snatched it, read it and shoved it back at Tox.

"Where's your driver's license?" The fat one's words slurred and spit shone on his slug-like lips.

"We don't carry our licenses. They're back in Poptún. We're missionaries," Fay said, as if that explained. "And you're drunk and shouldn't bother us!"

Oh God, I thought.

The heavy one yanked open her door. "Get out! Hurry up! We'll see if you're missionaries!"

"Fay, please don't make him angry," I whispered.

"*Cuidado, cuidado,*" hissed Tox.

We got out of the truck. I glanced across the road. A woman peered around the door of her thatched hut, holding two kids crushed to her legs. She disappeared from sight. No one would help us out of this. No one was around.

"Move!" the fat one screamed at Fay. "Show me your license!"

"I told you I don't have a license," Fay controlled herself with effort.

"How could you be driving without a license?" the other one yelled. "It's against the law. You're not going anywhere until you show it!"

"What are you carrying in this truck?" The heavier one moved to the back, fumbling with the vinyl flap held fast by a screw.

Tox opened the covering while the men crowded to see and started shoving boxes around roughly.

"Please be careful," Fay said, "those are our medicines."

They ignored her and flung our supplies on the ground.

The chubby one jabbed his stick at Tox. "You. Take this stuff out. Show us what's in these boxes."

I helped Tox open several. They contained our scale, thermometers and bottles of pink cough syrup. I could hardly make my hands function, they shook so.

I thought of the four bodies found along the road earlier that week. No one knew who the dead were or who had murdered them. People said the army or the police had killed them. Then we heard that two had been Nicaraguan tourists taken from a bus and shot. No one knew why. These men could direct me to do anything, and I would have to comply. The police in this country were the last people I would ask for help. They didn't maintain law and order, but kept the corrupt system going.

They finally calmed down and stopped yelling. But they insisted we couldn't leave until we showed our licenses.

It'd never occurred to me to carry my license. No one had ever stopped us. Naively, I assumed everyone knew who we were, even though we had no sign on our truck indicating we were a mobile clinic or worked with the church. We didn't

(below).

bring purses to the aldeas so we didn't bother to carry licenses either.

We debated whether to go back home, but the police wouldn't let us. They would confiscate the truck if we returned.

Fay (left) volunteered to stay while I went back to Poptún.

"They'll rip off all our stuff if we leave it," she said.

"I'll stay with you Fay...in case," said **Tox**

I started toward San Luís, at least an hour's walk away. I glanced back at Fay and Tox standing by the truck. The two men stood off to one side talking.

I hoped they'd be okay. Lord...let them be okay.

Further up the road, Don Antonio, who owned the bakery where we bought bread, was driving toward Poptún in his tiny blue Datsun truck. I had sent his daughter to a specialist for a fungal ear infection that wouldn't go away. Now, he stopped when I hailed him. The truck smelled of *pan dulce*, sweet bread, loaded in baskets in back. He was going to Poptún. I said a silent prayer of thanks. This ride would save me several hours of waiting for the bus.

I couldn't help thinking of the inconsistencies in this country. Fay and I should have carried our licenses, but even so, I had felt unnecessarily harassed and menaced.

Only a few months before, Mo and I had driven to Flores to renew the brake inspection permit on our Chevy Luv. Mo jumped out and said, "Wait here. I'll be right back." He hurried to the office.

He returned in a few minutes. "Good for another year." He handed me the brake inspection slip with a new stamp on it.

"Gee Mo, you mean they don't actually check our brakes?"

"That's how things are in this country," he said. He had paid for the brake inspection, but no one actually checked our brakes. The permit was only for the money it took in, not for the safety of our vehicles.

Car troubles were the rule in the jungle--that's **Tox**, below, fixing a flat on our truck with some recruited help.

In Poptún I hurriedly found Fay's license and grabbed my Washington and international driver's licenses. I'm never going *anywhere* without these again, I vowed. I ran to the bus stop and waited, anxious for Fay and Tox. The bus finally came and we lurched down the road. Two hours later, we drew close to the crossroads outside of San Luís. Sitting on the edge of my seat, I clutched the rusty rail, terrified of what I might see.

Our little mustard-brown truck remained where we had left it. Fay and Tox sat in it alone. I ran to them.

"What happened?" I said, relieved not to see any police.

"They got tired of waiting," answered Fay. "They left two hours ago."

I must have been hyperventilating because that tight feeling in my chest was gone. Tox and I held hands for a while. It was so good to see those two unharmed. Fay and I wondered later if the men had expected us to pay them off, a common way people dealt with police harassment. At the time it never occurred to us, and we wouldn't have bribed them anyhow. I felt disgusted and furious at the system that gave police control over everyone. But there was no one to complain to and no one who would do anything about it, either. By some miracle no harm had come to us, but it could easily have gone the other way. I can only imagine some guardian spirits were working overtime that day.

CHAPTER 19

LOS ANGELES
AND ITS
PROMOTER
APRIL 1979

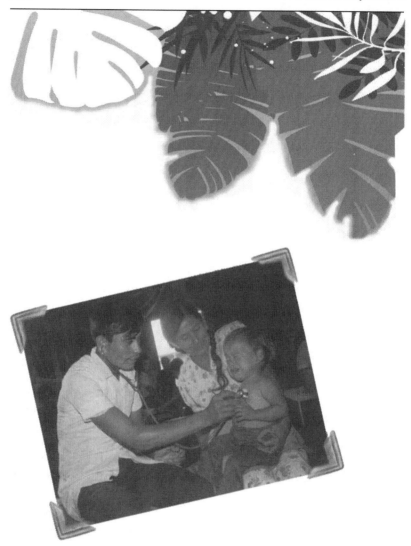

**After Fay and I had been visiting the aldeas for a year
and a half, we began our *promotor de salud* (promoters of
health) program to teach people to be mini-doctors.** In the
first group was **Jose Mario Balcarcel** (above) from
Macháquila.

To me, this was what our missionary work had been
aiming for all along. Now Fay and I knew the diseases and the
hardships of people's lives and could teach the promoters.

It was a relief to go to the aldeas this time, not for clinic, but to meet with the locals, asking them to choose one or two people from each village to study with us. As Fay and I traveled from place to place, the young men brought their guitars and home-made base fiddles, and sang and played

before and after the meetings. It was *muy alegre,* very happy.

We soon had several good prospects. Cansís, with a very cohesive community, chose two candidates. Yaltutú selected the wonderful catechist, Carlos Bran. From Boca del Monte, where I swear the children were as numerous as the parasites, came genial Mario; from Canchacán, our oldest candidate, Atilano Santos; and from Tanjoc, shy **Carmen Ché** (above). In most aldeas, we had no problems getting students.

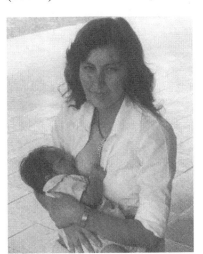

Rosa Imelda (left) was a candidate from Macháquila.

Los Angeles, with a tiny Catholic population, as miserable a place as I had ever had the misfortune to stay, had no possibilities. The settlement lay along a swampy plain; bugs, insects and mosquitoes infested the town in prodigious numbers.

One clear night we gathered in the Los Angeles

school with the same people who always greeted us. Don
Miguel and his wife, Doña Maria, and a handful of others.
Bugs circled the lantern. Mosquitoes stung through my long-
sleeved shirt and I began to scratch, as I always did when I
visited there.

We discussed each person who could study at the two-
year program. Although sessions were every two months, still
it was a considerable commitment for these people. Each class
meant sacrificing time from their fields. For that reason, most
students were teenagers without family responsibilities.

It looked as though Los Angeles wouldn't have a
candidate, which saddened me. Even this miserable place
should have a student, I thought, if only so someone could treat
the annual bouts of malaria.

Don Miguel, the catechist spoke up. "Señorita Elizabeth,"
he said, "since there's so few Catholics, it's difficult."

"What about the Evangelicals?" asked Doña Maria, a
chubby, good-natured woman who never missed a class. "They
get sick like we Catholics do!" She winked at us. "Speak to the
pastor," she continued. "He's a good man."

Fay and I hesitated. We served on a team of Catholics and
clinics were usually held in Catholic churches, except here in
Los Angeles where there was no official building. Perhaps the
Evangelicals had a church with a good zinc roof in this very
poor town and the Catholics didn't because they received
money from groups pushing the religion outside of town. Some
on our team spoke bitterly about the harm the Evangelicals
were causing and the enmity between the two religions. Fay
and I tried to be sensitive to that attitude. I, too, had viewed the
Evangelicals as obstacles after the pastor in Las Cruces
screamed all night, lamenting the death of a child. His church
was next to the building where I had attended a course. In La
Cumbre, the pastor said we gave out bad medicine and were
from the devil because we were Catholics. But once the people
began to trust us, I couldn't tell the difference between the

Catholic and the Evangelical patients.

These experiences were on my mind as we talked with Doña Maria and Don Miguel in Los Angeles. "Where's the pastor?" I asked.

"He's in the church. They're having their *culto*," Don Miguel said. He left to talk with the pastor. The culto was the nightly prayer meeting that went on until late in Evangelical churches.

Being born a Catholic, even to step foot in another church could be equated to watching an X-rated movie. I came from an era when participating in any other church's ritual used to be a sin.

I looked forward to attending the culto, as I'd always been interested in seeing what one was like.

Don Miguel returned. "The pastor said come right away. As soon as they're finished, you can present your idea."

Maybe we'd get a candidate from Los Angeles yet!

Fay, Tox, Doña Maria and I walked down the dark road, swatting vigorously at mosquitoes on our way. I bent over now and then to rake furiously at my feet. Los Angeles had a red bug that bit fiercely through any clothing. Even wearing thick cotton socks, I had the beginning of my third case of impetigo.

"I wonder what the guys will say if we have an Evangelical in our course," Fay said.

"Maybe they'll be upset, but we need someone from Los Angeles. Chacalté is too far from here and all Kek'chi. We'll never get a promoter from there," I said. Chacalté was the one place where Fay and I had failed. People there regarded us with hostility, as if we were the enemy.

I wondered, though, what would happen if we did get an Evangelical from Los Angeles. Would he or she go to mass? We wouldn't require attendance, but the student might feel uncomfortable and left out.

Our contacts with other religious groups were minimal. A couple Fay and I knew, Matt and Rosemary Ulrich, had worked in San Luís, Petén for 18 years. Rosemary was a nurse, treating as many as 100 patients a day. Matt spent those years translating the Bible for the Maya Mopán, a group of 2500 Indians.

Some on our team disliked the couple, maybe because Rosemary and Matt used terms like being "saved" and "knowing Jesus as their Savior," fanatical language for some main-line Catholics.

Fay and I ignored the rhetoric, enjoying Matt and Rosemary as the caring, dedicated people they were. I'll never forget how Rosemary visited Fay in the Center House in Guatemala City to bring a huge bag of books and favorite food after Fay lost her appetite during a bout of severe hepatitis.

Not far from Poptún, a group of Seventh Day Adventists opened a school in the settlement of Las Lájas. Soon, other projects followed—an orphanage and technical schools. We heard good reports about the work being done there.

Evangelicals set up new churches, seemingly overnight, on practically every street corner. I have to admit that at that time I did have some prejudice against Evangelicals, but one of our students proved me wrong. Once a person joined the Evangelical church, the decision could cause dissension within the family, especially if others refused to join. Two faiths in one home might even cause divorce, eviction of the un-accepting party from the house or denial of marital relations. Many pastors provided a caring presence to their congregations, giving them attention when someone was sick or died. This degree of ministry was sorely lacking in the Catholic church because of the scarcity of priests.

Some on our team had run-ins with the Evangelicals. In La Isla, a water-bound village far in the jungle where Fern visited, a man who became an Evangelical refused to give rides on his boat to Catholics, even to bring a dying girl to a hospital. The man doubled the prices to Catholics in his store, also disowning his wife and children.

The Evangelicals' successful efforts to entice converts from the Catholics fueled the war between the two groups. Some Evangelicals said Catholics were the antichrists, adored statues, confessed to priests instead of God and baptized children when they should have baptized adults. Sometimes there was dialogue when questions of land rights or water projects arose, but even today there is too much misunderstanding and animosity.

That night in Los Angeles, as we approached the Evangelical church, their singing and guitars made a pleasing sound in the quiet. I recognized the catchy tune, *"Alabare, Alabare."* "Praise. Praise." I liked that song. We tiptoed in, trying not to distract, but everyone turned to stare. This church looked like Catholic churches: wood boards, benches and a dirt floor, except here there was no altar, statues of Jesus, cross or candles, no pieces of colored plastic cut in zig-zags and strung across the room. Only a raised platform stretched along the front of the building.

The song ended. A man jumped onto the elevated stage. *"Hermanos y hermanas en Cristo,"* he began, pacing. After that I understood nothing. Used to the serious rituals of the Catholic church, where everyone behaved according to centuries-old patterns, I was both fascinated and repelled. The pastor's behavior seemed bizarre. His voice rose, his face turned red and his neck veins bulged. He waved his arms like a fighter minus the punching bag. It didn't occur to me in that moment that my own church's rituals might appear just as peculiar to Protestants.

"¿Esta enojado?" I whispered to Tox. The pastor certainly looked like he was boiling mad.

"No," said Tox. *"Es como son..*it's how they are."

Voices from around me shouted, "amen" and "alleluia." I cast a furtive glance at Tox. His upturned lips tried not to laugh. Fay's hand covered her face, not in prayerfulness, I'm afraid. Her shoulders heaved and little sounds escaped her.

Doña Maria rolled her eyes, gave me an obvious wink and fanned herself with a towel.

To keep from giggling, I swallowed hard. I've always had a tendency to laugh at the most inappropriate moments. I knew we couldn't laugh. What would everyone think? These were good, sincere folks. I made myself settle down.

Suddenly, the pastor dove from sight.

"Where'd he go?" I whispered to Fay.

He popped up again and didn't miss a step in his bounds across the stage. He must have been kneeling behind the pulpit.

"If he doesn't calm down, he's going to have a stroke," hissed Fay.

Everyone watched as if he was behaving normally. How long could he keep this up? His contortions on the platform went on for twenty minutes.

After another half hour of shouts and pacing, he yelled one more *Dios es Amor*! God is Love! Everyone shouted, "Alleluia!"

Then his face changed to a normal expression. "Tonight, brothers and sisters," he said quietly, "we have the pleasure of three honored guests to speak with us." He smiled as if he hadn't been shouting moments ago, then sat down among his congregation and faced us.

I didn't have time to think about his abrupt change as we walked to the front. A little self-conscious, I relaxed after I saw how each person listened with customary courtesy. Some faces were familiar from clinic. I was among friends.

Briefly, we presented the health promoter program. The pastor listened. Then he stood. "I think what the señoritas are proposing is a good idea. What do the rest of you think?"

A man raised his hand. "We need someone who knows about health in Los Angeles. We have many who are sick." Several others agreed. Throughout the crowd, people nodded and smiled at us. This was not a weird religious sect, but just the same, simple, respectful individuals I saw every day in our clinics.

"I'll take the matter up with the entire church and get back to you," the pastor said.

The next morning, he came by the school where we'd spent the night. He and Don Miguel were accompanied by **José Radino**, (below left) a tall, reserved, darkly handsome youth.

"I would love to become a promoter," José Radino told us. He smiled shyly when Fay and I reacted with enthusiasm. "My mother would be pleased if you joined us for breakfast. Can you come?"

Of course we would! How great not to have to light our stove.

We walked down the road to his home, a dirt-floored dwelling as clean and tidy as a house with a vinyl floor and painted walls.

On the way, Fay asked if José had attended school. "I have completed *primaria*, elementary school. *Me gusta estudiar*. I like to study."

His mother I'd seen in the clinic many times, her dark hair wound into a thick coil at her neck. She welcomed us now with a warm smile. We sat at their wooden table. Plastic cups hung from evenly spaced nails on the slat wall. She made a breakfast of scrambled eggs, hot black beans, fresh tortillas wrapped in a clean towel and sweetened coffee. José Radino waited on us. I could see he was an unspoiled and sweet boy.

José Radino turned out to be one of our best students. Unlike some of his rowdier Catholic classmates, he never goofed off. He joined in every aspect of the program, even played base guitar at mass. **Nicolasa** (left) and Juana, from El Crucero, our prettiest female students, giggled whenever he was around, for they had terrific crushes on him. But José Radino was oblivious of his charm. He was such a good young man. No one on our team ever mentioned he wasn't a Catholic. In the larger sense, it really wasn't important.

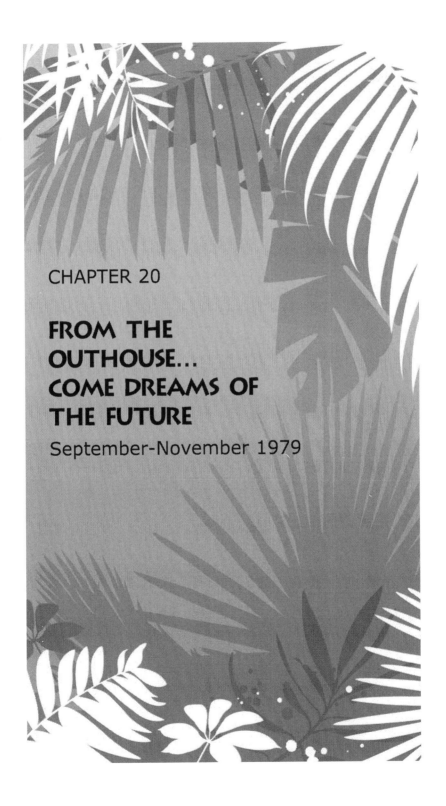

CHAPTER 20

FROM THE OUTHOUSE... COME DREAMS OF THE FUTURE

September-November 1979

Early in our visits to the aldeas, I taught a class on outhouses. That's **Julian Morales** (above) in front of one of the first finished ones. Many Kek'chi had never heard the word, so I drew pictures of them on a flip chart. I saw by people's blank stares that building a place just for relieving oneself was to them ridiculous, especially considering what shacks they lived in.

Everyone yawned with boredom, including me. I dreaded

these lectures, though I did get a few laughs when I showed how to dig a hole in the ground with a stick. Usually, the stick broke and barely made a nick in the hard-packed earthen floor. People leaned to look from their seats on the church bench, wondering no doubt what the crazy gringa was up to now.

Finally I stopped teaching that subject, as people could not seem to connect disease and relieving themselves wherever they liked. I dreamed out loud sometimes. "Wouldn't it be wonderful if there were outhouses everywhere...even the schools and churches?"

"Yeah," said Fay, with a hint of sarcasm, "and people were begging us to tell them how to build one."

Of all the towns we visited, only Las Cañas had an outdoor latrine.

Fay and I used it regularly. I had heard a story once about someone getting bitten by a snake, so I never sat down without imagining a reptile coiled to strike. No wonder both Fay and I suffered constipation when we weren't doubled over with the runs.

The outhouse was dark inside, but spiders and all sorts of bugs hung from the dried leaves. When I closed the door and slid the wooden peg across the opening, it felt as if something was in there with me. I tried not to breathe too deeply. The stench was awful. On hot days, the smell was so horrible we "went" behind the outhouse.

"Don't tell anybody," Fay would call from the bushes, "but I see why people prefer to go out here."

"At least it doesn't stink," I agreed.

Going outside had its drawbacks. Someone might see me squatting. We had to make sure to have a swatch of toilet paper in our pockets or we might have to use leaves, as the people did.

One day a bulldozer rumbled down the road and knocked down the outhouse. Oil had been discovered in the Petén. Big black pipes were laid alongside the road, the only sign of industry in that forgotten place. I couldn't help but think we were reaping the consequences for defecating behind it.

From then on, we went where everyone else went, wherever. But we wanted people to build outhouses to cut down on disease.

After the discouraging reaction to my class, I figured this was an idea whose time had not yet come.

A year and a half after we started our mobile clinic and health classes, Fay and I started our promoter program at the education center, which Mo had renamed Kerigma-Quetzal.(That's me at the front door, left.) It was located near the entrance to Poptún. Kerigma meant herald or preacher in Greek and Quetzal is the brilliant, red-and- green, long-tailed bird of Guatemala, symbolizing freedom.

Besides a large kitchen, dining room, two dorms, classrooms, the offices of health, literacy and leadership were housed there. Mo, Maria Dolores and Kay taught their leadership courses on the site, and Fern, church doctrine. Kerigma was like our convent and rectory—eaten up by termites and crumbling. Eventually, it would be rebuilt, long after I left the Petén. One functioning toilet and two broken-down latrines emitted a disgusting odor. Building new outdoor toilets during the second term in November would give us four new ones.

Students came by bus, walked or hitched rides. For some, the journey took a day or two. They arrived with cloth shoulder bags containing a change of clothes for the week, a notebook

and pencil, toothbrush and comb. Some were awestruck when
they saw Kerigma-Quetza (above)l. As decrepit as it was, to
them, the building was a castle. Many had never used a tap
with running water or a toilet that flushed. Even the dorms,
with their rows of crude wooden beds without mattresses, were
luxuries.

Meals were served in the dining room on rough plank
tables and benches. We had hired a cook, **Maria Elena**
(below). With the courses in leadership, literacy and now
health, she kept busy constantly. The usual meal was black
beans, tortillas and *queso*, white cheese, or *crema*, creamed

cheese. Students were
allowed as much as
they could stuff into
their slim stomachs.
Some young men
downed as many as
two dozen thick corn
tortillas at each meal.
Refresco, a sweet

beverage resembling Kool-Aid, was served to drink. Often, students ate greens that Leon grew in his garden, or other vegetables and fruits. The only complaint was that we served no chiles with their meals. Then one day, a student found green chile peppers, the size of almonds, growing wild on the grounds. From then on, they happily gathered the chiles before each meal, and with peppers in one hand and a tortilla in the other, scooped up their beans.

Women and girls were housed in one dorm and men in another. I loved seeing how much fun they had with one another and all the flirtations going on. At night, if Fay and I returned to give a class, we invariably found them together in one of the dorms, singing and playing guitars.

Promoter candidates were a mix of boys, family men, young girls and mothers. Fay and I were proud of "our" students. Never had I seen any other pupils so eager to learn. That's **Francisco Cuz**, left, our youngest student.

Over 60 students descended upon Kerigma-Quetzal in September of 1979. We taught the subject that we considered pivotal to improving their health: everything we knew about preventing parasites, which included boiling water, wearing shoes and covering food to keep off disease- bearing flies. If we motivated people to begin these elemental changes, they would no longer suffer from parasites, a major health problem. Teaching the classes was easy; we knew the subject backwards and forwards.

To spice things up, we added *competencias*, competitions, by dividing students into teams. **Guillermo** (left) answers a question. Groups picked names like *los liones*, the lions or *los torres*, the bulls. Questions were placed in a basket, such as: "Why is it necessary to boil water?" or "Name the symptoms of parasites." Teams with the most correct answers won pencils, notebooks or candy.

Competencias were one of the most fun aspects of our classes. **Isaias**, left, selects a question. Repetition helped even the slowest students learn. When I visited the Petén in 1989, Sheila Matthews, the nurse then in charge, still held competencias and the students still loved them.

One huge challenge was coping with teenagers intensely interested in one another. This was the first time they had tasted freedom away from their aldeas and families. Boys and girls were housed together for two weeks. Mostly, they exchanged flirty glances. Boys teased and girls giggled in groups of two or three about which boy was *más guapo*, the most handsome. Fay and I chaperoned, but it was rather like trying to keep magnets apart.

After I left, Fay solved the problem—at least she thought

she did—by housing the women students in the convent or her little house. Pictured above is a class on birth and delivery-- you can see how much the students enjoyed themselves. That's **Carmen Ché**, at the far right, who would go on to run the program years later.

Before Fay went home to Seattle in October of 1979 for a well-deserved rest, we planned our next course, teaching students to build outhouses. In four months, she planned to return to finish the program, which would take another year and a half. While she was gone, I was scheduled to teach the outhouse course.

Fay and I had appealed to the government for official sanction of our project. We talked with the doctors of Poptún, San Luís and Flores. The doctor from Flores said, "*Es una buena idea*. We have wanted to start a program for some time. We just hadn't gotten around to it." He shrugged, that gesture that meant what can one *do* in this country?

Doctors only gave their approval if we worked with their *technicos de salud*, health technicians. The alcoholic physician in charge of the Poptún hospital wanted to run the program.

Fay and I, talking fast and finagling, kept control.

Initially, six technicos worked with us. Two did not prepare for classes or come for meetings. One showed up drunk. We ended up with two who worked well, Manuel and Romeo. They proved a blessing. Both had built outdoor toilets and knew how deep to dig the hole and how to control odors.

Manuel, Romeo and I prepared lectures. By November, 1979, classes were in full swing. We had such fun, spending a lot of time giggling. Building latrines has its inherent humor.

When it was time to actually start construction, (left) I announced, "We need everyone's help. You girls can't just sit around while the men slave away. It wouldn't be fair. You women need to dig, too." I wanted to introduce them to the idea that jobs shouldn't be determined by gender.

This announcement produced consternation and raised eyebrows.

Nicolasa, a sixteen-year-old from El Crucero, raised her hand. "Seño Liz, digging trenches is men's work," and she tossed her mass of auburn curls like a princess.

The other women nodded, then looked at me.

"Who says it has to be that way?" I answered. "Women are as strong, if not stronger sometimes than men. Women have to *hacer las necessidades*, go to the bathroom, *tambien*, too." Several students tittered. "We're all going to help," I said. "Besides," I added, "in the States women do things like construction and engineering. And husbands wash clothes and diaper babies and cook." The women exchanged scandalized looks, as if I had told them to surrender making tortillas to men.

Some women only lifted a few shovels-full of dirt. Behind my back, they scrambled from the pit as fast as they could. Although the men did most of the labor, the women brought drinking water while they dug.

Carmen Ché, our only Kek'chi girl, was shy and spoke so quietly that I always asked her to repeat what she'd said. She was the only female who actually climbed into the excavation, letting the dirt fly while the others looked on in amazement.

Some students were particularly energetic, like Julian of Sajúl, a quiet family man with a handsome face despite his toothless smile. Julian shed his shirt and dug until sweat glistened on his muscled torso.

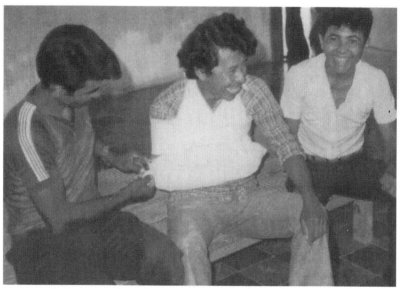

Another hard worker was **Macario**, (above, center, playing a patient) a catechist from Cansís. He was serious and dedicated. In one picture I took, he pushed a wheelbarrow piled with dirt, smiling as though it contained flowers.

Artistic students drew signs for the doors and instructions on how to dispose of paper, which couldn't be thrown in the latrine. Because it took up too much space, paper had to be burned in a barrel set in a large open spot behind Kerigma.

By the time classes ended, we had two new outhouses for women and two for men. They didn't even smell because we added chemicals to the holes.

When Fay and I had taught the first course on parasites, we set up a schedule for washing dishes. Men took turns, too, and swept the dorms and tidied the outhouses. At first, some refused. José Mario Balcarcel, a lanky youth, winked at Juana, who had a crush on him. "That's women's work," he said and slouched in his seat like John Wayne, pulling his cowboy hat over his eyes.

"If you don't help with chores, you're out of the program," we informed him. He straightened up fast and exchanged chagrined looks with the other males.

With over 65 of us, there was tons to do. To see the men washing up was comical. At first they handled dishes as if they were something repulsive. The boys giggled in embarrassment, but after a while they plunged their arms to the elbows in suds and enjoyed the camaraderie of the task. The wipers were even more hesitant, handling the plastic dishes like fine china, meticulously drying each cup.

Students were expected to motivate fellow villagers into building an outhouse in a public place, such as near the church or school. Each student was expected to set an example by constructing one at his or her own home. Later on, we'd try to persuade all villagers to build one. Though this program got off to a poor start, it eventually took hold, and continues to improve the health of many rural dwellers—all thanks to the humble outhouse.

CHAPTER 21

MUD...A LESSON
IN LOVE AND
COMMUNITY SPIRIT

DECEMBER 1979

**I couldn't have picked a worse time to travel than
December, when it rained so hard that rubberized ponchos
became sieves and even four-wheel-drive vehicles got stuck.**
The sky blanketed us in thick clouds. Cool, moist air blew in
through the truck's open window. I avoided puddles by
swerving back and forth across the slick road.

Beside me sat Lico, our literacy director. Next to him rode
faithful Tox. This would be my last trip into the jungle before I

left for the States. I'd sent a message advising the promoter students of our visit.

"I hope they got my note," I said to Lico.

"You know how the mail is," he replied, smiling with those curving lips that stirred something inside me. He had wavy brown hair and smoldering dark eyes. Together with his warmth and sensitive ways, no wonder half the women in Poptún were crazy about him. But Lico was more than a macho male. He worked long hours in the literacy program with the dedication of a missionary.

No one was waiting for us at the cutoff to Caín. Normally, aldea leaders sent a mule and a guide for the trip, knowing how hard it was to travel the nearly impenetrable roads. The route lay to my right, hung over by a canopy of bushes and trees. Quite usable during the dry season, it was now a sea of dark brown mud.

"We can turn around and go back," Lico said with his sultry voice. "Whatever you want. It'll be a rough trip."

"I didn't bring any food or water. How long do you think it'll take us?" I asked, fingering the bag of hard candy in my jeans pocket. Thank God for that.

"The campesinos make it in an hour and a half, but with the *camino tan malo*, so bad, it might take longer. *Talvez tres horas*, maybe three hours."

"I can do it," I said. "Come on. Let's go."

Tox flashed me a wide smile and handed me my backpack. I pulled on knee-high rubber boots from the truck, slung my Petri camera over my shoulder and tied a green rain poncho around my waist.

Fay had returned to the States, taking time off at home before she continued work here for another two years. Two months remained before I finished my contract with Maryknoll. I'd promised the students from Caín I'd come and couldn't let them down.

Lico and I walked side by side up the muddy road. We

rarely got a chance to talk. He came from Poptún. His sister, Lorena, was the excellent laboratory technician in the Poptún hospital, and his sister, Chita, worked for Mo and Kay as secretary.

"Someday I want to study law," he said now. "I enjoy teaching, but I think I could do more for people as a lawyer."

We were lucky Mo had hired Lico as supervisor of the literacy program. He treated everyone with kindness, and didn't consider himself better than poor people, like many Ladinos seemed to do. He even gave the students money from his modest salary.

Of course, he was amorous in that macho way. I thought he might have a crush on me. Flirting with him made me feel young.

This would be my first trip into the interior. Usually, Fay and I only traveled to the easily-accessible road towns. Since starting our program, we had tried to visit all students in their communities to show our support.

The first hour passed swiftly. A light rain started, like warm feathers tickling my face. I put on my poncho. The road climbed uphill. I began to feel hot and sticky, especially when the wind blew the rain against my face in stinging needles, plastering the poncho against me. I kept my head down. Soon, there were no more dry islands to find a foothold. Showers sliced my cheeks. I squinted at my feet.

I concentrated on avoiding the softer slime that sucked at my boots like something alive. Our pace had been slow and we hadn't gone far. Several times I almost fell, but Lico steadied me.

As we slogged through the mire, sweat tickled down my back. Before I'd come to Guatemala, I rarely perspired. In the Petén, I sweated like a sports nut. I sucked hard on a piece of candy, wishing for water.

Tox skimmed up the hill as if he had wings. The Kek'chi were so in tune with the earth that no terrain was an obstacle.

Beside me, Lico hiked sure-footed. He often glanced my way to make sure I'd negotiated the last step.

Dripping leaves slapped me. Gooey sludge covered the whole road. If I could just step more lightly, then I wouldn't sink in. But the mud fastened on my boots. I had to pull and wrench each step.

"How much farther?" I panted.

"It's quite a ways yet," Lico said with sympathy in his eyes.

I sighed and plodded ahead, resolved to get there somehow, proving to myself and to Lico I could keep up, even if he was ten years younger!

When I stopped to rest, Lico took my backpack. This helped. It had begun to feel like a boulder on my shoulders. Gasping, I followed behind his green poncho-wearing form.

Then my boot stuck. I wrenched it free, teetering on one foot. My arms flailed to keep from falling. My foot flew out of its boot and sank into the mud. A shiver of cold ran up one leg.

I could have *cried* in frustration. Lico steadied me while I tugged the boot free and swished the foot in a puddle. Chunks of mud plopped off my stocking. I slid my foot back into the boot.

Now I heard squiisshh...gluuuuuuuuunnnk, yank, yank with each step.

I knew what Fern had meant when Fay asked him one time how a trip had been, deep in the jungle.

"It was mud up to your backside!" Fern said.

Sometime during those hours, I stopped thinking. My heart pounded. Vaguely, I thought I might have a heart attack. Out-of-shape women could die like this. Engrossed in the world a few feet in front of me, I stumbled along, propelled by some force outside myself. Time and the jungle didn't exist, only the step I was in and the one ahead. My boots felt as though ten pounds of cement were attached to each. Five and one-half hours later, I staggered into Caín, and as if to mock me, the rain stopped.

Caín had been scooped out of the jungle. Banana palms and thick tropical plants sprouted everywhere. Thatched-roof homes were scattered around in the foliage, and here too, trails were mired in mud. What a desolate place. Everything gray and drenched and nothing but mud everywhere.

A woman emerged from a hut, amazed at our sudden appearance. A small boy and girl hung on her skirt. The children stared at my filthy pants and boots.

"Señorita, would you like to stay in my house? You can rest here," the woman said.

"Oh..*si...gracias...por favor.*" I collapsed into a hammock strung from a shelter outside the thatched roof dwelling. As if from a distance, I heard her ask my companions, "Would you like lunch?"

"*Si, por favor, muy amable,*" said Lico.

"*Muy cansada*, very tired," I whispered. Before I fell asleep, the thought that I should remove my boots and let my feet dry floated through my mind, but the idea was erased in a profound sleep.

I awakened that evening, amazingly refreshed. My feet felt wrinkled and I imagined the fungus growing between my toes. I wouldn't take off the boots because I had nothing to put on in their place, and walking barefoot in the parasite-laden mud wasn't a risk I wanted to take.

The woman served hot, thick corn tortillas with black beans and steaming sweetened coffee, which restored me like my mother's *pastina*, (tiny boiled pasta, butter and a beaten egg) when I'd been a sick kid.

Tox, Lico and I set off for the school, a crowd of children and adults trailing us. Caín was like all the other aldeas, with dogs, chickens and pigs roaming freely. This place had a special closeness like a house on a cul-de-sac.

The children waited at the school. Girls wore their best polyester dresses in flowered patterns of bright pink, yellow and red, hand sewn and falling apart at the seams. Their hair was wet and freshly combed. Some wore black rubber shoes but many were barefoot.

Encarnación welcomed us at the door. He touched me around the shoulders in the traditional Guatemalan greeting.

"Señorita Liz...you came," he said with his dimpled smile.

Encarnación was a star pupil. In addition to volunteer teaching, with his family he grew corn and beans in far-off fields. He had excelled in the promoter course, and found time for romance with his classmate, **Ana Victoria**, (below) a quiet girl who was the perfect foil for his outgoing nature. He was well educated for an aldea boy, having completed four years of

primary school. Sometimes I imagined what someone like Encarnación could accomplish in college. But there was no chance. Encarnación had immigrated to Caín with his family from the Atlantic Coast where land wasn't so available as in the Petén. On the Coast he received his schooling. Caín had only the school where he volunteered. He taught the children what he himself had learned, reading, writing and math. Encarnación looked at ease, even though we were here to check him out. In spite of few advantages, the people of the aldeas had an emotional confidence, evident in Encarnación's self assurance.

He lined up the children outside the school, placing the smallest ones in front. Each shouted out a song, even the littlest child. With their shining eyes, they were a delight to behold. The happiness these people exuded never ceased to uplift me.

We entered the school, lit only by a kerosene lantern hung from the rafter. The floor was hard-packed dirt. I sat down at a desk, ingeniously made from a tree branch stuck into the dirt, leaving two limbs spreading to both sides. A straight board balanced in the middle made a wobbly writing surface, but no one complained. Three children squeezed together at each desk.

Encarnación called on one child after another. Singly, they marched to the blackboard, recited, smiled and sat down. Encarnación controlled the class as a disciplinarian who expected their best and he got it. Joy permeated the atmosphere. Some children were shy, but that didn't stop them from reciting. They were so excited. How sad they had no books. Even Encarnación owned only a couple of books given him through the literacy program.

"*Buenas noches, todos*," Lico said. "We are happy with the tremendous job your teacher is doing. The children have learned much. They tell me he teaches you adults in the evenings, too."

Several heads nodded yes.

"Caín is one of the most supportive aldeas to the students." People beamed.

Afterward, Tox and I went to the Catholic church, where all community meetings were held. The other students, Ana Victoria and Miguel Angel were waiting there, along with a hundred villagers. Encarnación sat immediately with his *novia*, girlfriend, Ana Victoria. They snuggled close the rest of the meeting. Little kids played on the dirt floor.

Encarnación introduced Tox and me. "We didn't think you

would come...*con tanto lodo*...with so much mud," he said. "That's why even though we received your letter, we didn't send a guide or mules to meet you. No other gringo has come to Caín in December."

"I almost didn't make it," I told him, looking down at my filthy jeans and making a face. "How are things going for you?"

"We feel supported by the people," he said. "For the last course, the community gave us bus money and a sack of corn and beans."

Each village was expected to help students with expenses. Some sent donations of food for meals during the courses. In this way, communities would have a stake in student success. Their generosity might also have been because Ana Victoria was the daughter of Flavio, Caín's catechist. If anyone could inspire cooperation, Flavio did.

Now Flavio stood. His eyes, like dark pools of fire, the most snapping I'd ever seen. I remembered what Kay told me when Flavio attended a course Kay and Mo had given. Flavio endured malaria during the program and had a terrific headache, fever and chills. Yet he insisted on attending everything for he didn't want to miss any opportunity to learn.

"Brothers and sisters," Flavio began, "*Estamos muy contentos*, we are very happy, to have with us the Señorita Elizabeth and Salvador (Tox's other name). They journeyed such a long way to help us. We thank our good Lord who sent them. We must encourage the students so they will learn and help here in Caín. You know as well as I do how much we need someone skilled in these things. When it's time for the next health course, let's dig deep into our pockets and give a little something to our students. And let's not forget to tell them how glad we are they are doing this thing and studying hard. *Gracias a Dios!*"

He flashed a brilliant smile. I felt I'd been blessed by Flavio's words, too.

I stood and explained what the students would learn next, and how well their students were doing. People gazed into my eyes with total attention.

"What health problems do you have here?" I asked.

"As you can see, Seño Elizabeth, the children...*sufren de parasitos*, suffer from parasites and someone always has diarrhea," Encarnación said.

Yes, the villagers had pale faces, swollen bellies and scabbed sores on skinny legs, like people in every aldea. The miracle was that in spite of their poor health, they emitted joy of a kind I'd never experienced.

"*Es cierto*, that is certain," spoke up Ana Victoria, "and pregnant women often die during the birth. Many babies die in the first year." Ana Victoria was a plump, plain girl who hardly ever said anything but did well in classes.

"Our village is hard to leave during the rainy season. A promoter living here would be wonderful," said another woman.

"I was hoping you'd bring some medicines," Encarnación added hopefully, eyeing my bulging backpack.

"I did bring a few things."

But not nearly enough, I thought. Everyone crowded around as I spread packages of worm medicine, vitamins and antibiotics on the church bench. I wished I could have run a real clinic with a microscope and examining equipment.

Tox, working in his quietly efficient way, cared for those who wanted worm medicine. I concentrated on coughs and skin problems. In a few minutes, the supplies were gone, but no one seemed upset.

In fact, people laughed, smiled and compared their medicines. Maybe this visit was one of the more interesting events to happen here. I didn't mind the stares. I was used to being stared at. Besides, these were sympathetic looks. In spite of my fatigue, I felt a sense of accomplishment. I was needed. This was important work. People appreciated me.

That night, Tox, Lico and I stayed in the church, my first time sleeping in a hammock. It wouldn't have been bad if I could have kept warm. I didn't know you were supposed to put a blanket on the bottom to keep the cold from seeping through to your back. I shivered all night, worried I'd flip out if I turned over.

Having slept well, Tox and Lico arose in great spirits in the morning. I looked forward to the trip home, knowing I'd be riding a mule.

During breakfast, Flavio arrived to say a pregnant girl had been in labor for three days. She must get to a hospital soon, he said. I deduced she could easily become one of those women dying in childbirth I'd heard about last night from Ana Victoria. Flavio asked for volunteers to carry her to San Luís, where I'd left the truck. Although only a couple of miles away, it had seemed like twenty miles yesterday. They'd be lucky if anyone volunteered, I thought.

The man at whose house we ate breakfast promptly said he'd go, and by the time we left, six men and two women had joined us (carrying her through the mud, above).

A little later, with Lico and me straddling mules, we started out. (That's me, left, on what passes for a road.) I felt guilty while the volunteers plunged through the mud, but not enough to give up my mule. When the girl lay down on a canvas litter stretched between two poles, the men lifted her and the fabric folded over her like a sheet. One person held the pole at each side in a four-man lift. As my mule trudged through the mud, I looked back. The group had become fifteen. Along the way, more people joined. The men laughed and joked. Someone ahead was singing.

Rain began beating on us almost as soon as we started down the trail. The wide-brimmed straw hats the men wore didn't keep the rain from plastering sopping shirts to skin. No one had ponchos. A few wore colored plastic over their heads, held in place by a clenched fist under the chin, the plastic spreading out over their shoulders. Most went barefoot. I shivered in my dry clothes and wondered how they could stand it.

Several times, someone carrying the litter got stuck in the sludge. Along came another man to take his place, while the first wrestled his leg from the muck. I stopped counting the crowd at 30 people. More joined along the way.

Tears mingled with the rain on my cheeks. These Guatemalans kept amazing me. No one was congratulating himself on his charitable act, either. Yesterday's trip, which I would never forget, and probably would never again have to endure, was the life they faced daily.

My mule plodded ahead, its stick-like legs plunging into the puddles and out again like a machine. The motion made me rock in my saddle and the beginnings of a blister began to forming on the inside of my thigh.

We came upon a horse stuck to its belly in mud, heaving to wrench itself out. The horse was bathed in sweat, its eyes wild. Would anyone be able to get the poor thing out? No one stopped or gave the beast more than a passing glance. We were on a mission to save this woman. (That's me, below, visiting a different aldea on a mule in a lot less mud, later on.)

After two hours, we reached the road and our truck.

"Tox and I can take the bus or hitch a ride so you can drive her to the hospital," Lico said.

The men lowered the girl from the litter and she stepped out, looking pale. She wasn't in active labor, but this made me worry too. What if the baby was dead? Tox and Lico left to find a bus.

The girl climbed into the truck and sat by me. Her mother

followed.

The road was the usual ruts because of constant rain. It would be tricky driving.

"¿*Como se sientes*?" I asked the young woman as I started the engine.

"I am more or less good. The pains have eased a little," she said softly. She must not be past 15. She smiled shyly, then leaned on her mother and closed her eyes.

I drove slowly, but we still bounced. Muddy water splashed the windshield, and I put on the spray in a vain attempt to clear the window.

Thoughts of clean clothes, a shampoo and a long nap when we got back to Poptún were interrupted when the girl moaned. I darted a look at her sweaty face. Her hands clenched and her body arched towards her mother. Oh...God!

I tried to think how to deliver her on the road. I could rip up my T-shirt, and I had a Swiss Army knife. But please, God...help us make it to Poptún!

Then the mother gagged. "I've never been in a car before!" she gasped. With that, she hung her head out the window and threw up.

The girl groaned, an agonized sound that made my heart pound. I restrained a crazy impulse to laugh. What more could happen on this trip?

The girl's abdomen tightened under my hand. In another minute, her belly relaxed. A minute later another pain caught her. She writhed in silence.

"*Casi llegamos*, we're almost there," I said, my voice calm in spite of my inner turmoil, as we descended the hill on the outskirts of town.

At last, we reached the military hospital. Only then did relief come to me as she was whisked off in a wheelchair by the nurses. Later that week, news came the young woman had delivered a healthy baby girl.

After dropping her off at the hospital, I drove through the

mud-plugged streets. Poptún was a welcome sight with its stores and people walking by. I reflected on the events of the last two days, thinking I could write a book about these last three years.

When I arrived at the rectory, my jeans were so saturated with mud they could stand alone (left, with **Kay**). And I had been given another unforgettable lesson in love and community spirit.

I never saw the completion of our plans for, in February of 1980, I returned home to the States. Less than three years before, I'd thought I'd made a mistake in coming. Now, three years later, I wondered if I was making a mistake in leaving.

In the final year in Guatemala I'd felt more and more at home with the people. I had discovered that in our spirits, we were connected. I departed with a reluctant, sad heart

Back home in Seattle, I descended into the reverse culture shock that was normal for returning missioners. I could not reconcile myself to life in the U.S. To me, it was too materialistic.

I missed the students I'd grown to love, and ached for my fellow missioners with whom I felt as close as my own family.

A permanent sadness settled in my heart, as if someone I loved had died. Sometimes I even doubted whether my presence in Guatemala had meant much.

Fay must have known by the letters I sent her how
dejected I felt. She kept me informed about the program's
progress and had the students send me letters.

Then one day I received something special. "Remembered
friend," the note opened. "I miss you in our classes. I'll never
forget you...because you were interested in me as a person. I
have been able to get 21 people in Canchacán to build
outhouses. *Primero Diós*, first God, all will be building their
own.

"Your friend who will always remember you, Atilano
Santos."

Two other promoter candidates were instrumental in
getting the outhouse project going in Cansis. Fay and I selected
unpretentious Macario Cóc Chóc and José Bá of Cansís to join
the program. I had always liked Macario, who quietly urged his
fellow villagers to haul our supplies up that hill I dreaded to
climb. We relied on Macario's help with anything. He'd told us
from our first visit, "When you begin, remember me. I want to
be a promoter."

So many teeth crowded his mouth he would have been an
orthodontist's dream. I remember his smile of goodness most
of all.

We were delighted at the number of Kek'chi students,
whose villages had been neglected more than the poor Ladinos.
Six women qualified, an accomplishment for the aldeas whose
leaders were usually men. Our only Kek'chi girl, Carmen Ché,
came from Tanjoc. Kek'chi women were reticent and most
hadn't enough education. Carmen, though, was special. When
we stayed in La Tortuga, she came from Tanjoc to translate for
us. I thought at first she hung around because she was one of
the dozen ladies with crushes on Tox. They exchanged those
gleaming glances. I could almost imagine the unsaid words
passing between them.

Candidates needed one to two years of schooling, and had

to be chosen and supported by their community. In addition, they had to pass a simple reading and math test.

Macario passed easily. His cousin, José Bá, failed. We broke our rules to let José in because he was highly motivated. I doubted he could succeed in the program. Fay wanted to give him a chance. "I'll tutor him," she promised.

Another slow learner came from Ixbobó, Guillermo Reyes. Guillermo didn't *get* things. Thus began Fay's tutoring. At night, she drilled the slower or less educated students in reading and writing. Because of her efforts, some, including Tox, passed the *Sexto grado*, our equivalent of elementary school.

We finished the first course on parasites, euphoric with how superbly everything had gone.

Macario had found his calling. He knew the answers in class. He didn't goof off like some of the teenagers. He loved playing guitar and singing, his mop of Tiny Tim curls flopping over his eyes.

Fern attended classes, too, (below with **Julian Morales**). He'd always been interested in health. He amazed the students by loaning his rear end as an injection site when they

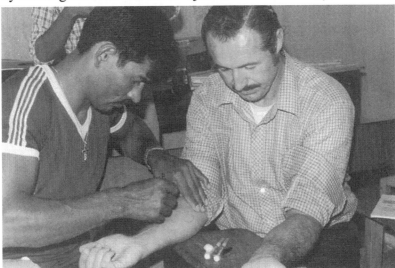

learned to give shots because they thought a priest wouldn't do such a thing.

Tox and a number of others dropped out. We were very disappointed. Tox was so talented, we had fantasized he might eventually run the program. We were like parents with a dream, which the child doesn't share. Instead, Tox went to work in the malaria prevention program.

When Fay and I first arrived in the Petén in 1977, we had seen the need for more health personnel to replace us. I wrote to Maryknoll and to my Seattle parish, St Patrick's, to recruit more help. Maryknoll promised more nurses, but not until after I left. In the meantime, we enlisted Dr. Evelyn St. Onge from Canada, who helped Fay finish teaching the first group of promoters.

After I left Guatemala, Fay and Evelyn taught first aid, baby and skin care, respiratory illnesses, intestinal diseases and reproduction. The curriculum took 16 weeks, spread over two years. Students journeyed to Poptún when they could spare time from the corn fields.

The last course was on sexually-transmitted diseases and birth control. Fay and Evelyn thought natural birth control or the rhythm method and condoms were the safest and cheapest methods. They taught how to wash out condoms, and after checking for holes, to re-use them.

Reproduction was *the* most popular course. Men listened spellbound as Fay and Evelyn explained women's physiology. Fertility was likened to the planting season, fertile soil and rain.

Evelyn took over the latrine project. She ordered 300 latrine kits from the Ministry of Health. The seats and floors were concrete, as termites would have destroyed wood. Catholic Relief Services and the Canadian consulate paid the three dollars each for hauling them to the Petén. Students would install one at their homes, helping to sell the idea to the community. The goal was a latrine at every house. Macario and José Bá supervised the installation of 26 units in Cansís alone.

After I left Guatemala in February of 1980, I returned to Seattle where I eventually bought my own little house and worked as a nurse in a nearby hospital in the newborn nursery and postpartum units. Rocking the newborn babies helped me heal from the loneliness and sadness I felt at leaving Guatemala. I'd been torn in my decision to leave—part of me wanting to stay and the other part wanting my own home and to adopt a child—something I couldn't do as a missionary in Guatemala. Eventually I worked in a clinic as a nurse practitioner, where I enjoyed using my Spanish and felt fulfilled serving our low-income Spanish speaking patients.
Fay wrote to me about the plans for the first graduation and I wished I could be there, but I couldn't afford the trip, as I had just purchased my house. Even from afar, I was thrilled about the terrific accomplishments of Fay and Evelyn and all the students.

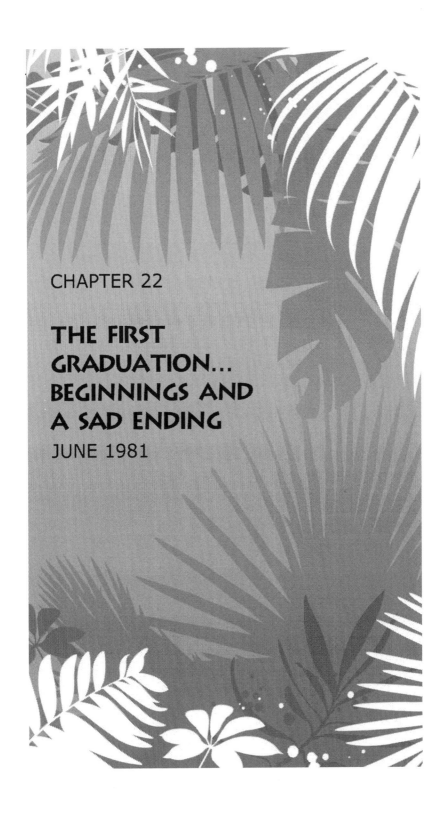

CHAPTER 22

THE FIRST GRADUATION... BEGINNINGS AND A SAD ENDING

JUNE 1981

   As June of 1981 approached, when the first class of
promoters was to graduate and receive their *tarjetas*,
government licenses, Fay wrote to me that they were
immensely excited. The students planned the graduation fiesta,
even hiring a marimba band for the *baile,* dance. Men
outnumbered women, so José Mario Balcarcel of Macháquilá
invited extras. He pleaded with Fay for two trucks. "Why two
trucks?" Fay asked.

"Some could ride in back," José Mario replied with a lazy smile. "We have to bring their chaperones, too!" José Mario was an excellent carpenter, a skill he would use unexpectedly before graduation ended.

There would be *caldo de pollo*, chicken soup, and tortillas. Chickens would be bought from the Devine ranch outside Poptún. Mike Devine, a U.S. citizen, owner of the Finca Ixobél near Poptún (now called the Hotel Ecological) was decapitated in 1990. Even to this date, mystery surrounds his death. His wife, Carol, hired private investigators, who linked his death to the government and the military. Rumor had it that Devine stumbled upon evidence of army involvement in drug trafficking and that his murder was ordered by Colonel Alberto Alpires, a Guatemalan officer on the CIA payroll.

I was thrilled when Mo, Fern and Fay sent funds for my air fare. "We want you to come to graduation," Fay wrote.

Tragically, I arrived in Poptún just one day after **Macario** died. (He's in the second row, far left, with his classmates and

below, taking an exam.)

Fay sobbed as she told me what happened. "Lizzie, it was so awful." We sat in the dining room of the rectory in Poptún while she told me the story.

It seems that Fay had been at Kerigma-Quetzal with the students, reviewing for the next day's exam. At 8:00 p.m., Fay, along with the student

Maria, her baby and Carmen Ché, got into the cab of the
Chevy Luv to return to the women's quarters at the convent.
Some of the young men asked Fay to drop them off at the
movie theatre on her way home. (Above, students are pictured
in the back of the truck.)

Fay agreed and they piled into the back of the truck,
covered by a canvas.

As Fay passed the hospital, she stopped to see how a
starving baby boy was doing. "I slowed down and turned into
the hospital parking lot," she continued, "but when I did, Maria
cried out, 'Seño!' I heard a commotion, so I stopped and
jumped out. Macario was holding his head and staggering."

"Oh, Fay," I said. How typical of her to visit a sick baby
after working all day.

Macario's new white sombrero had fallen in the dirt when
he jumped on the bumper as Fay drove off from Kerigma-
Quetzal. Riding on the bumper was forbidden. "But I was tired,
Lizzie...so I didn't remind the students of the rules. Besides,
the kids who hung around Kerigma-Quetzal had been playing
with the side-view mirrors. I couldn't see anything going on in

back."

"You must have been tired, Fay."

She nodded. "Macario didn't want to retrieve his hat from the ground when I was on the road, but as I slowed down, the students urged him to jump off. When he did, he slipped and hit his head on a small rock." Macario had hit his head on the ground when he fell from the truck.

He answered her questions intelligently, so Fay ruled out concussion. She saw no head wounds or blood coming from his ears. "But I was worried. I considered bringing him to that filthy hospital. Instead, I took him to the dorm at Kerigma and went to get Evelyn. She checked him over and he was okay."

Fay put Macario under the care of another student, Marcelino, a kind boy from the town of Dolores. She told Marcelino to send for her if there was a change, then she and Evelyn went home.

The next day Fay woke feeling agitated. Maria's little sister came running, saying, *"Seño, appurate. El muchacho esta muy enfermo!* Miss, hurry, the boy is very sick!" She voiced Fay's own fear. "It seemed strange, because no one had sent for us during the night. Maria's sister and I intuitively knew."

"How odd," I said. But I believed in intuition.

"We woke up Evelyn," Fay said, "and hurried to the school."

They found Macario in bed. He had vomited and was unable to urinate. "We knew we needed help. The hospital only has X-rays for teeth, and even that hardly ever works."

She and I had often despaired over the slovenly care there. The Poptún hospital wasn't capable of handling Macario's wound: bleeding inside the skull. His life was in extreme danger.

"Then what?" I said, thinking the military hospital across the road might have been able to treat Macario.

"We needed the commandant's permission to bring in a

civilian patient," Fay said. Evelyn stayed with Macario while Fay searched for the commandant. She found him in a bar, tersely giving orders into a hand-held radio.

"When I interrupted him, he was angry. But he gave his okay."

Fay described Macario's condition.

He told her without emotion, *"El muchacho se muere.* He will die."

When Fay returned to the dorm at Kerigma, they loaded Macario, mattress and all, onto the back of the truck; the students stayed with him. On the way, Fay had to explain to the guards that she had the commandant's permission to take Macario to the hospital. They made her wait while they checked with their commanding officers. Finally, accompanied by a soldier with an M-16, Macario was admitted.

"Oh Fay, you must have been going crazy."

She nodded, her mouth turned down in pain. Evelyn and Fay were greeted by an older sergeant, who said, "It's hopeless. The muchachos get in this condition by fighting. I have seen it often. He will die, or become *tonto*—a vegetable."

"We refused to believe him," Fay said.

After Evelyn and Fay laid Macario down in a bed, he said, *"Cobija,* blanket." He was shivering. Someone covered him. "I don't know if it was Evelyn or the base doctor who said, 'There's no pulse.' Even so, I was amazed when Evelyn began pressing on his chest," Fay said.

Fay asked Evelyn, "What are you doing?"

Evelyn kept on. Then he stopped breathing. In a daze, Fay started mouth-to-mouth breathing.

The doctor sent for a respirator. After a long time, it finally arrived. Evelyn succeeded in getting his pulse back, but Fay still had to breathe for him.

As she told me this, Fay had a faraway look on her face. Now and then, she wiped away tears.

After Macario was placed on the respirator, Fay tried to

secure a space for him on a plane to the capital. She was further sickened to learn that no planes could land in Poptún because of heavy fog.

While she was gone, the base doctor took an X-ray. Macario had a massive brain hemorrhage. When she returned, Evelyn said, "He's dead."

"Oh God, Fay...I'm sorry," I said.

For several minutes, she couldn't go on.

"I was overwhelmed by guilt, Lizzie. Such a fine young man."

"He *was* special, Fay...but it wasn't your fault." I knew even as the words spilled out that they couldn't ease her pain.

Slowly, Fay drove back to Kerigma to tell the other students the sad news.

When she parked the truck, they formed a semi-circle around her. "I was sobbing when I blurted out, 'It was my fault!'"

Joaquin said, "No, *maestra,* it was *our* fault because no one was supposed to ride on the bumper, but we let Macario do it anyway."

"Oh...Fay."

She went on. "Then 18-year-old Guillermo, you remember him, Lizzie, how we doubted he would complete the program? I tutored him in subtraction. Guillermo stepped into the group. 'What's all this stuff about it's *my* fault? No, it's *my* fault. This is *not* our fault.' He punctuated the air with an index finger. 'Instead of feeling guilty, we have only one job. Accept our *compañero's* death as *la voluntad de Dios.*'"

"How did you react to that?" I asked.

"We were all silent. Then the guilt rose like a bird with huge wings lifting its way to the hills."

Later, Fay spoke with his bereaved wife. The woman told Fay that Macario somehow knew he would die soon. Marcelino confirmed that. He said Macario had expressed concern for *la enfermera,* the nurse, because Fay was preparing

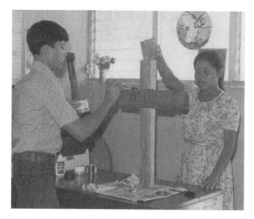

a fiesta and he would wreck the fun by dying. Marcelino added that Macario seemed at peace the night before he died. *"Bastante paz,"* Marcelino said. "Plenty of peace."

What a beautiful person Macario had been, sincere and honest. How unwavering his desire to be a promoter. They were right who said, "The best die young."

Graduation day dawned. The ceremony would be in the Poptún salón, next to the church. Facing the audience, was a table covered in the emerald green tablecloth for special occasions. And on it stood the two-and-a-half-foot pine cross that José Mario Balcarcel carved and **Carmen Ché** and **Adan Samayoa** (above) varnished. The students hung blue and white

paper streamers and all around were vases of peach gladiolas. In the front row sat Macario's widow, a pretty, dark-eyed young woman with their little boy, hair as luxuriant as his father's and a baby girl. Beside her, slumped in a posture of grief, were his father, mother and the rest of his family (left page, bottom). Like him, they had always attended classes in Cansís. The salón was filled with families. John Blazo, Leon and Pastora came. Parishioners Doña Hortensia, her daughter, Maria Edna, and the secretaries of all our programs were there.

Maryknoll sister Jane Buhlsbach, founder of the promoter program in Huehuetenango, was guest speaker. At that time, Sister Jane was beginning a promoter program in Sayaxché. I felt honored to be asked to speak, too, and rose to the podium to say a few words.

Fay (left with **Francisco Cuz**) and Evelyn handed out *tarjetas,* licences, to the 26 students, as well as to Fern. The women wore white blouses and blue skirts, the men and boys white shirts and dark pants. I felt like a mother watching her children graduate from medical school as they filed up with such aplomb.

Arms across chests, they sang the long Guatemalan anthem.

At the end, Carmen Ché bore the cross José Mario had lovingly carved and presented it to Macario's father, along with his tarjeta. His father accepted both with simple dignity. He kept his head bowed. Seeing the cross on his lap made me cry.

After the ceremony, while some of the students cooked dinner, the rest of us, filling three vehicles, drove the hour's journey to Cansís. The church (left) was packed. Pink and white streamers and red plastic cut in saw-tooth designs crisscrossed overhead. Mo and Fern celebrated mass. Mo's face was etched in sadness and Fern cried. Carmen Ché spoke the readings. Mo had known Macario through the leadership training course. He often said Macario was "one of the best."

Fern mentioned Macario had come regularly to him for confession. Many aldea people confessed whenever the priests visited for masses. In the States, individual confessions had dwindled, but not among aldea people. How typical of Macario to consider himself in need of confession. "Not that he had

much to confess," Fern added.

After mass, the townspeople, the family and the promoters carried the casket through the cornfields (left page, below). Gray mist and thick clouds hung overhead, as if even the weather mourned. Silently, we proceeded single file uphill and down, following the casket. The corn field rose in ankle-high fronds and the surroundings in green splendor. Ahead of me, Fay in her pink dress and a line of Kek'chi women in their plaid skirts wove down the path, preceding the girl students in their blue skirts.

At the top of the hill, where one saw the valleys from as lovely a gravesite as anyone might wish for, we circled the shallow hole. We buried Macario and threw flowers on the

casket: a wreath of yellow mums, lavender plumeria, and pink and red hibiscus (left). The students placed the cross on the grave. On it, along with his name etched in white letters "Macario Coc Choc 1959-1981" the students had glued the picture of him pushing a wheelbarrow loaded with dirt during latrine building—Macario of the joyful smile. Mo said the final blessing while José Mario and José Radino played the sweet tunes of the aldeas on their guitars. In one picture I snapped, Carmen Ché stands, dark eyes bleak.

We celebrated graduation that afternoon with a quiet fiesta. The students entered into the bittersweet joy of the moment. They prepared 23 chickens and plucked them outdoors near the kitchen of Kerigma-Quetzal, for the *caldo de pollo*. The cook made hundreds of corn tortillas and a cool pink drink. Every doctor from the hospital attended. There was, after all, rejoicing, but no marimba or dance. The students (below) had canceled the music to honor Macario.

Above, is the first class of Health Promoters--without one of the best.

FIRST GRADUATE PROMOTERS JUNE, 1981
Mario Balcárcel González, Machaquilá
Rosa Imelda Juárez de Campos, Machaquilá
Nicolasa Monterrozo Valensuela, El Crucero Chinchilá
Angel María Pesquera Salazar, Caín
María Cruz Mejía Oliva de R., Sabaneta
Marcelíno Cano Salazar, Cruce Dolores
José Alfredo Morales Marroquín, Cruce Dolores
Adán Samayoa Véliz, Parcelamiento San Antonio
Guillermo Reyes Gómez, Ixbobó
Francisco Cuz Caál, Chacté
Cármen Ché Choc, Tanjoc
Mario Carrera Alvarado, El Quetzalito
Roberto Pacay Xol, Chinchilá
Isaías Antonio Galicia Arévalo, Ixbobó
Hugo René Ortíz Cardona, El Quetzalito
Oscar Baudílio Santiago C., El Cruce Chinchilá

Juana Soto Ruíz, El Cruce Chinchilá
José Mario Estrada Sánchez, Boca del Monte
Julián Morales Flores, Sajul
Victoria Maldonado Ruíz, Caín
José Radino Hernández de Jesús, Los Angeles
Angel Custodio Aquino de R., Caserío Suculté
Carlos Humberto Brán Perea, Yaltutú
Encarnación Hernández Flores, Caín
José Bá Cac, Cansís
Atilano Santos Alvarado, Canchacán

CHAPTER 23

ANOTHER TRIP, ANOTHER MASSACRE

JANUARY 1989

I returned home to Seattle that June of 1981, and continued to reflect on the *why* of Macario's death. When I left Guatemala in 1980, my heart was broken. I was so deeply attached to our team, to the students, to the people of the aldeas, that I could barely function. I felt half alive.

This dislocation was a common experience among missionaries, especially when they resumed their former lives and became isolated from other missionaries, as I was. Life in the U.S., with its hectic pace and materialistic focus, was too dispiriting after Guatemala.

In 1984, I adopted my little girl, **Maria** (left), who was born in Guatemala in 1983. When Maria came, all else stopped. She had so many needs, it was all I could do to work and care for her. I was suddenly a single parent with a special needs child.

At one month of age, Maria and 30 others were rescued from a home where children were sold on the black market. She was placed in the state-run orphanage, El Hogar Eliza Martinez, in Antigua. There, she languished for a year until the courts pronounced her available for adoption. She suffered measles, parasites, chicken pox, several bouts of pneumonia, as well as depression, common among institutionalized children. Thirteen months old when I heard about her, Maria was hospitalized with pneumonia. The social worker with whom I had been corresponding assured me that she was "*muy linda, very beautiful,*" and that she needed only a mother. Those words were all it took for me to bond with her, though we had never met. I couldn't foresee that during hospitalization, Maria would suffer a stroke, leaving her with a partially paralyzed left side, a seizure disorder and a developmental lag. Her condition would require every ounce of strength, money and faith I possessed. I will write her story someday.

As years passed, I kept thinking of all that had transpired in Guatemala. Memories seethed within. I had to tell the story. I cut down my work to four days a week, then joined the Seahurst Writers, who met in the library near my home, and began writing again. Writer friends gave me tremendous support and invaluable criticism.

Through correspondence, I heard the health promoter program was going well, and that Sheila Matthews and MaryBeth Bathum, nurses who had taken over after Fay and Evelyn left, expanded it even further.

Though the violence persisted, even affecting the Petén, I

longed to go back. As a visitor I thought I would be safe.

I returned to Guatemala in January of 1989 with Maria,
who was then 5 years old. Brother Ron Rinella drove us to San
Mateo to visit my old friend Father Fern. Fern had moved from
Guatemala when his life was threatened shortly after the first
promoter graduation in 1981. He worked in Nicaragua for
several years. Then, when priests were no longer being
murdered in Guatemala, he returned, but not to the Petén. He
couldn't be sure it was safe for him there, where the
commandant still lived and retained power. No one knew if the
military would retaliate against the church again. Maryknoll
assigned Fern to San Mateo in the mountains of
Huehuetenango.

In the mid-1980s, the army forced men to guard gates at
the entrance and exit of towns in the highlands, where many
rebel groups worked. This was the civil patrol. I saw some of
these checkpoints when Ron Rinella, Maria and I passed
through on our way to San Mateo. They were frightening.

As we approached a town, Ron slowed the vehicle and
stopped in front of the rough gate blocking our way. Soldiers
watched us closely. I held my breath while a civilian in fatigue
pants and a white shirt opened the barricade and motioned us
through with an Israeli-made Fal rifle. The soldiers swung the
barrier shut after us. Feeling we could be shot without doing
anything wrong, I resisted the urge to look back.

Even if the civil patrol members sympathized with the
guerilla cause, they didn't dare show it, or their lives were in
danger. The military claimed it didn't force anyone to join the
civil patrol, but everyone knew that was a lie. My bias lay with
the guerillas. They were supposed to be on the side of the
people.

Once safely in San Mateo, Maria and I strolled to the
market. Smoke hung in the air above the Chuj women's wood
fires. Not a face glanced up as we walked past. These people

were more reserved than those I'd worked with in the Petén. They ignored anyone who wasn't a part of their world. Massacres by the army and disappointments in the rebels, who didn't come through with their promises, followed by army repression, left them suspicious.

Garbage odors wafted through the air. The town dump festered next to the market. Baskets of yucca, corn, onions, and gunnysacks of black beans were displayed. Women sat cross-legged in the dirt behind their wares awaiting customers. Some *palanganas*, plastic basins, contained gray salt. Salt existed in the town from the golden age of the Maya, about A.D. 600 to 900. The salt, thought to have medicinal values, was mined from a spring near San Mateo and boiled into six-inch chunks.

Maria and I passed women selling *pan dulce*, sweet bread. Other stalls contained corn tortillas, tamales and eggs. *Dulces*, home-made caramel candy, were covered with flies. One man sold live chickens and turkeys. Another stall offered every kind of house ware made of plastic.

Looking down from the market, the church dominated the scene. One of Guatemala's oldest, it may have dated from the 1500s, when Spaniards conquered the country and forced Christianity on the Indian people. I remembered seeing the tall adobe structure with its dark, medieval entrance in *National Geographic* magazine. The bell tower resembled the ginger-bread facade of a Victorian house. Eight-foot-thick stonewalls kept the inside cool and dark.

Near the market was the mayor's office, where a constant flow of men hurried in and out. I wondered what was going on. Later, back at the village rectory, I asked my old friend Father Fern Gosselin.

He said that in recent days, buses, beer, rum and Coca-Cola trucks had been robbed by the guerillas, who lived off the people. If someone didn't give voluntarily, the guerillas took what they needed. Perhaps the army was responding to this extortion.

"The army ordered a sweep for guerillas," Fern explained. "All the men from San Mateo and the other towns have to go." He sighed. "Who knows what'll happen."

"But why do they have to go?" I asked him.

"The army forces them. They have no choice. Most don't even have guns, just machetes. You know how the people are. They'd much rather be left alone."

If anyone helped the guerillas, he or she would be reported to the army and subsequently tortured or killed, unless the person could be used as bait to catch guerillas. The army hooded such victims, brought detainees to the checkpoints and forced them to identify any guerillas passing through. Sometimes the person pointed to someone who had nothing to do with the guerillas. To avoid being killed, anyone with knowledge of the guerillas immediately told the local army commander.

During the late 1970s and early '80s, guerilla groups tried to awaken the people to fight for their rights. Guatemala was torn by the unequal distribution of land and by the inhuman conditions under which the majority of people lived. Most property was owned by a tiny upper class or the military.

The government, run by the army behind the scenes even with a civilian president, wanted nothing to change. Since 1954, when the CIA and the army manipulated the overthrow of Guatemala's first democratically-elected president, control of the country had been in army hands. Anything that threatened army power was eliminated. That meant, of course, the guerillas. Indians mostly kept out of politics in the past. But in the guerilla organizations they saw for the first time a chance for a better life. How many Indians joined the guerillas is unknown. Even if they never joined as combatants, many supported the rebels. For the army, sympathy for guerillas was a distinct threat, because Indians made up over 60 percent of the population.

As the guerillas persuaded more Indians to support their

cause, the army retaliated. Wherever the military heard of guerilla activity, it bombed the town. Thousands of innocent people were massacred. Many fled to the mountains, living in miserable poverty, with no durable food source, because the army found any hidden cornfields and destroyed them. Indians became exiles in their own country.

Back at the rectory window, I was anxiously waiting for Fern to return. Except for my daughter, Maria, napping in the back bedroom, I was alone. Fern had left abruptly when men pounded on the rectory door at lunchtime, asking for help with villagers injured by guerillas. I wiped dishes, worried about Fern's safety.

From my view at the window, the church was visible (above), so ancient no one knew when it had been built. Limestone and mud walls resembled a crumbling yellow birthday cake with pink trim. Mist shrouded the town of 5,000 Chuj Indians, 8,000 feet high in the Cuchumatanes Mountains. Suddenly, a hundred or more men crested the hill and

poured down the slope facing the church square. I froze. Down
the grassy steps they spread, like an army of ants erupting from
an ant hill.

Two villagers, brown capes flapping as they leaped from
one terraced step to the next, carried a man by his arms and
legs. Their voices grew louder as they raced toward me.
Sensing their panic, I ran outside.

I had been dreading something horrible after Fr. Fern
drove off, winding his white Toyota Land Cruiser up the dirt
road leading out of town, past the somber, pine-covered
mountains. He would bring any injured men to San Mateo's
clinic. I'd felt uneasy seeing him go alone. Even the air seemed
charged with danger.

The old Chuj women squatting near the church stopped
praying and now watched the men shoot down the hill.

I threw open the door of the adobe clinic. "Justa!" I
shouted to the clinic nurse. "They're bringing the injured."

Justa hurried from the back ward where she'd been
tending a woman with a stubborn bone infection. The nurse
said nothing, but her eyes widened in alarm. She moved a
wooden IV pole to the exam table. I could have screamed
watching her move so deliberately. I had never visited before
and didn't know where supplies were kept. My mind screamed,
"hurry, hurry!"

I wished Fr. Fern was there, but Justa and I were the
only ones to cope with this emergency.

Voices outside grew louder. The men I'd seen racing down
the hill burst through the clinic door, staggering under their
load. What seemed half the village squeezed in after them, the
women's *huipiles*, traditional costumes, a nightmare of color.
Everyone pressed close, as Guatemalans do. These people were
as quiet as those I'd worked with in the Petén jungle twelve
years earlier in 1977, when I first met Fr. Fern. I couldn't help
thinking how those in power had made them suffer. In the 500
years since the Spaniards conquered this country, things hadn't

changed much.

The villagers clacked strange Chuj words, soft whispers, clicks and rustles. I didn't have to understand them to sense their fear.

"Over here," I directed.

They laid the wounded man on the exam table as if he was a beloved child.

"*Por favor*, please...you must leave," I told the crowd and urged them toward the door. We couldn't care for our patient with dozens of people crowding around. A handful refused to go, staring at him with wide eyes and frozen expressions.

He was maybe 25, with a shock of lush black hair. He lay still on the rusty exam table. A red-and-white bandanna soaked with blood was wrapped around his neck. His pants were splattered with blood. I took his pulse; his skin felt as smooth as cool satin. The strong heartbeat reassured me. I longed to tell him how sorry I was. His eyes pleaded, "Save me!" In that moment, without words, something rose between us and I cared deeply what would happen to him.

I tried to start the IV, but only made a lump bulge under his chestnut skin, since this kind of old-fashioned inflexible needle rarely stayed in veins for long. The villagers watched intently.

Justa prepared another needle and in moments the IV flowed.

The patient suddenly sat up and pointed to his throat. I unwound the sodden bandanna. Blood clots and flesh splattered to the floor. His jaw had been shot away. Shards of bone and parts of teeth hung where his chin had been.

"*Dios*, God," breathed Justa.

I restrained the sob rising in my throat.

"Ahhh," a woman sobbed, "ahhh."

"*La esposa*...his wife," someone murmured.

She stood at his feet, tears coursing down her brown cheeks, rubbing and caressing his callused foot in her slim hand.

Tears blurred my eyes and the lump grew in my throat until I couldn't swallow.

"*¿Mamin Dios tas yuuj?*" a woman asked.

"That means, 'Why did this have to happen?'" explained Justa.

Who could answer such a question?

A bullet had penetrated his shoulder from front to back, but his breathing was normal. He'd be disfigured the rest of his life if he survived. His eyes shone, that vibrant dark gaze of the Guatemalan people.

Justa and I carefully dressed his wounds. When we finished, I touched his wife's shoulder. I wondered if they had children.

Silent, unmoving, she regarded me, as though his fate was in someone else's hands now.

I tried to think what to do next. Maybe transport him to Huehuetenango, the closest hospital. But the road was so stony it seemed designed to shake the teeth right out of your mouth. He wouldn't survive.

I ran outside and spoke to Byron, Fern's helper. "Let's ask at the mayor's office...maybe they can take him to Barillas." Byron's mouth tightened. I wondered if he was remembering how his own father had been killed by the guerillas.

We hurried up the hill to the mayor's office. "Please," I pleaded, "you must help us...isn't there a car...could you call the military...we have to get him out of here."

There were no phones. Fern, the pastor of the Catholic church, and his co-worker, Brother Ron Rinella, owned the only two vehicles.

Men in the mayor's office radioed Barillas, but couldn't get through the static. They promised to keep trying. Barillas was an hour and a half away, near the Mexican border. From its airstrip, our patient could be flown to Guatemala City, but it might be hours before a vehicle could come to pick him up.

Byron and I rushed to the clinic. "Fern can drive him to Barillas when he gets back," I told Justa.

"No, you and Brother Ron *vayan ahora*...go now," she said. "Quickly, so we only have to care for one at a time. The people say...*que hay mas,* there are more. I'll stay here for the next one."

Justa functioned as well as any emergency room nurse, with only correspondence training. She'd gained experience caring for the injured when she worked in San Mateo in the early 1980s during the massacres when groups opposed to the government flourished. The Guatemalan army retaliated against the dissidents by burning down whole villages, murdering thousands. Sixty-five were killed from San Mateo alone, and another 700 from nearby towns.

I found Ron Rinella outside, the Maryknoll brother who repaired things around the parish.

"Hey, wait a minute," Ron said, when I told him what Justa advised. "Calm down. I don't wanna go blasting off with the guerillas out in force."

I couldn't blame him for being hesitant.

We talked it over and he agreed to transport the injured man to Barrillas.

"Justa says I should be with you in case something goes wrong on the road, but I'm afraid for my daughter. What if the guerillas come while we're gone? Should I take her with us?"

"No," said Ron. "It's best she stays here. Worse could happen on the road. Bring your passport."

I ran outside again, concerned for my five-year-old Guatemalan daughter. I'd adopted Maria in 1984, when she was an infant, after completing my contract as a missionary in the Petén.

Now groups of San Mateans milled outside. Someone said, "They're coming closer."

How strange to fear the guerillas; I'd always thought they were on the people's side. But townspeople had been hurt; I couldn't ignore the threat the guerillas represented.

I tiptoed into the bedroom where Maria peacefully slept, her hair a black fan across the bed, her eyebrow a perfect curve against her brown complexion. I had returned to Guatemala, thinking of working here again, and I wanted to see how Maria would fare, back in her birth country. Now those yearnings seemed insane. Should I go with the injured man? I could hardly think for the frantic beating of my heart.

Only minutes ago, San Mateo had been a quiet mountain town. Now we were all at risk. Why was it that the most horrendous things happened while I was in Guatemala? I had jeopardized Maria's life bringing her here. But I had to help this injured man.

I rummaged in my suitcase for my passport and stuffed *quetzales*, the Guatemalan currency, into my pocket.

Back in the clinic, which reeked of blood, I checked on our patient. His pulse was still strong, his lungs clear.

"I want to live," his eyes begged.

"I'm going to help you," I told him silently.

From outside voices swelled, some speaking Chuj, others Spanish. People shouted. A man burst through the door, "*Otro*...another one," he hollered.

Rapidly, Justa and I moved the first patient on a canvas stretcher to the cement floor.

I opened the door to villagers carrying an unconscious man. He'd been shot twice in the back. The villagers laid him tenderly on the exam table. I dressed his wounds, a futile gesture. There was no surgeon and no blood transfusions. The IV Justa started didn't last. It seeped into the tissues. He'd probably die before we got back from Barillas.

"He's an ex-soldier," someone whispered.

What did *that* mean? He was young, like the other one.

I rushed outside. Ron drove his tiny bright blue Suzuki close to the clinic and removed the front seat. Several men carried the man with no jaw while people surged around us.

Women were crying. The stretcher just fit. The man's wife squeezed beside him, settling on her heels. Thick blue fabric with a magenta thread swathed her waist. Her poncho-like cape flowed from the shoulders in a brilliant red-and-yellow rick-rack design. I assumed her circumstances were like the other villagers: poverty, illiteracy and no opportunities. How could she stand this new trouble?

The Chuj girl whose mother had the bone infection stood at the door. "Juana...watch Maria," I shouted. "Don't let her go outside."

As we set off, a friend of the injured man offered to come with us. We took turns holding the IV bag high over the patient's body to help it drip. The crowd parted. Ron drove up the road, lurching over rocks, inching along. Our injured man groaned.

His friend told me what happened. *"Pensamos que el ex-soldado empezo la cosa*...we think the ex-soldier opened fire. The guerillas thought we all had weapons and started shooting. But none of us had guns except him. I had only my machete, and what is that against a gun?"

"They didn't look like we Guatemalans," he continued. "They were bigger. One man was blond, and there were tall women, with long straight hair. One even wore pants."

The injured man's friend shook his head. He wasn't used to women dressed like men. In San Mateo, Chuj women had worn the traditional *huipiles* for centuries. The few Ladino women of Mayan and Spanish descent wore polyester dresses. None wore trousers. Ladinos, considered a higher class of Guatemalans, were a mixture of Mayan Indian and Spaniards who conquered the country in the 1500s.

"Maybe they're from another country," I said. "Is anyone from San Mateo a guerilla?"

He shook his head. *"Pero no, ninguno de nuestra gente pertenece a esta gente*...none of our people belongs to *them.*"

He was so vehement, he could be fearful I'd report him if

he sympathized with the guerillas. In Guatemala, it was dangerous to openly support resistance to the government. *"Orejas,"* spies, were everywhere, looking for local people aiding the rebels.

Guerillas were dedicated to changing the corrupt Guatemalan political system. They lived in the hills, hid from the army and occasionally ambushed a military patrol. Up till now, there had been few problems between them and townspeople. Guerillas of one country sometimes helped movements in other countries. Could these today be Cubans or Nicaraguans? Was that why they'd fired on these helpless San Mateans?

The men of San Mateo had no choice. The army forced them to hunt the guerillas. I hated how the innocent suffered the worst, caught in the middle between two ideologies.

The situation was much more complicated than I'd ever guessed, much more menacing. People were out here with guns, maybe aimed at us.

We crept along the empty road, my body crashing into the Suzuki's sides as the wheels thudded against each foot-deep rut. My arm ached holding the crazily swinging IV bag. We met Fern coming toward us with a Chuj man who had a bullet graze on his cheek.

"People say eight men were killed or injured," Fern called.

"I'm going with this one to Barillas. Take care of Maria," I reminded him as we lurched by.

An hour passed. We continued at a cautious pace, stopping a few times for me to check our patient's pulse and IV. His wife had covered him with a thin cloth that barely reached his knees. Every few minutes, his eyes showing terror, he struggled up as though he couldn't breathe. The bullet might have punctured a lung, or perhaps blood had seeped into his airway.

High mountains rose from the road, robed in emerald pine

and fir trees. They cast menacing shadows in the late afternoon sun. Dark green shades of the *palo negro*, dark wood, (so hard it is used to build houses), were mixed with clumps of cedar, mahogany, oak, chicle and coaba trees. Cut logs were stacked along the road. Fern had once said the townspeople were forced to cut down trees on orders from the army, leaving a bare swath on each side. In this way, the army hoped to prevent ambush by the guerillas.

The sky was clouded over, and I felt a penetrating cold. The far mountains were veiled by a misty haze. They resembled the elegant Swiss Alps, until I glimpsed dark shacks stuck into the hillsides. Some peaks were dusted with snow.

In rural Guatemala, people popped up everywhere, no matter how isolated the spot. Now, no one was to be seen. Ahead and behind us, the road stretched lonely and barren.

Goose bumps tingled up my arms. My heart beat faster. "Ron," I whispered, "someone's watching us..."

"Guerillas are thick around here. Up there," he pointed, "is the valley of the guerillas. This whole section belongs to them." He swept his arm in an arc. We were traveling right through their territory. Ron speeded up. Ahead lay a clearing, a route to Barillas, other highland towns and the Ixcán, an undeveloped part of Guatemala where guerillas were active.

Quietly, Ron and I said the Our Father and a Hail Mary. I had never prayed so fervently. After that I felt more peaceful, as if nothing would happen to us.

I thought about how someone's hand could move so quickly on a gun. What it could do to someone else. One minute with his life before him. Then a bullet tearing into his back. His children without a father. I never wanted to see a gun again.

Finally, we passed through the military checkpoint in Barillas. Soldiers escorted us to the clinic.

Our patient was lifted from the bloody stretcher. His arm had swollen as if pumped with air. Once more the IV had

seeped into the tissues instead of the vein. I couldn't help
thinking, as I had many times before in Guatemala, how good
medical supplies and decent care would have made a huge
difference to everyone.

A doctor appeared and while I explained what had
happened, he removed the old IV to insert a new one. The
injured man and I exchanged a parting look that made my
throat tighten.

His wife stayed at the clinic. I never saw either of them
again. And when I went back to Guatemala City, no one had
heard of what had happened. In Guatemala, these killings were
hardly newsworthy.

Ron drove us back to San Mateo, faster this time, through
mist so dense our headlights sent only a feeble glow into the
blackness. When we slowed, I got the same creepy feeling as
before. Someone was watching. Anything could happen. God,
please....

Except for a few *quetzales*, I hid my money in my
underwear. Fern had told me the guerillas, poor as any of the
townspeople, stopped vehicles and took food and money to
survive. Thank God nothing happened on our return.

When we arrived back in San Mateo at eight that night;
another man, his knee shattered by a bullet, lay moaning in the
clinic. After treatment for shock, Justa had injected him with
Neo-Melubrina, the only painkiller she had. It only took the
edge off his agony. The plan was to transport him to Barillas,
too, but he'd have to wait until a truck with those smooth
Mercedes Benz engines traveled through. Then he could lie on
a mattress in back.

Another man had died in the mountains before
townspeople could bring him to us. The *ex-soldado*, the
unconscious man shot in the back, was dead too.

I ran to the rectory and hugged Maria, feeling how
precious she was. Everything was calm now.

Today's memories would torment me forever. We'd leave

San Mateo; I'd tell everyone I knew. But this chaos was Guatemala. This same violence could happen tomorrow in some other town. And few but the perpetrators and victims would know.

I lay in bed that night consumed by sadness for the wounded and the dead, agonizing and wondering why tragedy afflicted people whose lives were much harder than mine.

The next day the sun shone through mountain haze which mitigated the heat. Through the kitchen window I watched people gather for the funeral. Quiet hung over the town. Old Chuj women, faces wrinkled like unironed fabric, sat in front of the church burning little piles of *ocote*—heartwood—that sent up a rich pine scent. They chanted over incense and candles, feet digging into the dirt, part of the scenery, yet uninvolved.

They may have been invoking the spirits to the god of the dog, or San Simón, who wasn't a Catholic saint, but an invention of the Indians. San Simón has many followers; some Indians consider him more important than Mayan gods or Catholic saints. People dress San Simón in a business suit and sunglasses and pour *aguardiente,* the local moonshine, down his throat into some enclosed container, praying for abundant crops or care from offspring when they grow old. These Mayan people mix Catholicism with their ancient religion. They had everyday gods, like the cat and monkey, some on saint's days. The god of corn symbolized sustenance. Corn, eaten daily in tortillas, was as important as life itself.

The church sat seemingly propped in the flat part of a bowl. Everything else was on a hill, either above or below. Above, the San Matean women stood along the pink, latticed wall, their bearing erect, dressed in their finest *huipiles,* the richest most brilliant colors I had ever seen. Each also wore mounted on her head, high swaths of fabric in bright pink, red and yellow. Younger women and girls wore blue or green skirts

of brighter weaves. Older women had black, gray or maroon.
Most women carried a baby slung on her shoulders and two or
three barefoot kids clutching her hem.

A single file of men gathered with dignity and without
haste to stand against the other wall above the church (above).
Younger men straddled the concrete wall. Below, grassy steps
tiered down to a basketball court. What a gorgeous picture the
men would make in their brown wool capes and pale straw
hats, but I felt I would be exploiting them to take their
photographs now.

Apart from everyone else, a group of soldiers waited on
the basketball court flanking the church, their ever-present
guns slung casually over their shoulders. Thinking how the
army was responsible for yesterday's deaths and injuries, anger
squeezed my heart. Now they come with their guns, I thought,
since the unarmed are already dead.

I wondered if the townspeople felt as angry as I did. They
didn't show it. Fern told me they concealed their rage when
something happened they could do nothing about.

Down the hill, village men bore the coffin. The pine box

dipped from one side to the other with each step, as the pallbearers negotiated the rocky ground. People watched solemnly, as if they were inside the church.

I couldn't help thinking of funerals back home where pallbearers rolled the casket on wheels and the mortician took the body away so we didn't have to see it. In the remote towns of Guatemala, the dead must be buried within twenty-four hours. Nobody can afford embalming.

Behind the pallbearers plodded a group of villagers. "*La familia*," whispered Justa, while we watched from our window. Slowly the cortege filed through the entrance. Another family followed. Painted on the second casket in white were the words, "Jose Manuel Hernandez, *ex-soldado*."

So death was what being an ex-soldier brought one in Guatemala.

The church bell tolled, a mournful sound. In the bell tower a man pulled hard on the rope. This job was an honor reserved only for the *Comité*. The Comité were parish men with prestigious roles, similar to deacons. No women were allowed to ring the bell.

Perhaps a couple of hundred townspeople stayed on the hillside above the church.

"Why aren't they going inside?" I asked Justa.

"*No es la tradición*," she said. Many San Mateans were *costumbre* Indians; they followed Mayan customs more than Catholic rituals and felt inadequate in the church. Also, when soldiers were present, the Catholic Church wasn't safe. Too often, because a person was Catholic, he or she was persecuted or killed.

There was an eerie feeling that this ritual dated back to biblical times. Everyone knew his or her role. I sensed I must not intrude.

Near the grassy steps, the old women in their faded *huipiles* beseeched their gods as if nothing had changed. Perhaps for them nothing had. They prayed as if little else

mattered. Only a few years before, they had witnessed more
deaths. I couldn't help but conclude that the Indian population
was cannon fodder, both for the army and the guerillas.

I knew what the army had done: massacres a thousand
times worse than yesterday. But watching this funeral, I was
reminded of guerilla bullets destroying the jaw of an innocent
man. From now on, I couldn't side with either group. I would
sit with the people, in the middle, rejecting the objectives of
both sides. Although I believed people should be free to change
their government, ideology that promoted violence seemed a
contradiction. Never had I been personally affected until now.

Yesterday changed my thinking about war forever.

I walked into the church. Hazy light came from the sun
through the doorway, windows near the sanctuary, and dozens
of candles on the floor along the sides. At the end of the long
aisle, Fern intoned the final blessing at the altar. From the
rafters, hung embroidered cloths trimmed in white and pink
lace. More old women bent over lighted candles along the front
and side aisles, their *huipiles* like jewels in the dark. They
chanted in a low hum, like mourners in a sick room. Incense
permeated the air. Seeming to envision all over again the man
whose jaw had been blown away, I wanted to cry and walked
outside.

Only several children crying pierced the silence. The bell
tolled again. Out trudged the men carrying first one, then the
other casket, followed by the little group of family. Those
lining the plaza above the church waited until the procession
wound its way up the hill by the marketplace, then joined.

"Want to go to the burial?" asked Juana, the pretty Chuj
girl who'd watched Maria for me yesterday.

"Yes, I'd like that."

We climbed the hill following the crowd. Juana's feet
skimmed the dust, while I puffed up the steep incline.

At the top of the grassy hill, soldiers dug shallow holes for
the coffins. At least they were helping with that. Their guns

were propped in the dirt around the excavation. Except for their uniforms, and a hardness in their expressions, they looked like any of these villagers.

They could have been conscripted into the army against their will, perhaps while innocently enjoying a Sunday in their hometowns. Fiestas were favorite places for "round ups," forcing boys 15 to 18 years old into the army. Unless a family had money or power, or the boy was already married, he must enter the army even against his will. Some married at 15 to avoid service. They were forced to submit to the indoctrination that turned them into savages who would not flinch as they ripped open a pregnant woman's stomach with bayonets. Young boys were made to watch torture, and beaten until they could torture others easily. On the first day of conscription, one boy was paired with another, then they were compelled to hit each other until blood was spilled.

Maybe José Manuel Hernandez, ex-soldier, had been high jacked into the army. Had he fired the gun that precipitated the killings of yesterday?

Up on this hill, with the town lying brown-roofed below, everything seemed peaceful. The people gazed at me as if I was an odd thing. Even so, when I smiled, they responded with warm smiles that lit their faces. I liked the Guatemalan people so much. Something in their characters appealed to me. Was it their dignity, their strength, their courage, their ability to live in the moment?

I expected a graveside ceremony, but there was nothing except the digging of graves. Fern told me the work would go on for hours. Later, townspeople would place food around the grave so the dead person would have nourishment.

With a persuasive smile, a Chuj woman approached. "You like tablecloth?" she asked in Spanish. "I have beautiful woven *mantel*, very cheap. Come, I show you."

She took my arm. I felt ashamed to leave the burial, but let her lead me down the mountainside. At the bottom of the hill, I bought a tablecloth for $25, with the same star-within-a-star weave of the women's *huipiles*, the design so complex, it must have taken months to make. It is beneath glass now, in a handsome gold frame and mounted on a wall in my home, easily the most beautiful thing I own.

That night, when Fern and Ron and I talked, they too wondered about the shootings. This part of the highlands had been relatively free of violence for some time. In a way, they were not surprised, because Guatemala was never without upheaval for long.

Fern told us that on the day of the killings, the army had ordered trucks loaded with soldiers to set a trap for the rebels. The men of San Mateo and neighboring communities were ordered to initiate the sweep, which caught the guerillas by surprise. Instead of running away, as they usually did when the army attacked, they fired on the civil patrollers. We were guessing. No one knew for sure how the carnage started. When I went back to Guatemala City, I found out that nothing appeared in the newspapers. Other Maryknollers in the Center House hadn't heard of the killings. Except for two dead men, the injured, and their families, the violence might never have been.

Two days later, Maria and I rode with Fern in his Toyota jeep crammed with sick Indian people from around San Mateo, including Juana's mother. Her leg felt mushy, the skin shiny and black, possibly a fungal infection. Fern carried her in his arms into the hospital clinic in Huehuetenango. From there we took a bus back to Guatemala City, and on that journey I kept reliving the deaths and disaster. I couldn't shake my helplessness.

Years before, when Ron Hennessey, the former regional superior of Maryknoll, had served in San Mateo, the army conducted brutal massacres. But life had been fairly quiet recently. While Fern worked in San Mateo, there had never been an incident like the clash of the civil patrol and guerillas I had just witnessed. The killings in San Mateo reflected what was wrong throughout the country.

I kept wondering if there could be a reason that I witnessed the death and injury of the civil patrollers. In the mysterious ways of God and his perfect timing, had He wanted me there?

CHAPTER 24

LIFE GOES ON
IN POPTÚN
FEBRUARY 1989

Next, we flew to the Petén in a small plane. With Maria on my lap, I sat next to the pilot, trying to ignore the clouds whizzing by, reading Bert and Ernie books aloud to distract both of us from dwelling on the unnerving sight outside the window. Flying low over dense tree tops, the tiny four-seater felt like a paper airplane, trembling in the wind. We arrived in Flores, where Maryknoll priest Al Goebl, then pastor at Poptún, picked us up and drove us on to Poptún. FYDEP, the

National Enterprise for the Promotion and Economic
Development of the Peten, had finally made a decent road.

In Poptún, I met Maryknoll lay missioner, nurse Jane
Redig. She had just arrived to teach in the promoter program.
Poptún no longer had that look of a place at the end of the
world. In the eight years since my last visit, modern frame
houses and stores had been built. The church had been painted
and the rectory was well cared for. Fr. Goebl renovated the
convent from concrete blocks, even using the beautiful floor
tiles from the old convent for the new building.

I stopped in the chapel where I'd cried many lonely tears.
The same weavings adorned the room. These walls were no
longer chewed up by termites, but clean and painted.

Down the hall in the pharmacy, **Rosa Imelda** (below with
my daughter, **Maria**), a student from the first class of
promoters, filled prescriptions. Studying had been hard for
Rosa, yet here she was, ten years later, a backbone of the
project.

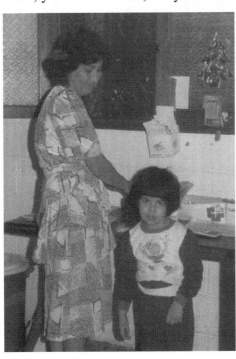

Carmen Ché, now
married, arrived,
plump and smiling.
She was a teacher in
the program.

"Seño Liz, you
must come to the fiesta
tonight at Kerigma-
Quetzal. We've
planned something
special," she said.

I was desperately
tired and would have
liked a day to recover
from the trip, but how
could I refuse?

After supper, Jane

and I rattled to Kerigma-Quetzal in what had been Mo's vehicle. By then, it was 11 years old, and the door wouldn't open on the driver's side.

In the classroom, young men and women sat at desks as other students had years before. A hand-lettered sign decorated with flowers posted across the blackboard proclaimed, *"Bienvenida, Seño Liz!"*

Carmen amazed me. (The sign is above, with **Maria** and I). I felt in awe of her, as if our roles were reversed.

"We are happy to have Seño Liz with us once again," she said. "I remember Seño Liz and how she helped start this program. When she came to La Tortuga, I helped her and Seño Fay. *Si no fuera para ellos*—if it hadn't been for them, we wouldn't have this program today. Let's give Seño Liz a hand."

Everyone stood and clapped for a very long time, with those remembered smiles of affection. I felt a tightness in my throat.

Then some young men played and sang the songs from years before. Their faces regarded me with warmth and sincerity making the tears come. In no other place had I felt so accepted, so loved, so appreciated. Why had I ever left? *This* was where I belonged. I vowed to return to Guatemala someday.

When the music ended, Francisco, Tox's friend from Chacté, another original student, rose. The class that night was on neurological disorders. He asked me to speak to them.

I told them of my daughter Maria's seizures, the medication that controlled them and how someone like her could be helped. Though delayed, she was learning, drawing comparison to those with disabilities who were hidden away. When Fay and I had still been in the Petén, we visited a home in Boca del Monte, where a child with the twisted limbs of polio was kept in a dark room, huddled on the dirt floor, with no chance to learn and no therapy for her disability. Now, several students raised their hands to tell about people who might have untreated seizures and neurological problems. I described what could be done.

Francisco was another marvel. As I listened to his skilled teaching, it was apparent he was no longer the bumbling teenager who had irritated me in the aldeas, but a vital leader.

Beside me sat a young man who looked familiar. He leaned over and whispered, *"Recuerde a mi, Seño?* Remember me? I am from Las Cañas. When you and Seño Fay visited, I was ten years old. Now I'm a promoter." He beamed, as proud as any high school graduate. Then I recalled how I had known him. He was Baby Maria's cousin.

What Fay and I had begun grew in ways never anticipated. We were afraid our hard work would go up in smoke when we left. Sheila Matthews initiated classes in Kek'chi for those students. Now 120 promoters were actively employed, and there were two more groups in formation. I didn't have to worry that everything would end when we Americans departed. The promoters were propelling everything forward themselves.

After class, we enjoyed *pan dulce,* sweet bread and *chocoláte*, hot chocolate, which the students prepared, followed by a hilarious skit. These students, all leaders— Carmen, Francisco, Rosa and a young man named Angel

Custudio—exuded confidence. They had needed only a chance.

I learned José Bá, Macario's cousin, who had seemed one of the least likely to graduate, was working regularly as a promoter in Cansís.

I asked Sheila Matthews how the latrine project had fared.

"Well," she said, "we still have a long way to go. Installing latrines and using them isn't as popular as we'd like."

"That hasn't changed," I laughed.

"But now there's cholera in the Petén," she went on, "so people's attitudes might change. *One* aldea has a latrine at every house," she added. Most villages had some latrines, which was a far cry from the single latrine in Las Cañas when Fay and I were there.

The success of the promoters thrilled me. They would forge ahead, no matter what. A chapter in my life had closed and I could go on to the next.

However, Guatemala's violence and injustice do continue. Sometimes, when I meditate over the cruel situation there, I feel hopeless. Will the carnage never end? But then I am reminded of the people of the Petén, of their hope in spite of all obstacles. I'm convinced Macario isn't dead: his spirit lives on.

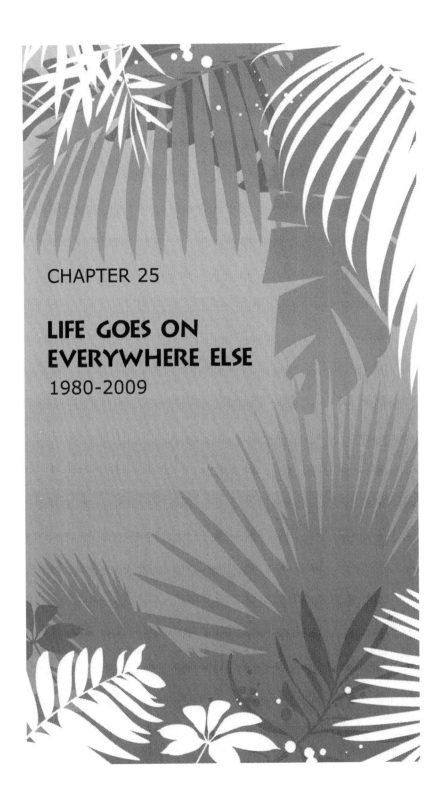

CHAPTER 25

LIFE GOES ON EVERYWHERE ELSE

1980-2009

   **Now that 30 years have passed since my years living in
Guatemala, I've reflected on my own metamorphosis.**
Nursing in the jungle changed me. I never would have adopted
a child from Guatemala had I not fallen in love with
Guatemalan children. And because of Maria's needs, I've
entered the world of special needs children. A unique world,
peopled by the special folks who help special kids; dedicated
physical therapists; outstanding teachers; Maria's neurologist,

Dr. Stephen Glass, the best pediatric neurologist west of the Mississippi; and parents, like me, of differently-abled kids. My life is much richer because of **Maria**. Often difficult, because being a single parent isn't easy, but tremendously rich. (That's us in our Guatemalan finery.)

When I returned to the States in 1980 after my years in Guatemala, it took me awhile to find a satisfying job. I flailed around for awhile, even considering a director's job in the Archdiocese of Seattle Mission office. Good thing I didn't get that job, because I'm a hands-on type. When I finally found a job that fit, it was working with low-income, Spanish-speaking people, which energized me.

Every job I had after Guatemala involved speaking Spanish. I loved using the language with our patients at Sea Mar Clinic where I worked as a nurse practitioner for seven years. At the Health Department where I worked for ten years, the staff asked me to translate when someone Latino came in. (That's me at work in the Health Department, left.) My spirit somehow connects with theirs. The same was true in my next job in school nursing, where the staff called on me to translate for Spanish-speaking parents and students. I discovered that I like working with the poor more than with any other group.

Without realizing it, I became politically active. My politics—which were never extreme—shifted over time, and now my friends probably call me a bleeding heart liberal. In the early '80s, I joined NISGUA, an organization in solidarity with Guatemala. We raised funds to heighten consciousness about Guatemala's plight. I helped sell the brilliantly hued textiles woven in Guatemala. I also joined GUASO, a Seattle group dedicated to helping the people of Guatemala. I gave talks and slide shows to school children and different parishes about my missionary experience. I was impassioned to tell people about the suffering, courageous Guatemalan people.

I even developed a calendar teaching health concepts using pictures of the promoters and shipped hundreds to the Petén. Pan American Airways transported them free of charge. (That's me packing them up, left.) Fr. Joe Kramis, pastor at St. Patrick's church, where I'd been active before Guatemala, helped me send boxes upon boxes of donated Campbell's soup to the Petén. I became incensed when I learned of President Reagan's deal with Iran to bring arms against the people of Nicaragua and our government's support of the military in El Salvador. I hated the U.S. policy which supported the dictatorship's of President Lucas Garcia and Rios Montt, president of Guatemala after Lucas Garcia.

I wanted desperately to share my experiences in Guatemala, and joined various writer's groups, even winning a grant from the Seattle Arts Commission to finish this book. In high school I wanted to write, but thought I had no talent and never pursued that dream. However, my adventures in Guatemala were so profound that I forgot my fear and wrote.

Then in 1994 I met Jennifer Harbury. Jennifer is a

Harvard educated lawyer with lots of Guatemalan refugees as her clients. Fascinated by their stories, she traveled to see their actual situation. In the mountains, she met Everardo, a guerilla fighter leader. Incredibly, they fell in love and married. A few months later, Everardo was captured in an encounter with the military and disappeared. A witness escaped and told Jennifer that Everardo was being tortured in a clandestine prison. (That's **Jennifer**, above, during one of her vigils in Guatemala.)

Jennifer decided to stage a hunger strike in Guatemala City to focus world attention on her husband. She hoped the army would free him. I was moved by her plight, by her passion for Everardo. I longed to stand by her and help during the hunger strike. I was torn, though, because what right did I have to leave my daughter Maria? But everything worked out. I got leave from work, my friend Mark helped pay for my trip and my mother agreed to care for Maria.

So in October, 1994 I spent a week watching over

Jennifer, checking her blood, taking her blood pressure, urging her, as nurses do, to drink the electrolyte fluid she needed to stay healthy. All sorts of media people interviewed her. My friend Fern later sent me a picture from the *New York Times* of me taking Jennifer's blood pressure. Sadly, we learned that while Jennifer endangered her life by fasting, Everardo was killed by the military long before the hunger strike began. His body was never found and to this day, no one knows exactly what happened to Everardo.

My interest in peace went beyond Guatemala. Before Iraq was invaded, I joined protesters who paraded Seattle's streets. Because of my experiences in Guatemala, I'm convinced that no war is a good war and that this war is a mistake. I joined the Southend Neighbors For Peace and Justice and joined with them in many activities, including marching as a group in my town's Fourth of July Parade. I stand with our group at our main intersection, holding signs protesting the war. I believe it's important that I speak up and remind people that our soldiers are dying daily, sent to Iraq because of lies. Every day I check an online site that lists more and more dead, and I feel tremendous sadness. I grieve for the maimed and the thousands upon thousands of Iraqi dead and injured. As the war continues, I post the numbers of our American dead in my living room window.

Sometimes I ponder my direction in life following Guatemala, and it seems I've taken a completely different turn in the road than if I had never gone there. I wouldn't change that path for the world.

Now I live in the town of Burien in south Seattle, in my little house with gorgeous Guatemalan weavings on the walls, with my daughter Maria, who has now turned 26. Despite her disabilities, she amazes everyone with her accomplishments, which include singing in a choir, working at a newspaper where she cuts out ads and mails them to businesses, walks to

Burien listening to music on her Walkman, and enjoys playing softball in an adaptive recreation program. She's a good worker at home, getting the mail, putting out the garbage, washing dishes and vacuuming.

I still work occasionally as a nurse in schools near home. I love camping (in an RV now), still read voraciously, enjoy writing, walking, yoga, and getting together with friends and family.

I've stayed in touch with many of my companions from my years in Guatemala.

Fay Hauer resumed her first profession of teaching, in Toppenish, WA to be home summers with her adopted daughters, Azucena and Ana, as they were growing up. She taught at-risk Latino youth and now is semi-retired, but works some helping kids with homework. She loves gardening, helps care for her elderly mother and revels in being a grandmother now that Azu has two children. Fay and I stay in touch often, but don't get to see each other as much because she lives farther away.

Kay Studer lives in Seattle with her husband, a former Spanish priest. She received her master's degree in counseling and works in an agency for Latinos. She and her husband worked with groups in solidarity with Guatemala for years and hope to develop a couples counseling service. We remain as close as sisters.

Fern Gosselin cared for his ill parents until they died and then promoted Maryknoll's missionary program in the States. He worked for years on Siberia's Sakhalin Island and for a time in South Korea. Semi-retired, he now lives at Maryknoll, NY, and grows a large garden and contributes the harvest to food banks. He helps with bringing elderly Maryknoll priests and brothers to appointments.

John Blazo is very active giving presentations on mission work in schools and parishes in New York and Pennsylvania. We enjoy talking often, keeping up with who is doing what.

His home base is Maryknoll, NY.

John Fay lived for years at Maryknoll's St. Teresa's residence for elderly and ill priests and brothers in Maryknoll, NY. He died in 2003.

Leon Cook remained in Poptún longer than any Maryknoller, until he was in his 80s, gardening and recycling. Although now confined mostly to a wheelchair, he remains cheerful. He lives at Maryknoll, NY.

Mo Healy and **Maria Dolores Cheng** (left) married. They recently retired from a project for the poor elderly in her town of Santa Lucia Cotzumalguapa on the Pacific Coast of Guatemala. Though Mo is in frail health, when we visited them in April, 2009, they had just come from bringing sandwiches to jail inmates.

Pastora Lira, who worked with John Blazo in catechesis, returned to Nicaragua and married a soldier injured in the Nicaraguan revolution.

Mecca Mendez, our cook, married Hermelindo Póp, Fern's translator. They had four children and are now grandparents to five.

Marina, our laundress, was abused and killed by her common law husband.

Lico Retana, head of the literacy program and my companion on the *Mud* trip, became a lawyer.

Tox became a driver in the military. He lived in Cobán, Guatemala. Before going to Guatemala this April, I wrote, wanting to see him but never heard back. With Tox's ambition and abilities, it wouldn't surprise me if he somehow made it to the States. I hope we meet again someday.

Carmen Ché (left with Fay in 2009) and Rosa Imelda, students in the first class of promoters, headed the flourishing health program for years. Rosa Imelda only occasionally helps out now because of health issues. Carmen is now the energetic director, with help from Domingo Pop, Chabela Reyes and Elvia Milian. Carmen instigated programs such as the midwife, natural medicine and dental promoter programs.

Recently, Carmen visited the aldeas with Padre Demetrio and the health team. They saw over 70 patients in one day. They trekked through the jungle, gathered natural herbs and cured a woman of second and third degree burns using herbs and tomatoes. She was left without scars.

About four years ago, my 95-year-old mother came to live with Maria and me. We expanded my little house, so Mama had her own space. It was a sad time, though, because she couldn't garden as she had all her life, and lost her independence. Gradually, she deteriorated, and was on Hospice. Maria, God bless her, helped me greatly with Mama's care, but caretaking took a toll on my health. When **Maria** graduated from high school, (following page) I promised her a trip to Guatemala. She hadn't been there since 1989, at age 5. Because of my own health issues, and because we were now taking care of Mama, we were unable to take Maria's graduation trip.

Then on January 2, 2009, at 99 years of age, Mama died.

It was sad losing her, but she lived a long and worthwhile life. So Maria and I could finally take our long-delayed trip to Guatemala, and Fay decided to come too. We were immensely excited and scampered to prepare. I bought gifts for Carmen and the health team, office supplies like sticky-notes, pens and pencils for the promoter courses, Seattle t-shirts and m & m's. Sheila Matthews, who directed the program after Fay and I left, sent me a boxful of empty medicine bottles for Carmen to use in the pharmacy.

So after 20 years, I was off once again to Poptún, eager to see how many of my old friends and former students we could round up.

CHAPTER 26

COMING
FULL CIRCLE...
BACK TO POPTÚN
APRIL 2009

I can hardly believe I'm in Guatemala again with my old friend and fellow missioner, Fay and my daughter Maria. It's just 10:30 a.m. and about 90 degrees, with humidity to match. (That's **Maria** and I in Guatemala City, above, with **Maria Edna Castellanos**, center.) We were excited to visit with Maria Edna and see her doing so well. She's come a long way from her days as a child cleaning our slides and helping us out. Now she's bilungual and works as an

administrator in the healthcare field. She took us out for a very nice dinner while we were in Guatemala City.

Carmen Ché (left), a student in the first class of promoters, now heads the still flourishing program. She offered to pick us up in Guatemala City. When I see Carmen waiting for Fay, Maria and I outside the gate of the Center House, the 20 years since I last saw her gather in that tight hug we give each other. She looks spectacular—coffee brown skin, gleaming black hair pulled back in a silver clip, and a white, strong-toothed smile. We both cry.

Thirty years ago we crossed the Rio Dulce by ferry on our way to Poptún. Now we drive the paved road to Poptún, arriving late at night. In the morning, it's a good thing Carmen takes us around town, for I don't recognize much. The church is painted gold and yellow and is still the town's centerpiece. Native plants surround the church perimeter and a fence keeps the cows out. I no longer see chickens wandering and pigs and cows lumbering along the streets. The streets of Poptún

(below) are paved! More businesses, more people, more cars, lots of women and girls of all ages on motorcycles and not a helmet in sight. Interestingly, there's no military presence in town, as there was 30 years before. Now there's a park across from the church where kids play basketball and people gather.

Once again the convent is a wreck. There are no more American missionaries or priests in Poptún, and without women in residence to maintain the place, the jungle climate has overtaken it. There are holes in the window screens, tons of mosquitoes, the sink leaks and the toilet doesn't flush. For the first couple of days, I take the back off, and plunge my hand in to lift that ball-like black thing, and even then half the time it still won't work, so now I go outside to the *pila*, fill a bucket with water and dump it in the toilet. Garbage is strewn all over: an old toilet on the patio, a grimy kitchen with filth that rivals what we experienced in 1977. My hand runs into cobwebs in the dish cupboard; there are locks everywhere, even on the dish cupboard, because people steal. We wash our clothes in the *pila* as we had years ago. There are only one lemon and two orange trees left. The papaya bushes are gone, but there are red flowering plants along the rectory patio. Padre Demetrio, the current pastor, tells us that blight destroyed most of the fruit trees. It's hotter now, because cattle ranchers whacked down many pine trees and other foliage.

Despite all that, everyone is so amiable and welcoming; the health team and people we've run into in the market are all happy to see us. Padre Demetrio's a really good guy, but he's by himself. He can't do it all. Plus, there's only so much money. He's the typical missionary, taking care of others before himself. Fay and I are furiously making plans to clean the joint up, just like we did thirty years ago. We haven't changed much.

We pass by the house of Francisco Cuz who now lives in Poptún by the cemetery. His black eyes gleam at seeing us. I remember him as a skinny kid, but now he's hefty and diabetic. Calling his family of five children together in the main room, we all sit around. A modest-sized TV, a computer tower with monitor and a stereo sit in a large wooden display case.

"Listen to Seño Fay," he says to his kids. "I want you to hear what she and Seño Liz did. They gave me a chance."

Fay says, "When your dad was only 14, he told us he wanted to be a promoter. We thought he was too young. And yet the community chose him as their candidate."

Francisco wipes tears from his chubby cheeks as Fay talks. His wife and daughter cry too. (**Fay, Maria** and I visit with **Francisco**, far left, with his family, above.)

"When I visited in 1989," I tell him, "I was amazed at Francisco and how he had become so confident and capable as a teacher." I didn't add that Francisco had been somewhat of a rascal at the age of 14. When he helped Fay and me in Chacté, he spent more time asking questions than working. Who would dream he'd become the family man sitting next to me now.

His house has a tin roof, wood slat walls for air circulation, one bedroom where everyone sleeps on beds or hammocks with mosquito netting. His house in Chacté thirty years ago had been the typical Kek'chi dwelling—a thatched roof with slat wood sides and a dirt floor. Francisco tells us he's had malaria and dengue fever, acquired in Poptún, because many more mosquitoes infest the town than before. We're taking our anti-malaria medicine. Years working in the promoter program helped him get the administrative job in healthcare that he has now.

Francisco invites us for a meal later that week, and we go with Carmen. His wife makes *caldo de chompipe* (turkey soup), with yucca, *guiskil,* Guatemalan zucchini, another vegetable I don't recognize and tortillas. Now everyone seems to have those big 5 gallon jugs of bottled water.

Then we ride in his truck to the Río Macháquila. I ride in back, on the wheel-housing. His oldest daughter hands me a folded sheet to sit on, but it doesn't pad much. We bump along and I hang on hard. My daughter Maria wants to ride in back, so we stop and I climb out. Francisco puts down the cement block for my petite Maria to use as a step. She climbs up and sits on the wheel housing, giggling and delighted. A bunch of people sitting in the back of a truck is something you'd never see in the States.

Styrofoam cups, rotten fruit, paper and beer cans litter the river. Hundreds of people splash around in that terrible beige water, swimming, probably swallowing water and yet enjoying themselves immensely. Like years ago, they swim in their clothes, which cling to them, only modestly revealing. Thirty years ago, a few clusters of women washed clothes or bathed in their clothes in the river. Then, the water was clear.

It's so hot and the nights are horrible, the hot sheets protect a bit from mosquitoes, but make me sweat. I feel dehydrated, sweating until drops drip down into my waistband. I'm glad I brought Bacitracin, Desitin, and Hydrocortisone ointments, which I slather on Maria and me over itchy mosquito bites.

Holy Thursday at church is joyful; we see Mecca, our former cook. She never used to go to church. Her warm hug makes me cry again. I had forgotten the nurturing hugs people give in the Petén.

On Good Friday we start to climb the hill with the three crosses on top, (left) a Lenten tradition, but it's way too hot, and we turn back. Can't believe how many people attend the *Semana Santa* (Holy Week) activities, compared to the handful who used to participate. I think it's because of Padre Demetrio. He has such a pastoral presence. He greets everyone and they respond with genuine smiles as he strolls the streets of Poptún. People seek him out constantly. In the seven years he's been here, he's pulled the community together. There's a harmonizing choral group, guitars, violins, lots of young people as altar servers, singers and in the procession. The choir sings on tune, not like thirty years ago when Doña Elmira screeched along with a couple of other off-tune ladies. For Easter, the church is packed with people, sitting on the side aisles, standing in back and on the steps, all very happy.

People invite us for dinner and lunch. At Mario Castellano's home we wash our hands with the harsh cleanser Comet. As when we lived here before, the days are filled with

funny moments, like using Comet. His mother, **Doña Hortensia**, (left with **Fay**) is still very active in the church and just like years ago, we see her running to church constantly. Mario, along with his sister Maria Edna, helped us when they were kids, washing our truck, cleaning slides and dirty thermometers. Mario confides to Fay, "The money you paid helped us survive. You'll never know how much it meant." Mario now owns a pharmacy.

All three of us have had diarrhea. Imodium helps, some. Now I just have occasional cramps but carry toilet paper, because just like back then, you can never count on toilets with toilet paper. Funny, at Francisco's house, I ask for the bathroom. He directs me to a door. I open the door, which reveals a concrete latrine—and out stalks a chicken.

We lunch at Carmen's house, and it's delicious, with *caldo de pollo*, chicken soup, tortillas, rice, mashed potatoes, macaroni salad, lemonade and watermelon. Her house is the cleanest so far. She shows us proudly around. There's no toilet but she has a room set aside for it.

"How much would a toilet cost, Carmen, pipes and everything?" I ask.

"About 900 *quetzales,* ($120 American money)," she says.

I'll send money for one when I can. She works so hard, bringing us papayas and tortillas, takes us all over. Anybody who arrives, she serves them with respect and caring. She's often on her cell phone. Promoters call her constantly from far-off aldeas, asking advice and help. She never stops serving. Carmen's mother died just three weeks ago after a long period suffering with cancer. I feel badly that our trip came at this time, but we had already purchased our tickets. Carmen assures us that our presence is actually helping her. I do feel some resonance with her situation, as my own mother also died so recently.

One night, a Kek'chi promoter and a midwife arrive from an aldea far into the interior. They bring a newborn baby and take her mother to the hospital. After the mother gave birth she got a uterine infection. The promoter and midwife talked the woman's husband into letting them bring her to the Poptún hospital by bus. An accomplishment, because far in the interior, people are distrustful and don't always follow the promoter's advice. The mother is admitted, but they won't let the baby stay or let the mother breastfeed, since she's receiving antibiotics that could pass to the breast milk. The promoter and midwife come looking for Carmen. Because it's Holy Week, there's no one caretaking Kerigma Quetzal, the center where people usually stay when they come from the aldeas.

Carmen settles them in the room next to mine. The baby girl is an alert and contented six-pounder, carried in the traditional cloth sling down the midwife's back.

They lay her down on the bed and Fay and I run around boiling water for the formula they brought with them. I tell the couple her name should be *chulita*, little cutie, but they say they will name her Elizabeth. All night I listen for the baby, waiting for her cry, but she doesn't. She seems perfectly okay, and takes formula really well. The next morning Carmen comes and we go to the *mercado*, where I buy a tiny pink baby sweater, onesies and baby formula. We visit the mother at the hospital and she's pale, wan and very thin. I found out later that both she and her baby survived, and she was able to breast feed her infant.

One of the doctors shows us proudly around the new Poptún hospital (left) which is clean, organized, with almost every service imaginable. Carmen tells me that patients have free care, unless of course, the hospital equipment is broken down. Then they must pay a private doctor for medicines, x-rays or special exams. Still, what a metamorphosis from the old hospital, a slovenly place I wouldn't bring my worst enemy to.

Before the promoter and midwife leave for their aldea,

they meet with Fay. She convinces them to ask breastfeeding aldea women to wet nurse the baby. We rarely saw good outcomes using formula. In the aldeas it's too tough to maintain cleanliness for bottle feeding. The promoter wants Fay to help with his son's educational expenses, which Fay agrees to do.

Carmen shows us around Kerigma-Quetzal, the educational center where we taught promoter classes. The grass is macheteed, corridors swept. Kek'chi nuns from Alta Verapaz built a convent on one corner of the property. We meet the mother superior; she's a black-haired, dark-eyed beauty of only 32 dressed in an immaculate Kek'chi *traje*.

I ask Carmen if they still have the picture albums.

"*Si, como no*," Carmen says. She takes from the shelf a pile of dusty, dog-eared albums.

I am filled with nostalgia as I look at the pictures, many of which I snapped, of the aldea people and the promoters.

"Here's Maria Cristina." says Carmen, showing me a black and white photo of a darling girl in Kek'chi *traje*. "She's now a promoter and a midwife."

"Oh my God, I took that picture," I say.

"Maybe we'll see her tomorrow," says Carmen, giving me that million-dollar smile and hug.

We visit the aldeas two days in a row. In Dolores, Marcelino, now a grandfather, still works as a promoter of health. He's become a dental promoter too, trained in basic dentistry by visiting

American dentists. One grandchild has yellowish-green snot dripping into his mouth, but both grandchildren wear Pampers! We had lunch there— delicious lemonade from their own fruit, a tomato-cucumber salad and a hunk of charbroiled meat, almost burned, that I thought at first was frijoles. We visit his clinic, a simple but decent building bearing a sign: *Casa Dental* (left). **Marcelino** proudly shows us his yellow vinyl dental chair, a compressor, and dental tools (below, with **Carmen** playing patient).

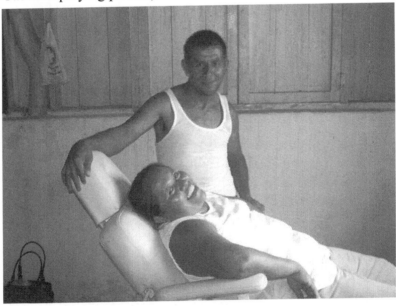

"I charge 25 quetzales for fillings, 25 for extractions and 30 for cleaning," he says, almost apologetically. Between $3 to $4 American money.

"We need equipment for all the dental promoters," says Carmen. "Every time the dental promoters in other aldeas want to hold a dental clinic, they must ask Marcelino to bring his, which means he must go through us for a vehicle to bring his tools to their village. "It's complicated."

At hearing this news, Fay and I exchange looks. "We're going to get you equipment for each of the dental promoters," she says.

"*Gracias,* Fay," Marcelino says. He accepts help graciously, not as though it's expected, but with no insincere protestations. Marcelino calls Carlos Bran, from Yaltutú, on his cell phone, but Carlos is far into the *milpa* and can't come. There used to be only one public telephone in Poptún and now amazingly, everyone seems to have cell phones.

We try unsuccessfully to find José Mario Balcarcel of Machaquilá. We hear he's a cattle rancher. We pass by the home of José Mario Estrada of Boca del Monte. His wife informs us he's working in the *milpa*.

The following day we head for the aldeas of San Luís with Carmen and Padre Demetrio. He drives a high-off-the-ground red pickup. Our low-to-the-ground Chevy Luv used to scrape and thud against the rutted roads of the Petén.

Next, we head for the home of Guillermo, who worked for years as a promoter. He was the slow one who Fay tutored, who we never thought would make it through the program. He said, when Macario died, that our duty was to accept Macario's death as the will of God. **Guillermo** cares for his mother (below) who suffered a stroke six years ago. Along a rocky, unpaved trail, we come to Guillermo's place—a shack, really—with a dirt floor and scrawny dogs running around. There stands Guillermo, grinning happily. He wears a dirty,

 ripped t-shirt and his left eye is half-closed. His mother sits in a wooden Adirondack chair, he's just been combing her hair neatly into a bun. She wears a clean pink housedress. Her right hand lies useless in her lap and she can't speak clearly.

Nevertheless she smiles lovingly at her son.

We visit awhile and then make an excuse to leave. We are so touched by Guillermo's circumstances, that we rush off to the nearest store and buy a couple of boxes of food; rice, sugar, soap, cooking oil, a comb for his mom and a notebook and pens for him. We tell Guillermo, "These are for your mom." We don't want to embarrass him by giving him too many things, but he seems grateful and he smiles when he sees the pens and notebook.

"I had a wheelchair for her," he says, "but it broke." No wonder, there's no sidewalk, only rocky ground. She's unable to stand so he must lift her.

"I lift her chair and all," he says. I see how that would work, because when a person has a stroke, their limbs can flop all over. But, she's a stocky lady. I can't imagine how Guillermo manages. I glance inside the house, which is a shambles. If cleaned up, the yard would be a pretty place, with large shady trees.

"I feel alone," he says. "My brothers and sisters live far away and don't help much. I can't work anymore, because I take care of my mother."

When Carmen says, "There may be a nursing home built soon in Poptún. Maybe your mom could live there."

Guillermo says, "I'd never do that. My mother doesn't want to live in one of those places. That's ok, I'll take care of her."

We ask about Isaías, who worked with Guillermo in Cansís.

"He died," says Guillermo. Isaías developed a drinking problem, and died in a motorcycle accident. Fay and I are so sad, because Isaías was one of the best—intelligent, responsible, warm.

"Do you like coconuts?" Guillermo asks. We nod and he promptly climbs a tree and whacks off several golden coconuts, then trims off the tops with his machete. The milk is slightly

sweet, sticky and warm. Apple trees bear a fruit shaped like a
pear and are a delicate pinkish red—less sweet than our apples,
but delicious. We snap a picture of Guillermo in his apple tree,
smiling a radiant smile. (There he is whacking the coconut,
above.)

As we leave, Carmen promises to tell the other promoters
of his circumstances so they can visit. She'll be in touch about
another wheelchair. We pile into the truck, drinking from
dripping coconuts, and making a mess in the truck with the
juice as we bounce over the ruts.

Our next stop is Cansís, which I don't recognize because
of all the houses and businesses. When we visited with our
mobile clinic and classes, there hadn't even been *one* store. We
turn onto a rocky road to a house perched on a cliff where
Macario's widow lives (right). Macario was in the first class of
promoters and died tragically after falling off the Chevy Luv
the day before graduation in 1981.

From a bag, Fay takes out Macario's notebook, the list of
26 latrines which he and Jose Bá helped install in Cansís, and

pictures of Macario. When his widow sees these keepsakes for the first time, which Fay stored safely for thirty years, she cries quietly, wiping her eyes with her apron. Then up roars a young man on a motorcycle, wearing a name tag, which says he's a teacher. This is **Macario's son**, (below) who was just 3 when

his father died. He accepts those pictures and caresses them with his eyes. He opens the nutrition notebook his father colored with crayons, all neatly within the lines, turning each page as if he were reading a holy book. He takes the list that Fay gives him of the latrines his father had been instrumental in installing in Cansís, and as he reads, tears trace down his cheeks. We sit there together. Fay and I sigh, wiping our eyes.

"I've never seen a picture of my father," he says. That I am overwhelmed with sadness but yet a certain closure underestimates how I feel. Carmen, whose mother died less than a month ago, escapes outside.

The circle seems closed. His father's tragic death at age 22 seems mitigated. Now his son might know his father in a new way, and see the worthwhile life his father led.

I feel as I felt then, blessed. On this trip, I've seen men cry without restraint. Francisco, and now Macario's son. And almost every time I hug Carmen, tears well. Where else can I get these wonderfully warm embraces, kisses upon kisses on the cheek, joyous smiles, attitudes of faith and hope?

Macario's widow makes us lunch, *caldo de pollo*, the luxury meal of the aldeas, with hot, thick tortillas, fresh off the *comal*, a round flattish pan for cooking tortillas. Later, I ask for the bathroom. The oldest girl shows me outside, and points to a ramshackle latrine perched on another cliff above the house. She takes me by the hand up the steep hill, because I slip over the rocks and slide backwards. The latrine has a piece of plastic and a gunnysack covering in front. She pulls together the gunnysack and plastic to shield me from people passing on the road below and hands me a roll of toilet paper. I sit on the concrete latrine, but then I drop the toilet paper, and it begins to roll down the hill. While grasping the curtains closed in one hand, she quickly grabs the rolling toilet paper. Restraining a hysterical giggle, I file this episode in my growing repertoire of bathroom stories. I wonder what this family does when it rains, or at night? How can they possibly scale this cliff in the dark?

We stop at the home of José Bá. His sister cries when Fay hands her José's photos. He died in Guatemala City, caught in a crossfire, in the wrong place at the wrong time, presumably by the drug gangs that now terrorize Guatemala. We learn that Julian Morales died of an illness. That makes four in the first class of promoters who have passed away; Macario, Isaías, Jose Bá, and Julian. All before the age of 40. It's not fair, I think.

Next we stop in La Cumbre, where we consume another *caldo de pollo* lunch, with those lovely thick tortillas, tamales and a delicious drink from a fruit tree. We meet some of the current crop of promoters who I wish I could talk with longer, because I can see what bright men they are. Then here comes

Maria Cristina Xol Chub (left), promoter and midwife, whose picture I took when she was 9 years old (see Page 141.) I brought her a copy. She had never seen it. She covers her face in embarrassment while practically the whole village passes the picture from person to person, while teasing her in Kek'chi.

I ask about her work as a midwife.

"Now few women die during childbirth. The babies live too," she explains. She gave prenatal care to a woman expecting twins, and the woman delivered safely in the Poptún hospital.

"I even did a version." (The baby is turned in utero if it's breech.) "I don't do that much as it's dangerous," she says.

"Do you have a blood pressure cuff and stethoscope?" I ask.

"No, we don't have that kind of equipment."

I must find a way to send her a blood pressure cuff and stethoscope that is just taking up space in my closet.

Carmen taught these midwives. Many speak Kek'chi and never had schooling. So during the midwifery courses, she teaches them reading and writing. Where there had been none, there are now 70 midwives working in the aldeas! Many midwives also cultivate aldea gardens and have little tiendas where they sell medicines. There are 25 promoters who practice herbal medicine. **There have been eight graduations, with a total of 180 promoters, and 125 promoters still practice. Knowing that the humble program we started so many years ago has continued to thrive, fills me with deep satisfaction and joy.**

(Left, that's me with former Promoter **Adan Samayoa**, now the proud owner of a hardware store.) Adan was only 15 when he entered the program and was one of the youngest students.

The rest of the time in Poptún flies by. One night, Padre Demetrio, Rosa Imelda, Domingo Pop, Carmen's helper in the health program, Carmen, Fay, Maria and I walk through the streets of Poptún looking for a pizza joint. When we tell the young woman at the counter we'd like pizza, she says, "I'm sorry, we have no pizza." Only in Guatemala, I think. We parade down the street convulsed in laughing.

We have a meal at Chabela Reyes' home, who helps Carmen in the health office. Chabela graduated from the fourth class of promoters. Her daughter and Domingo's son showed great potential for learning. When Cuban doctors worked in town, they chose the son and daughter to attend medical school in Cuba. Both are now doctors. Domingo's son works in Sayaxché, Petén. From *no* medical programs, now the sons and daughters of promoters are doctors.

Fay says and I agree, "I can't stay another night in that wreck of a convent." We're not self-sacrificing missionaries anymore.

We pack our bags and stay the last two nights at the Finca Ixobél (below). Carol Devine has developed the Finca into the *Hotel Ecological*, a lush, serene setting, with good food, home-made bread, fans and mosquito netting in the rooms. Her husband Michael was beheaded in 1990. Carol says the mystery of his death has never been solved, although everyone suspects it is somehow connected to the military.

On our last night, Carmen, the health team and Padre Demetrio gather with us at the Finca. Carmen brings a huge pan of homemade tamales steaming in flavorful broth, wrapped

in palm leaves. I eat three of the giant things and they are luscious. Other than Italian food, the best food ever created. The health team present **Fay** (left, with **Carmen**) and I with beautiful Guatemalan woven cloth; red with an interwoven silver thread and handmade wooden plaques inscribed *Recuerdo de Programa de Salud y Parroquia. Poptún, Petén. 4/18/09.* (Memento from the Health Program and Church, pictured below with **Fay** and **Padre Demetrio**.) Even **Maria** gets a hand-carved wooden cup, made in Poptún (above right, with **Carmen**). Everyone is happy; joy infuses my spirit.

The next morning, dear Francisco carries our suitcases down to the truck and sees us off. He gives me his cell phone number. Padre Demetrio drives and Domingo and Carmen accompany us.

As I promised Maria, we visit Tikál (below). Besides the ancient stone edifices of the Mayas, we see monkeys high up in the trees and strange gnarled shapes of unusual trees

and exquisite yellow-tailed birds. When we embrace in that final hug with Carmen and leave from the airport in Santa Elena to fly to Guatemala City, I feel unshed tears tighten my throat. I am so filled to the brim with the myriad emotions of this trip, that I'm speechless.

Before we leave for the States, Mo Healy and Aidé, now married, (we knew her as Maria Dolores when she was still a nun) visit us in Guatemala City. It's a joyful reunion, even though Mo is now in frail health.

Everything about this trip is memorable. I'm so glad that Maria is now 25 and understands more. She says to me, "Mom, I want to live here. This is my country. But," she adds, "I don't want to live in the convent." Of the three of us, she's had the most mosquito bites. She wants to live at the *Finca Ixobel*. It's natural that Maria feels that connection to her homeland, but I had to tell her that I'm no longer physically up to living in Guatemala. She accepted that reality and does understand that she isn't able to live there independently.

The trip wouldn't have been nearly as fun without Fay. It's fitting that having worked so hard together many years ago, we returned together.

Fay and I are awed with what the promoters have accomplished. Carmen is a gifted leader. Who would have imagined this shy girl from Tanjoc leading as she does, magnificently. I thought, as I did when I visited in 1989, that all the promoters needed was a chance. Talent lay within them. Fay and I were the catalysts, but they grew in ways we never imagined. They don't need us anymore, but that's a good thing. Fay and I agree, as we leave Guatemala, that we had a fabulous time.

As I muse over this trip on the plane back home to Seattle, I'm grateful for the emotion-filled days we spent with Carmen and the health team, in awe of their work and the quality of their dedication. Carmen has been hospitable, gracious, warm, extremely thoughtful and happy while doing it. Fay and I decide to help with the health program needs, and they're many: Francisco's son wants funds to complete high school, and Padre Demetrio needs help to fix up the rectory and convent.

We'll return in another two years, and keep in touch by email. I didn't know what to do with my life after Mama died, but now I do. I'll be involved with the people of the Petén and help them as much as I can, part of a living continuous circle from me to them and back again. **For it's my great joy to recognize again that Guatemala is in my blood—forever.**

Made in the USA
Charleston, SC
10 September 2010